Rabbi Eliezer Berland

One in a
GENERATION

VOLUME I: FROM HAIFA TO UMAN

B.R. LEVY & Y.D. BERGMAN

ACKNOWLEDGEMENTS

The authors would like to extend our deepest gratitude to the *Knishta Chada* newsletter; the *Kav Hamida* Breslov information line; the authors of *Lahavot Eish*; the Shuvu Banim International website; Rav Rachamim Bracha; and the publishers of the *Hitchadshut* newsletter for sharing their content with us, which helped us greatly in the preparation of this book.

We'd also like to thank photographers Nachi Weiss and Shuki Lerer for permitting us to use their images; ECM for their translations from Hebrew to English; Y. Mayer and A. Teitelbaum for their editorial assistance; Raphael Albinati for his attention to detail and design; and the donors whose contributions helped this book to see the light of day.

May Hashem continue to bless them all in their endeavors to spread Rebbe Nachman's light in the world.

Lastly, we'd like to thank our spouses and families for their patience and encouragement, and *Hakadosh Baruch Hu* for giving us the tremendous privilege of being able able to share this book with the English-speaking public.

B.R. Levy & Y.D. Bergman

TECHNICAL NOTE:

All the Hebrew words in this book have been italicized for ease of reference, and can be found in the glossary at the back of the book.

DEDICATIONS

This publication was made possible through the generous contributions of the following people:

Daniel Orlowski:

Dedicated for the ilui neshama of:

L'Iluy Nishamot

Yitzhak Ben Boruch

Zelda Bat Boruch

Bella Bat Yitzhak

Chone Ben Yitzhak

Viktor Ben Yitzhak

Peretz Ben Yaakov

Asya Bat Yitzhak

Ilya Ben Simcha

Sue Reiss:

May Rav Berland have more and more success in his holy work, and may his holy message spread to all of Klal Yisroel until all of us are ready for redemption.

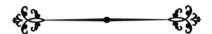

Mary Mandel:

Dedicated in loving memory of:

Avraham Beinish Ben Golda Shprintza and

Miriam Chaya Bas Bracha

May this be an aliyah for their neshamos.

This is dedicated l'ilui nishmat Raziel Feivish ben Hadassah.

May we all do teshuvah from love and bring Mashiach quickly and pleasantly in our days.

Meyer and Elisheva Fhima:

Dedicated in loving memory of Esther Bat Masouda.

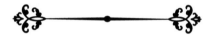

Isaac Farin:

Thank you for helping me tap into the deepest depths of my soul! Lots of love!

Stella Croning:

For Rivka Levy & family.

Gilson Arruda:

Dedicated to the beloved and holy tzaddik, Rav Eliezer Berland.

Dedicated for the hatzlacha of Nachman ben Tsipora, and to hasten the geula.

Ronen Hazan:

Thank you Rav for teaching me ultimate humility!

Meirah:

To the Tzadik, Rav Eliezer Berland, Shlita,

Thank you for our precious diamond,.

This Book is Imozik

הַסְכָּמָה לַסֵּפֶר

זֶה הַסֵּפֶר פִּלְאֵי פְּלָאוֹת וּמְסוּפָּר בּוֹ עַל נִסִּים וְנִפְלָאוֹת
שֶׁלֹּא הָיוּ מִימוֹת עוֹלָם וְעַל עֲבוֹדַת ה' שֶׁלֹּא נַעֲשׂוּ כָּמוֹתָן
בַּדּוֹר הַזֶּה לָכֵן כָּל הַקּוֹרֵא בְּסֵפֶר זֶה יִזְכֶּה לְהִדָּבֵק
בַּעֲבוֹדַת ה' בֶּאֱמֶת וּבִתְמִימוּת אֲמִיתִּית

בִּזְכוּת רַבֵּינוּ הַקָּדוֹשׁ וְהַנּוֹרָא
וּבִזְכוּת הַתּוֹרָה הַקְּדוֹשָׁה וְהַטְּהוֹרָה
עַבְדְּכֶם הַנֶּאֱמָן
אליעזר ברלנד

Haskama for the book

This book wonder of wonders contains stories of
miracles and marvels that did not exist from the
beginning of creation, and service of Hashem the likes of
which have not been done in this generation. Whoever
reads this book will merit clinging to the true service of
Hashem with simplicity and sincerity.

In the merit of our holy and awesome Rebbe

And in the merit the holy and pure Torah

Your faithful servant,

Eliezer Berland

CONTENTS

PROLOGUE

Few people in the English-speaking world ever heard of Rabbi Eliezer Berland before the Rav started hitting the headlines for all the wrong reasons, back in 2012.

For the English-speaking public, and particularly those who live outside of Israel, their first impressions of Rabbi Berland were the false, deceitful media accounts of his departure from Israel, apparently as a 'wanted man'.

In Volume II of 'One in a Generation', we will tell the true story behind the terrible, false accusations levelled at Rabbi Eliezer Berland, and reveal the people and the motives behind one of the most scandalous, politically-motivated libels in the history of the modern State of Israel.

But before we do, there is another story that must first be told. It's the story of a young, sincere, deep-thinker from Haifa who became a respected learning partner of the revered Steipler Gaon, Rabbi Yaakov Yisroel Kanievsky in Bnei Brak, before discovering an obscure branch of chassidus called *Breslov*.

When Rabbi Berland first came to Breslov, the chassidus was dying on its feet. It barely had a few hundred adherents, mostly centered around the Yiddish-speaking enclave of Bnei Brak. Rabbi Berland single-handedly breathed new life into Breslov chassidus, re-instituted many of the core Breslov practices that had been neglected for decades, and attracted thousands of new followers to this 'dead chassidus' in the space of a few short years.

From a very young age, Rabbi Eliezer Berland has devoted his life to sharing the sweetness of observant Judaism, and the beauty of Torah, and the light of Rebbe Nachman with as many people as possible.

The stories of the Rav's self-sacrifice, incredible devotion to Torah and *mitzvos*, miracles performed for *Am Yisrael*, and over-arching love for his fellow Jew would fill many, many volumes.

Here, we bring the reader just a taste, a bare minimum, of the many wondrous stories that could be told about Rabbi Berland's devotion to *Hashem*, commitment to Torah and love of the Jewish people.

It's our hope that when more people understand who Rabbi Eliezer Berland actually is, then they'll also understand the real context of the next, incredible part of the story that will be told in Volume II.

B.R. Levy & Y.D. Bergman

Jerusalem, 10ᵗʰ Kislev, 5778

FROM
HAIFA TO UMAN

IN THE BEGINNING:
HAIFA TO KFAR CHASSIDIM

The boy who would grow up to be Rav Eliezer Berland was born in Haifa on 23 *Teves*, 5698 (December 26, 1937), to Chaim and Ettia Berland[1]. Chaim Berland had recently moved to *Eretz Yisrael* from Poland, while Ettia had come to the Holy Land from Hungary, where her family had been followers of the *Rahak*, Rebbe Yoelish of Satmar. The couple met and married in Haifa, and found a place to live in the Carmel neighborhood of the city. The couple's first child was Eliezer, who was later joined by his brother Yechezkel, and his sister Leah.

Chaim Berland left Europe a few years before World War II because he said he could see the Holocaust coming[2]. As a former Polish native, he strongly believed in the Jewish imperative to rebuild the national home of the Jews on the holy soil of *Eretz Yisrael*. But he differed from the other Zionists who were making Aliyah at that time in his belief that without a strong and enduring connection to the Creator, "Jewish nationalism" by itself wouldn't be enough to sustain the Jewish people in Israel.

Chaim Berland worked as a partner and baker at one of Haifa's cooperative bakeries, while Ettia worked for a coffee wholesaler. The 1930s and 1940s were years of deprivation and hardship across the world but, while it couldn't be said that the Berland family was particularly well-off, the members of their household always had food to eat and the basics they needed to live—which couldn't be said of many other families during this period.

Helping others out was one of the Berland family's mottos and, when Ettia wasn't working at the coffee wholesaler or raising her children, she kept busy with a number of volunteering projects. Her concern for the needs of the Jewish people was deeply etched onto the Berland children, and continued to shape their attitudes and decisions over the coming decades.

Religious families were few and far between in the Haifa of the 1940s, and most of the Berlands' neighbors in the Carmel community were *Mapainiks*[1]. Come May

---

1   *Mapainik* is a colloquial term for a member or supporter of the Mapai, the historical name of the Israeli Labour Party. It's used to refer to 'old school' members of the Labour party in Israel who were wedded to a strongly secular, anti-religious type of Zionist ideology.

1ˢᵗ—Labor Day—the Carmel would be festooned in red to celebrate this national holiday of the workers, while Jewish holidays were celebrated with much less fanfare, if at all.

Young Eliezer Berland felt a spiritual lack in his surroundings from a very young age. Even as a three-year-old boy, Eliezer was mocked by his friends for being the only religious boy in his playgroup[3]. It was only much later in 1952 that Rebbe Boruch Hager of Vizhnitz founded Ramat Vizhnitz in the city of Haifa, and began the religious rehabilitation of Haifa. But until that time, it was rare to find an outwardly religious Jew in the city.

THE ODD ONE OUT

While the Berland family was considered *dati-leumi-masorati* (traditional national religious) and not *chareidi,* young Eliezer was drawn to the *chareidi* way of life from a very young age.

For example, in the *Bnei Akiva* high school that he attended, Eliezer was the only boy who insisted on wearing his hat to school in order to keep his head covered, which at that time was considered extremely odd behavior.

"They threatened to beat me up if I kept coming in my hat, but I kept wearing it anyway," Rav Berland remembers. "The *menahel* used to yell at me, and he'd ask me why I insisted on being different from the other pupils. He told me that wearing a hat wasn't something that the Torah itself commanded us to do; it wasn't a *d'Oraisa.* But I told him that I was still going to wear my hat to school."

His younger brother, Yechezkel[II], followed his example and started wearing his *tzitzis* over his shirt. Under the guidance of his older brother, he left *Bnei Akiva* high school and moved to Rav Yaakov Edelstein's *yeshivah* in Hod Hasharon. "Yechezkel had never learned *Gemara* before in his life, but when Rav Edelstein tested him, he understood it all," recalls Rav Berland. "He had a brilliant, analytical mind; to this day, he still does.[4]"

II   Yechezkel today is Rav of the Israeli town, Nehora

DISCOVERING *GEMARA* AT AGE 9

Rav Berland once described his childhood in these words: "When I was nine years old, I discovered the *Gemara*. And from then, I haven't left it for a moment. I don't understand why people don't learn it; after all, it's so very enjoyable."

When the Rav recalls that he and his *Gemara* were inseparable, he means literally. On one occasion, young Eliezer was taken on a sailing trip with the rest of his class. While his classmates reveled in the experience of being at sea, young Eliezer sat on the side of the boat with his *Gemara* and learned Torah instead. When the other children from his class saw him absorbed in his studies, they yelled at him: "What?! Even here you're still with your *Gemara*?!'" and wanted to throw him overboard, to finally get his head out of his holy books.

On another occasion, the Rav's class was taken to a local theater in Haifa, where the Rav and his classmates were shown a movie. Again, Eliezer took his *Gemara* along with him and sat there with a small flashlight, absorbed in the words of the Sages and oblivious to his surroundings.

Years later, the Rav explained that the spiritual light was exceptionally strong in that movie theater because he'd been learning Torah in a place where no one had ever done a *mitzvah* before. There were many sparks of holiness there that were just waiting to be revealed by a young boy learning *Gemara* by the light of a flashlight while the rest of his class watched a movie.

The Rav's love for Torah was so great that as a boy he would stay up all night learning. Rav Berland's sister remembers that, when their mother would tell him to put on pajamas and go to sleep, he would respond: "two minutes". Then, when everyone in the house was sleeping, he stayed up engrossed in his studies.

When his sister woke up in the morning, she would see his pajamas neatly folded in exactly the same way that they'd been left the night before, and Eliezer would be sitting and learning already, after the *vasikin davening*.

In addition to his precocious Torah learning, Eliezer's sense of right and wrong was also unusually well developed. A relative recalled that, when the Rav was a six-year-old boy, he asked an older girl to help him cross the street. As soon as he got to the other side, he fell over and scraped his whole face. "Even at the time, Eliezer felt that this had happened to him as some sort of punishment because he'd held a girl's hand. From that time on, he decided he needed to distance himself from girls.[5]"

ROWING AGAINST THE CURRENT

Eliezer came of age in a country drunk on the promises of political Zionism, where religious observance was derided and scorned.

The "modern Jew" of Ben Gurion and his fellow Zionists was a pioneer who would stand his ground and fight hard to defend his right to life. What had happened in the Holocaust would never happen again! God and religion were pushed out of the picture by those who preached that political independence and military might held the keys to redemption.

Where Judaism could be used to inspire loyal followers, or financial contributions from Jewish patrons abroad, it was tolerated—but certainly not encouraged. So, the young Eliezer grew up in a city where the main "religions" being practiced were Jewish socialism and political Zionism.

SAVED FROM THE HOLOCAUST

Rav Berland's parents had moved to Israel from Europe some years before the Holocaust began, but the family they'd left behind was decimated. Most of their European siblings and relatives had perished. When Eliezer was seven years old, he met some of his surviving cousins who had come through the Holocaust and moved to Israel. These relatives had lost their faith as a result of the suffering they'd endured, and proclaimed that "there was no God in the Holocaust."

This idea troubled Eliezer profoundly, and his thoughts often turned to the suffering that the Jewish nation, including his own relatives, had endured during World War II. When he was 10 years old, Eliezer finally had an answer for his relatives: he told them that one tiny burn in *Gehinnom* is more painful than all the crematoria in Auschwitz.

The lad told his stunned relatives that the great Jewish souls who had perished in the Holocaust must have asked to be sent down to this world, to be born into a generation of destruction, rather than having to endure the suffering of *Gehinnom*. And their request had apparently been accepted.

THE VIZHNITZ CONNECTION

A few years after the founding of the State of Israel in 1948, Rebbe R Boruch Hagar, zt" l, the *Mekor Boruch* of Vizhnitz, founded the Ramat Vizhnitz neighborhood in

Haifa. From that time on, the teenage Eliezer Berland started davening at the main Vizhnitz *beis midrash* every *Shabbos*.

One of Rav Berland's childhood friends from those early years in Haifa, R' Yosef Gensler, now a Vizhnitzer *chassid* who lives in New York, recalls the impression that the 15-year-old Eliezer made on him when he saw him in *shul*: "The first thing that struck me about him was how serious he looked," he recalls. "You could see that he was a deep thinker, and that he had a lot of thoughts in his head. Externally, he dressed the same as all the other boys, but he was always deep in thought."

R' Chaim Weiss, another childhood friend, describes how the young Eliezer used to pray in the Vizhnitz *shul* of Haifa: "The Rav used to stand on the left side of the *bimah* at *shul*, and when he bowed he used to bend down until the floor, with his eyes fixed only on his *siddur*. All the local kids, including me, would come and look at him, because it was such a strange sight to see someone so engrossed in their praying in the Haifa of those days. We all wanted to come and see it."

R' Chaim explains that the young Eliezer always wanted more than the superficial, materialistic endeavors his peers were pursuing. "Everyone that saw him saw how serious he was. He was always looking for something deeper. Everyone knew, even from those early days, that Rav Berland was someone who was always working on himself, and who wanted to improve himself and to become better. So naturally he came to *daven* in Vizhnitz which was the most powerful *minyan* in Haifa at that time, but eventually he went on and we didn't see him anymore. It was clear to everyone who knew him that this boy was never satisfied with a basic connection to *Hashem*, and that he was always searching for deeper and more meaningful ways to connect to his Creator. I'm sure that this is the character trait that brought him to where he is today."

TALKING TO *HASHEM*

R' Chaim recounts how the Rav used to go for long walks and talk to *Hashem* on the mountains around his home in Haifa, long before he'd even heard about the Breslov practice of *hisbodedus*, the practice of talking to God in one's own words.

"He used to go and seclude himself in the mountains outside of Ramat Vizhnitz, and sometimes he'd encounter a secular youth group doing activities in the same area," recalls R' Chaim. "Even then, Rav Berland used to do his *hisbodedus* out loud, and it was audible enough for others to hear him. Once, some of the members of this secular youth group came over to tell him that he was really bothering them with all his praying, and that he should go away. So, the Rav climbed even higher to the top of the mountain, so that he could carry on talking to *Hashem* without upsetting anyone else. Most people would be afraid to walk around in such secluded places by themselves, especially at that time—but the Rav did all of this when he was just 16 years old!"

SEARCHING FOR THE TRUTH

Young Eliezer was preoccupied with searching for truth. At 16 years old, he was taught Darwin's theory that human beings are descended from monkeys--an heretical deception that's still being taught today. As was his practice, the teenager thought about the idea a great deal, and prayed for God to give him clarity, until he realized that the theory of evolution is completely impossible.

Eliezer reasoned that if evolution has actually occurred in the past, there should still be beings who were 'half man, half monkey' walking around, because natural processes of development are cyclical. A fetus 'evolves' into an adult, and a seed 'evolves' into a plant. If humans truly came from monkeys, there should be evidence of this cycle of evolution all around - and clearly, there wasn't.

Around the same time, the 16-year-old Eliezer spent months pleading with God to show him which religious tradition was the true one. During one of his midnight *hisbodedus* sessions on Shiloach Street in Haifa, Rav Berland described how the heavens opened, and he experienced some sort of Divine revelation that the Torah--and only the Torah--was the truth.

From that point on, he made sure that his parents' home was run according to the strictest halachic standards[6].

The teenage Eliezer also began to make greater efforts to guard his eyes on the street, long before he was formally introduced to the concept. One of his cousins, Liki Miller, used to tell her friends: "I have a cousin--Eliezer Berland—who is so religious that when he goes out to the street he takes off his glasses, even though he has such a high prescription that he often walks into poles! And all this, just so he shouldn't look at women.[7] [8]"

Once, someone asked him: "What's wrong with women?!" Rav Berland replied: "There is nothing wrong with women, just as there is nothing wrong with milk and meat, or wool and linen. You just can't mix those things together."

THE "COMPOSER"

The well-known artist from Chevron, Baruch Nachshon, has been a good friend of Rav Berland for almost 65 years. The two met in the Yavneh School in Haifa when Rav Berland was 16, and Baruch was 14.

"The Rav was in the same class as my older brother, and he told me one day that he had a kid in class with him who was a real 'composer' type", he says. This piqued Baruch's interest, and he decided that he wanted to meet this unusual kid who'd been nicknamed "the composer".

"I didn't really know how to approach the Rav and break the ice, so in the end I just went over and slapped him," and that's how they got to be friends.

"The Rav's nickname was a reflection of the fact that even then, his classmates could tell that there was something very lofty about his soul," explains Baruch. "He was a person who was looking for God, even before anyone else was really talking about such things. When someone is on a higher level, especially in school, their classmates don't always know how to express these things, so they give them nicknames like 'the composer.'

"We were together in school for a little while, and then the Rav went to learn in the yeshivah at Kfar Chassidim. I went to see him there during Chanukah, and we lit our Chanukah candles together. Even today, many decades later, I can still remember the light, warmth, and happiness that I saw reflected on his face."

The two young men kept up a correspondence for many years. "I could tell that he didn't have a lot of money at that time, because he'd use a pencil to write to me instead of a pen, as was standard in those times. He'd sign the bottom of his notes 'Eliezer,' and all his letters were telling me to strengthen my *emunah*, and to keep on learning."

The two were such good friends that they also occasionally went on trips together. "One time, we went on a trip up north to the Galilee," recalls Baruch. "We climbed up a whole load of mountains, and the whole time we were just talking Torah. The Rav then took me to the forlorn towns on the Lebanese border; he spoke to the people there and strengthened their spirits. It was an unbelievable experience for me. I remember it until this day."

THE YESHIVAH IN KFAR CHASSIDIM

Between the ages of 17 to 21, the teenage Eliezer spent three and half years at the Lithuanian yeshivah Knesses Chizkiyahu located in Kfar Chassidim, a small pastoral community near the city of Haifa. It was there that Eliezer first met the renowned Torah leader Rav Eliyahu Lopian, *zt"l*, who he became very close to.

Knesses Chizkiyahu Yeshivah was founded by Rav Noach Shimonowitz, one of the foremost students of Rabbi Boruch Ber Leibowitz, *Rosh* Yeshivah of the Kaminetz Yeshivah in Belarus. Rav Shimonowitz was a native of Poland and a Holocaust survivor, and upon arriving in Israel he decided he wanted to open a yeshivah in the fledgling State of Israel, in order to try and regain some of what had been lost from the pre-war Torah world.

At that time the Chazon Ish was living in Bnei Brak, so Rav Shimonowitz went to visit him to get a blessing for his new endeavor and to ask the Torah sage where he should open the new yeshivah. The Chazon Ish advised him to open the yeshivah in the north of the country, which at that time didn't have any Torah institutions at all.

When Knesses Chizkiyahu moved from the city of Zichron Yaakov to a large campus at Kfar Chassidim at the end of April 1955, it was the crowning moment of Rav Shimonowitz's life. Sadly, the *Rosh* Yeshivah only had a brief time to enjoy the fruits of his labor. Just five days later, Rav Shimonowitz suffered a massive stroke and passed away.

"I never met him," Rav Berland recalled. "He passed away on the 5th of Iyar [1955], and I was still in the Bnei Akiva school in Kfar HaRoeh at the time. It was Israel's Independence Day [Yom Ha'atzmaut] and everyone went to get wild and drunk. But I just couldn't, so I stayed inside and learned while everyone else was celebrating outside. So, there I was, in the *shiur* room of the Kfar HaRoeh yeshivah when the news arrived that Rav Noach Shimonowitz had passed away. I started crying like a little child when I heard, even though I didn't even know him. To this day, I don't know why I cried...Every time I remember it, I start to cry. Everyone else went out to party and I stayed to learn and to cry about Rav Noach's passing.[4]"

"IF YOU DON'T STOP YOUR BRAIN WILL POP"

Eliezer Berland joined Knesses Chizkiyahu a month after it opened in Kfar Chassidim, in May 1955. After Rav Shimonowitz passed away, the yeshivah's *Mashgiach*, Rabbi Eliyahu Lopian, stepped into the gaping void and asked Rav Shimonowitz's brother-in-law and co-founder, Rabbi Raphael Eliyahu Eliezer Mishkovsky, to become the new *Rosh* Yeshivah.

Even at this relatively early stage, the other students at Knesses Chizkiyahu recalled that Rav Berland would learn for 20 hours a day. Fifteen years later, Rav Feival Lebel, one of the Breslov elders, travelled from Mea Shearim to Rav Eliyahu Lopian at Kfar Chassidim, to learn a little more about Rav Berland's roots. Rav Lebel asked him if he remembered a boy called Eliezer Berland. Reb Elyah answered excitedly: "R' Lazer! How can I forget him?! I myself can testify that he learned 20 hours every single day! We've never had a *bachur* at the yeshivah who learned 20 hours each day, like Reb Lazer!⁹"

Indeed, the Rav's industrious approach to learning Torah started to worry the yeshivah staff a little; they were concerned that their gifted student would burn out if he didn't find a way to properly contain and channel his love of learning. One day, Rav Mishkovsky called him over and told him that he needed to take things a little easier.

"Rav Mishkovsky told me I had to take a break from my learning and go out to the fields a bit, to get some fresh air," says Rav Berland. "Back then, I didn't even know that there was any such thing as Breslov *Chassidus*. I'd never heard about the formal practice of *hisbodedus*. I came from other places. But my *Rosh* Yeshivah told me to go out to the fields every day for two hours.ᴵᴵᴵ 'If you don't do that,' he told me, 'either your head will explode or a vein will pop⁴.'"

THE THREE-HOUR WALK TO YESHIVAH

Dutifully, the young Eliezer followed his *Rosh* Yeshivah's instructions—and rediscovered the practice of talking to *Hashem* every day in his own language. Rav Berland found the experience of communicating with God in the fields surrounding Kfar Chassidim so pleasant and uplifting that he decided that from that point on, he was going to walk the whole way from his home in Haifa to the yeshivah every single day, while talking to God—nearly a three-hour walk each way!

This arrangement suited the young Eliezer Berland very well: While he was walking through the fields and orchards between Haifa and Kfar Chassidim, he could happily talk his heart out to *Hashem* for hours. At the same time, he could avoid the

---

ᴵᴵᴵ   Rav Mishkovsky didn't necessarily intend for Rav Berland to be spending this time immersed in personal prayer, but the Rav saw it as an opportunity to return to the earlier practice of talking to God that he'd begun in Haifa.

public buses and the challenge of dealing with the immodestly dressed women he'd otherwise encounter.

Apart from these daily "personal prayer" breaks, Rav Berland's days were filled with learning Torah and he quickly became known among his classmates as a Torah genius and *masmid*. During his three-and-a-half-year stay at Knesses Chizkiyahu, the Rav also become very close to the yeshivah's *Mashgiach*, Rav Eliyahu Lopian, who was affectionately known to his students as "Reb Elya".

RAV ELIYAHU LOPIAN

Rav Lopian had joined the yeshivah in 1952, while it was still in Zichron Yaakov, and was considered one of the giants of the contemporary *mussar* movement. He had a huge impact on the nascent yeshivah and the many hundreds of students who passed through its doors.

In his youth, Rav Lopian had learned at many of the great yeshivos of prewar Europe, including the Lomza Yeshivah and the Kelm Talmud Torah of Rabbi Simcha Zissel Ziv. Rav Lopian moved to England in 1928 to head the Etz Chaim Yeshivah in London's East End. Twenty-two years later, in 1950, he fulfilled his lifelong dream of moving to Israel.

Rav Lopian was already 74 years old when he made *aliyah*. Initially he rebuffed all requests to teach *mussar* in a yeshivah setting, preferring to teach privately. But, after a meeting with the Chazon Ish in Bnei Brak, he decided to take up an offer from Knesses Chizkiyahu to become the yeshivah's *Mashgiach Ruchani* at the advanced age of 76.

From the moment he arrived on the scene, he became a magnet for young students. He took a great deal of interest in them, including one new arrival named Eliezer Berland. "He was a very humble, modest person, and I become very close to him", recalls the Rav. "I'll never forget how he used to *daven*, with such power and with such tears—he'd literally be crying into his *siddur*!"

Reb Elyah was responsible for teaching the yeshivah students *mussar* and would give a daily lecture on the topic to his students. During the class, the young Eliezer Berland would sit on the first bench at the front of the room, to be as near to his teacher as possible. "When Reb Elya used to learn *Shaarei Teshuva*, he'd start to cry very loudly, and then I would start to cry with him," he recalls. "The whole yeshivah would tremble from his *mussar* discourses."

For his part, Rav Lopian frequently asked his young student to stand up and address the yeshivah. Even then, the young Berland would always begin his discourses with the words: "We are living in the last generation of exile, and the first generation of the redemption![10]"

"THE ANGEL OF DEATH IS WAITING FOR YOU!"

Rav Berland once reminisced: "Rabbi Eliyahu [Lopian] used to give very rousing lectures and held his students to very high standards. Some of the other students didn't really understand what he was trying to do, and they used to make fun of it. But I sat there in his lectures gulping down every word he said and thirsting for more.

"I got such a big dose of *yiras Shamayim* [from Rav Lopian] that if I hadn't come closer to Breslov afterwards and learned the Torah of strengthening and encouraging oneself, I don't think I could have lasted the distance because of all the *yirah* I had.

"Rav Lopian once told us: 'When you step out through the doors of the *beis medrash*, know that the Angel of Death is waiting for you at the entrance, waiting to trip you up! The Angel of Death is on the streets, to burn up everything you just learned over the last 10, 12 or even 18 hours! Know that the Angel of Death is to be found on the streets, and beware of him!'

"I had the privilege of learning with Rav Eliyahu Lopian for three and half years," continues the Rav. "He instituted a kind of 'rule' that we shouldn't go out on the streets. At the end of the day, we'd all come from regular schools, but he managed to raise us up. He simply wouldn't let us go out on the streets without a thousand warnings, and a thousand rules.

"Rav Lopian once yelled at his students in Kfar Chassidim, 'If you're not learning Torah, I know what your head is filled with! If the pit is empty of water, it's full of scorpions and snakes![IV]'

"Rav Elya once told me, "*Chazal* say that a person who repeats something in the name of the originator brings *geulah* to the world. The 'originator' is HaKadosh Baruch Hu. A person has to know that everything belongs to *Hashem*: our wisdom, our brains, our strength, everything. Someone who recognizes that, and who lives with that constantly, brings about a redemption for himself and for the world."

IV   From Rashi in Bereishis 37:23

MESIRUS NEFESH **FOR TORAH**

While at Kfar Chassidim, Rav Eliezer Berland quickly began to develop a reputation for being unusually committed to learning Torah. Rav Avraham Coch zt" l, a contemporary of Rav Berland's at Kfar Chassidim, recalled:

"When I was at the yeshivah at Kfar Chassidim we didn't have air conditioners, and we also didn't even have any fans. On *Tisha B'Av*, it was really hot, and the *beis medrash* was in a shack, which was even hotter than the main building. After noon on the fast of *Tisha B'Av*, who had the strength to go and learn in heat like that?

"But Reb Lazer sat there in the *beis medrash* and learned, as though he was at the beginning of the *zman*. He sat there on the floor and learned diligently [of course, only things which are allowed to be learned on *Tisha B'Av*][11]."

THE IMPORTANCE OF AVOIDING *BITUL TORAH*

Rav Dov Yaffe was the *Mashgiach*[V] at Kfar Chassidim when Rav Berland was there. He once told Rav Yosef Chaim Assulin, the *Mo"tz* of Rav Nissim Karelitz's *beis din*, that on Fridays Rav Berland would go visit his parents in Haifa. As the *Mashgiach*, he spoke to the Rav about it, and told him not to make a habit out of it, as it involved a lot of *bitul Torah*.

The Rav replied, "It makes no difference if I'm in the *beis medrash* or learning while traveling, so there's no danger at all of me wasting the time I could be learning Torah."

Rav Assulin says, "Rav Dov Yaffe said to me in amazement, 'Who could say something like that about himself?' Nevertheless, after a couple of months the Rav stopped his visits home on Fridays. Rav Dov went to ask him, 'If you said there's no danger of *bitul Torah* from making the trips, then why aren't you fulfilling the *mitzvah* of honoring your parents?'

"Reb Lazer responded, 'In terms of the level I'm learning Torah at now, it would be *bitul Torah*.' Rav Dov was amazed by the words of this teenager, and they made a very big impression on him."

V   When Rav Lopian passed away, Rav Yaffe was made the Menahel Ruchani in his place, a post he continued to hold until his passing in 5778.

LEARNING THE *MISHNAH BERURAH* 50 TIMES IN A ROW

Rav Yehoshua Dov Rubinstein recounts: "I met someone who had learned in Kfar Chassidim, so I asked him if he knew of Rav Eliezer Berland, and he told me, 'Sure, I know him! I learned with him. But to tell you the truth, we thought he was an odd boy. He didn't talk to people so much, and he never came on the trips with us, or talked about the news and politics. He just sat in front of his *sefarim* day and night — he was just learning the whole day and the whole night.'"

Rav Rubinstein continues, "This man told me that when Rav Berland was in Kfar Chassidim, he went through the entire *Mishnah Berurah* 50 times."

"HE DIDN'T EVEN KNOW THERE WAS A WAR GOING ON"

Another contemporary of the Rav's at Kfar Chassidim, Rav Yehuda Melamed, recalled that while all of Israel continued to be obsessed with politics and military campaigns, all the Rav was interested in was learning Torah.

"When we were *bachurim* at the yeshivah in Kfar Chassidim during the Sinai War of 1956, he had no idea that a war was going on, he was so engrossed in his studies," he says. "All the other students used to go off to listen to the news by the neighbors who lived next to the yeshivah, but he didn't even know there was a war going on!"

Rav Melamed knew the Rav from their school days in Haifa. He recalls: "Another time, we went on a school outing in the Galilee, and we picked fruit from one of the fields to eat [without asking permission first]. A long time afterwards, when the Rav had already moved away from the yeshivah at Kfar Chassidim, he went back to the area to check where we'd been on that outing so that he could go and pay some money for the fruit that we'd eaten."

ACTS OF KINDNESS

Even though the Rav's commitment to learning Torah was so unusual, what made him stand out from the crowd even more at Kfar Chassidim was the kindness and consideration he regularly showed to his fellow Jew. The only thing that was guaranteed to get the Rav to put his holy books down was the chance to help one of the other students.

One of his fellow students recalls: "I was a younger *bachur* than the Rav, and I came to the yeshivah at a later time than everyone else. I arrived at the yeshivah at Kfar

Chassidim on a Friday, and the place was empty. There was just one student there, who was learning *Gemara* with enthusiasm and zest: Eliezer Berland.

"When he saw me, he immediately got up and welcomed me — a new student — and went to get me a full plate of food. Even today, I can't forget the incredibly warm welcome he gave me."

Another of the Rav's former classmates, Rav Aharon Golbanzich, *zt"l*, said that when he learned in Kfar Chassidim with the Rav, it was known in the yeshivah that, if one of the students was sick, he'd go to Reb Lazer and ask him to pray for him. "Reb Lazer would shut himself into his room with a *sefer Tehillim* and complete the entire book of *Tehillim*," he said. "He'd come out with his eyes red from crying, and the student would get well."

Rav Golobanchich continued, "On Fridays, the Rav would receive a cake from home. The usual way of the world is that you give a slice to the others, then keep the rest for yourself. But by Reb Lazer, it was the opposite: He took a slice for himself, then distributed the rest of his cake to everyone else."[VI]

AVOIDING THE ARMY

Despite the Rav's reputation for being a student with good *middos*, fear of Heaven, and an unparalleled thirst for Torah learning, he continued to be regarded as a difficult student by some of the teachers and even by some of his classmates.

The Rav said in later years that he'd spent many long hours praying in the fields around Kfar Chassidim to be able to avoid going to the army—something which was extremely controversial, even at that time.

All the young men of army age who were learning in the yeshiva were still required to go the enlisting office to request a formal deferment. The Rav felt that spending long hours at the enlisting office was *bitul Torah*, so he ignored the letters he was being sent by the army. This caused some controversy with a few of the Rav's peers, who were concerned that flouting the army's formal deferment process could lead to the army making trouble for them, and the yeshivah.

Rav Golobanchich said, "We went to the *Gaon* Rav Eliyahu Mishkovsky, *zt"l*, who was then the *Rosh* Yeshivah, and a student of the Rav Shimon Shkop, *zt"l*, and told

---

VI   As told to Rav Yosef Chaim Assulin, the Mo"tz of the beis din of Rav Nissim Karelitz.

them that there was a student in the yeshivah who didn't want to follow the army's rules, and that he was potentially causing the other students problems as a result.[VII]

"Rav Eliyahu asked us who it was, and we told him, 'Lazer Berland.' Then he told us, 'Lazer is something else. Lazer is a *baal emunah*, and I don't interfere with *baalei emunah.*'"

As has always been his way, the Rav went to great pains to try to smooth things over with his detractors and opponents, even at that relatively young age.

Rav Yehuda Melamed recalled: "There was another student at Kfar Chassidim who was tremendously jealous of the Rav and tried to prevent him from doing all sorts of things. Once, the Rav got a cake from home, and he gave the whole thing to this student."

HOW THE RAV NEARLY GOT KICKED OUT OF YESHIVAH

On another occasion, the Rav's zeal as a young man for maintaining the highest *halachic* standards almost got him kicked out of the yeshivah. Rav Nissan Shuv recalls that one time, Kfar Chassidim received a new bread machine for their kitchen.

"Rav Berland decided that it needed to be *toiveled* in the *mikvah*. So, in the middle of the night, he took a screwdriver and disassembled it piece by piece (it was a large machine), and snuck out the window to take the pieces to the *mikvah*. Then he had to reassemble it, so it took him a long time.

"When we came down in the morning, he was caught red-handed, and the yeshivah administrators wanted to punish him—even though the machine still worked perfectly afterwards. They even discussed throwing him out of the yeshivah, except the Chazon Ish had spoken very strongly about not throwing people out of yeshivah at that time."

Rav Yehoshua Dov Rubinstein continues the tale: "They discussed what to do with him, because they'd also had other problems with Rav Berland, because he wouldn't learn the *sefarim* the other boys were learning. He'd learn whatever *sefarim* he wanted to learn, and wasn't following the yeshivah's curriculum.

VII   If the Israeli government had decided to make an example out of Rav Berland, they could have come down hard on Yeshivas Knesses Chizkiyahu, including reducing the yeshivah's funding and / or giving them a fine.

"'They realized it was a big question, and they decided they needed to go and ask the yeshivah's *Mashgiach*, Rav Elya Lopian, what to do. Rav Lopian was a huge *talmid chacham*, and he lived on top of the yeshivah. They didn't bother him with all their questions, but this was a big problem, and they didn't know what to do, so they decided they had to ask him. When they told him what had happened, and that they were considering kicking the Rav out of yeshivah, he replied, 'Lazer Berland?! Don't dare touch him! This is a boy who is a *baki* in the entire *Shas*!'"

THE HOLIEST BOY IN YESHIVAH

Rabbi Yaakov Moshe Shpitzer was one of Rav Berland's contemporaries at Knesses Chizkiyahu, and has known the Rav for more than 60 years. He recalls:

"Rav Berland was regarded as the holiest *bachur* in the yeshivah. It's impossible to describe the persistence and determination he showed even then with regard to his learning. His conduct was held up as an example to the rest of the yeshivah."

Rav Shpitzer continues: "People used to talk about the steely determination he showed in his *avodas Hashem*. He would stand on his feet for hours, learning out loud, and he just used to study and study. He also used to pray out loud, too, with complete *mesirus nefesh*.

"The other *bachurim* in the yeshivah used to treat themselves on Fridays before Shabbos by going to the beach. I once asked Rav Berland why he never used to join us, and he replied, 'Don't talk to me about all that stuff.'

"I never once saw him teasing someone else, or heard him speak badly about another person. I never once saw him sitting with the other boys outside the yeshivah after our studies and spending his time chit-chatting. I only saw Rav Berland engaged in holy matters and Torah learning. He really threw himself into his learning with an enormous amount of energy."

"ONE DAY, YOU'LL BECOME A BIG *ROSH* YESHIVAH!"

Toward the end of Rav Berland's time in Kfar Chassidim, he was talking with Rav Elya when the *Mashgiach* suddenly told him, "One day, you'll become a big *Rosh Yeshivah*!" But it would still take a few more years—and some huge changes in the Rav's spiritual direction—before Rav Lopian's stunning prediction would come true.

BNEI BRAK: PONEVEZH, VOLOZHIN, AND THE STEIPLER GAON

At the age of 21, two momentous things occurred in Rav Berland's life: He entered the Ponevezh Yeshivah in Bnei Brak, and he met and married his wife, Tehillah Shaki. The new Rebbetzin Berland was the daughter of Rabbi Shalom Avraham Shaki, a Yemenite immigrant and member of the National Religious Party. Shaki had made *aliyah* to what was then called "Palestine" in 1914, just as World War I—which redrew the whole map of the Middle East—began.

Rav Shaki was a deeply religious man, and worked as the headmaster of various religious schools before entering politics. The Rav once explained that his father-in-law, Rabbi Shalom Avraham, used to fill up all his spare time with reciting *Tehillim*, which is how his daughter had gotten her name.

When Tehillah was still a young child her father used to tell her, with more than a hint of prophecy, "You are going to marry someone who's going to spend a lot of time praying in nature, on the mountains and hills, and who's always going to be singing to Hashem and thanking Him. And you're going to have to go and find him in those mountains and hills."

A few years later, that's exactly what happened. The couple happened to meet each other at one of the holiest mountains in Israel, at Meron, at the grave of Rabbi Shimon Bar Yochai.

Rav Nachman Horowitz, the grandson of Rav Shmuel Horowitz, *zt"l*, describes the young couple's fateful first encounter: "Rav Berland had come to Meron to pray, and while he was there he happened to start reciting the *birkas hamazon* blessing out loud, with a lot of *kavanah*. And it took him a long time to finish it... At that moment the Rebbetzin arrived at Meron with a *kvittel* for Rebbe Shimon asking for help to find a good *shidduch*. When she heard the Rav reciting the grace after meals she immediately said, 'That's my future husband!'"

The people accompanying the Rebbetzin tried to dissuade her. "They told her that the young man she'd heard praying was only doing that sort of thing there, at Meron. They told her that after the wedding he'd probably just recite the grace after meals for a minute and half. But the Rebbetzin understood that this wasn't the case, and that's how the *shidduch* of the Rav came about," explains Rav Horowitz.

When she returned home from Meron, the Rebbetzin found out who that young man was, and began the formal *shidduch* process.

THE RAV WANTS TO KEEP HIS EYES SHUT

As with all matters of holiness, Rav Berland was very concerned about conducting himself in the correct way when it came to meeting his *shidduch*. Rav Horowitz takes up the tale:

"The Rav's son-in-law once told me that he'd seen in the Rav's writings to the Steipler that before he went out on the *shidduch* with his potential wife, he'd asked the Steipler if he could keep his eyes closed during the meeting—even though he was still a single man! The Steipler responded with his customary sharpness. He told the Rav, 'If you're going to keep your eyes closed for the rest of your life, then it's also permitted for you to close your eyes during that meeting.'"

But the Rav's questions regarding the right way of going on *shidduchim* and getting married didn't end there.

"The Rav once told us before his marriage, he'd been a *talmid* of Rav Elazar Menachem Mann Shach," continues Rav Horowitz. "The Rav described how when he got engaged, he asked Rav Shach what to do, because he really wanted to recite the *Shemoneh Esrei* prayers for a very long time, especially on the day of his wedding. But at the same time, people would be waiting for the *chuppah* to begin, so what should he do?

"Rav Shach told him that on the day of his wedding he was a king, and that he could do what he wanted. The Rav took Rav Shach's answer to heart and told us, 'From then on, I was the student of Rav Shach in these matters.'"

TALES FROM PONEVEZH

After his engagement but before he was actually married, the Rav started learning at the *kollel* of the Ponevezh Yeshivah in Bnei Brak, home to some of the biggest Torah figures of that era, including Rabbi Ben Zion Bamberger, Rabbi Yechezkel Levenstein and Rabbi Chaim Friedlander. "I learned *b'chavrusa* with Rav Chaim, and I also slept in his house," the Rav recalls. On another occasion, Rav Berland remarked, "I drew from the wellsprings of Rav Yechezkel's fear of Heaven for five years."

He continued to learn Torah with his customary diligence in the Ponevezh Yeshivah, spending every hour of the day bent over the holy books. One of the Rabbonim of Haifa, Rav Shmuel Heller, recalled that one Purim, some of the Rabbis at the Ponevezh Yeshivah came over to Rav Berland and told him that it was Purim, and he needed to go outside with the other students and dance a little, in honor of the holiday. The Rav told them that he couldn't bring himself to leave his *Gemara*, even when they told him that they'd pour water all over him if he didn't get up and dance. Even then, he still couldn't close it.

"WE NEED TO BE LISTENING TO HIM"

After his wedding, Rav Berland continued to mentor some of the younger students. At that time, it was customary at the Ponevezh Yeshivah that *chassanim* would be invited to a special *"mussar conversation"* with the Ponovezh *Mashgiach*, Rav Yechezkel Levenstein, *zt"l*. On one occasion, the Rav accompanied Rav Shlomo Zalman Grossman,[VIII] who'd just become engaged, to Rav Levenstein's room for the "chat", and entered with him.

For a while, Rav Levenstein didn't say anything to either of the two young men. Finally, Rav Grossman spoke up and said, "I'm due to get married", but still, Rav Levenstein stayed silent. After a few more minutes, the younger man spoke up again and asked, "Why is the Rav not saying anything?"

Rav Levenstein looked at him for a moment before replying, "You and I, we both need to be listening to him," then pointed to Rav Berland.

Rav Levenstein was a giant in Torah and many of his conversations and lectures had already been published in a number of books. He was also extremely careful not to encourage even a hint of arrogance among his students. Once, when a student brought him a cup of tea, he remarked to him as he was leaving, "Be very careful that you don't start to get arrogant because you just brought the *Mashgiach* a cup of tea!"

Rav Grossman later commented that some of the people who heard this story contacted him to find out whether it was really true. "I told them that it was!" he said. "And not only that, I told them that I could write at least three books' worth of stories about Rav Berland, from his days at the Ponevezh Yeshivah."

VIII   Currently the Rav of the Israeli city of Elad.

VOLOZHIN AND THE STEIPLER GAON

After his wedding, the Rav moved from the Ponovezh Yeshivah to the Volozhin *kollel*, which was under the supervision of one of the leading *tzaddikim* of that generation, Rav Yaakov Yisrael Kanievsky, otherwise known as the Steipler Gaon.

The Steipler Gaon was a world-class scholar, the head of two yeshivos in Bnei Brak, and author of many highly-acclaimed Torah works, including his *sefer Kehillas Yaakov*, an epic 10 volume commentary on the Talmud. His Torah discourses were so highly acclaimed that the Chazon Ish decided to make a *shidduch* between the Steipler and his sister Miriam, even though he'd never actually met him, solely on the basis of that first *sefer*.

Rabbi Kanievsky had been born in the Ukraine, but later moved to Poland before making *aliyah* to Israel in 1934, where he settled close to his brother-in-law, the Chazon Ish, in Bnei Brak.

Even before he arrived in Bnei Brak, Rav Berland had been in regular correspondence with Rav Kanievsky as a young student in Kfar Chassidim, when he used to write to the *Gadol* to ask him many of his halachic questions. "I used to ask him things about whether it was more important to cut off the *tchup*[IX] or to grow a beard. I had a huge *tchup*; no one could compete with it. The Steipler replied that I should first cut off the *tchup*, and then grow a beard after my wedding. We exchanged a lot of questions and answers in writing. But it all got lost."

10,000 *TESHUVOS*

Over the course of their relationship Rav Berland asked the Steipler thousands of questions about the correct way of following even the smallest letter of the law when it came to *halachah*, and many of these questions were written down. Some of these *halachic* rulings contained some very novel ideas from the Steipler, and the correspondence was kept in a number of special binders in the Berland home for many years, until they were somehow misplaced a few years ago.

Aside from the more basic and intricate questions on *halachah*, Rav Berland also corresponded with the Steipler on many of the more difficult passages contained in the Talmud.

IX   A *tchup* is slightly longer hair at the bangs.

One time, the Rav commented, "It's such a shame that I didn't preserve all the Torah correspondence that I shared with the Steipler on the *sugyos* of *Shas*. If I'd have kept everything, today we'd have today a few more volumes of the Steipler's Torah insights."

Another time, he said, "I wrote down 10,000 *halachic teshuvos* that I received from the Steipler. Most of them got lost, but a small part of them now reside with some of the Steipler's grandchildren."

"CONTINUE TO PRAY WITH ENTHUSIASM"

One of the questions Rav Berland asked the Steipler was what he should do about the fact that he was praying with such enthusiasm and fervor, when he knew that he was making a spectacle of himself in the Lederman shul and drawing unwanted attention to himself, as a result. The Steipler told him not to pay any attention to the matter and to continue to pray with his heartfelt enthusiasm. Sooner or later people would get used to it, and then they'd stop paying any attention to him.

After the Rav moved over to the Volozhin Yeshivah, the relationship that had begun as a written correspondence deepened into a very strong connection between the two men. The 60-year-old Steipler surprised many of the expert, elderly Torah scholars of Bnei Brak by taking the young 20-something *avreich* from Haifa as his regular learning partner.

LEARNING *B'CHAVRUSA* WITH THE STEIPLER

For around four years, Rav Berland learned *b'chavrusa* with the Steipler. "I was completely attached to him," recalls Rav Berland.

When they learned together, they studied all the most difficult sections of the *Gemara*. They used to learn every day during the hours of the midday break, from 1 p.m. to around 3 p.m., and would sit and learn *sugyos* of *Shas*, *Choshen Mishpat* and *halachah*. The duo's meth-

The Steipler's courtyard in Bnei Brak, as it appears today.

od of learning was to start learning from the beginning of the *sugya* and then continue all the way through to the *poskim*.

The Steipler was an extremely humble individual and lived as simply as possible, despite his awesome stature as the *Gadol Hador*. Once, when the Steipler and Rav Berland were learning the *sugya* of the *Shehechiyanu* blessing at the Steipler's home, they were seen going down to the building's courtyard together, where some fruit trees that the Steipler's wife had planted were growing.

There was a guava tree and some pomegranate trees there, and the Steipler—the spiritual leader of the generation — picked a guava fruit so that he and Rav Berland could make the *Shehechiyanu* blessing together. The tree was full of dust, and the Steipler's clothes got filthy from touching it.

WHAT DOES THE STEIPLER SEE IN RAV BERLAND?

At that time, many of the people in Bnei Brak were curious as to why one of the undisputed Torah leaders of the generation had taken such a big interest in the young *avreich* from Haifa. As word spread about the way the Steipler would go out of his way to honor his young learning partner, their curiosity grew even stronger.

The Steipler was not known for freely honoring his students and colleagues, out of concern that it could go to their heads and cause them to fall into the terrible sin of pride. Yet, he would stand up in honor of Rav Berland when Rav Berland came into the room. In another example of the great esteem in which the Steipler held the young Rav Berland, he once described him in a letter written to Rabbi Aaron Berlin[X] as *"HaRav HaGaon Rav Eliezer Berland, shlita"*—even though he was still a young *avreich*.

In those days, the title *"Gaon"* was reserved for very few people, and was very rarely bequeathed on others, particularly not by the *Gadol Hador*. Even other famous Torah sages of his generation weren't given the title *"Gaon"* by the Steipler.

In another letter[XI] the Steipler referred to Rav Berland as: *""The precious young avreich, genius in Torah and fear of heaven, our master and teacher Rav Eliezer Berland, shlit'a"*.

X   Now the Rav of a flourishing Breslov community in Flatbush, NY.
XI   This letter was printed in the book Avnei HaMenora.

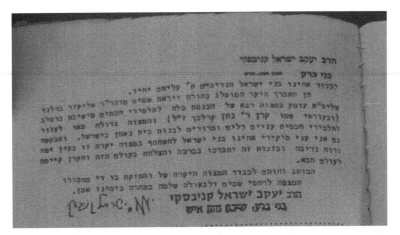

הרב יעקב ישראל קניבסקי

בני ברק

לכבוד אחינו בני ישראל הנדיבים ח'' עליהם יחיו.
הן האברך היקר המופלג בתורה ויראת שמים מוהר''ר אליעזר ברלנד
(ונקראיר) שמו קרן ר' נתן קרלבך ז'ל) והמצוה הכמים חשובים פיסים ברסלב
לתלמידי חכמים עזרים דלים ומרודים לבנות בית נאמן בישראל, מאד לעורר
גם אני בני מיקירי אחינו בני ישראל להשתתף במצוה יקרה זו בעין יפה
ורוח נדיבה ובזכות זה יתברכו בברכת והצלחה בעולם הזה והזן קיימת
לעולם הבא.

הכותב וחותם לכבוד המצוה היקרה של ותמיכה בו די מסורו
המצפה לרחמי שליח דלנצולה שלמה במהרה בימינו אמן.

הרב יעקב ישראל קניבסקי

בני נבון שבע מם איש

""The precious young avreich, genius in Torah and fear of heaven, our master and teacher Rav Eliezer Berland, shlit'a"

As news spread of the special treatment the Steipler was according the young *avreich*, at least one other young man in Bnei Brak, Rav Dovid Chaim Stern, plucked up the courage to ask the Steipler what he saw in Rav Berland.

"He was a young man while the Steipler was the *Gadol Hador* and much older than him. They were study partners, learning many hours together each day, so I was interested in finding out what he had to say about him", explains Rav Stern. "The Steipler told me, 'You should know, he is an expert in the entire Torah, a holy man and a *tzaddik*!' That was the testimony from the mouth of the *Gadol Hador*. And it's clear as day that the Steipler had true *ruach hakodesh*. There is no one who argues about this."

At this time, Rabbi Moshe Cohen, the *gabbai* of the Lederman shul, was also learning at the Volozhin Yeshivah in Bnei Brak. He once described to his grandson that, when he used to go and visit the Steipler, he noticed a big notebook on his desk. He asked the Steipler about it, and he was told that the young Rabbi Berland would write his halachic questions in the notebook, and the Steipler would then write back his response, and then the other people in the yeshivah would come to look at the questions and the answers, so that they could also learn from the exchange.

(The Steipler was extremely hard of hearing, as a result of a bout of typhus in his childhood, which meant that typically his visitors would write down their questions for him to read in advance, before coming to see him for advice. When it came to Rav Berland's queries, the Steipler would keep a copy of both the questions and the answers by his desk in order for others to be able to learn from their exchange.)

Once, R' Moshe Cohen went in to see the Steipler just after Rav Berland had been in his room, and the Steipler told him in Yiddish, "Rav Berland has a lot of *yiras Shamayim*."

THE STEIPLER STOOD UP FOR RAV BERLAND

Rav Yehoshua Dov Rubinstein has known the Rav for more than 50 years, from the time they learned together in the Breslov Yeshivah in Bnei Brak. He begins: "It was known that Rav Berland learned *b'chavrusa* with the Steipler, and when I got engaged, Rav Berland came over to me and told me, 'Since your father is a prominent member of the Breslov community, we need to help you raise funds to marry you off properly.'

"The Rav then took me to a number of places in Bnei Brak, and one of the addresses he took me to was the Steipler. To this day, I'm grateful to him for getting me in to see the Steipler for that one single time in my life that I merited to see him. And I was astonished to see the amazing love and respect the Steipler had for him. Here you had the elderly *Gadol Hador*, the Steipler, but he gave tremendous respect to the young *avreich*, Rav Berland.

"The Steipler stood up in respect of Rav Berland, which amazed me. Then, I remember exactly the words the Steipler said to him, in Yiddish. He said, 'Reb Lazer, I just got a new set of *Mishnayos*, and I want to give you my old set, as a present.' The Steipler wouldn't say that to just anyone!"

IT'S FORBIDDEN TO ASK RAV BERLAND FOR MONEY

Before long, Rav Berland developed a reputation in Bnei Brak as the place to go for anyone who needed financial help, and many, many people showed up at his door asking for money. The Rav freely gave whatever he had, and never asked people to repay the money he'd lent them—which meant that all too frequently, he didn't have the money he needed to cover his own family's needs.

One of the Rav's grandchildren told over the following story that he'd heard from one of the Rav's daughters: "Already as a young man, the Rav was incredibly generous," he said. "He used to immediately distribute all the money that he came by to needy people, with a very generous hand—so much so, that usually his *kollel* stipend never even made it home. The Steipler's daughter saw what was happening and started giving the Rav's *kollel* stipend (from the Volozhin Yeshivah) straight to the Rebbetzin, so that the family would have enough for its own needs."

Rav Moshe Cohen, the *gabbai* at the Lederman shul, remembers: "At that time at the Volozhin *kollel* in Bnei Brak, whenever anyone asked the Rav for monetary assistance, the Rav would do everything in his power to help them. People started to take advantage of the Rav's good heart, until the Steipler, *zt"l*, arranged for a note to be put up in the *kollel* that it was forbidden to ask Rav Berland for money."

"YOUR RAV MARRIED OFF MY SON!"

Rav Shlomo Gabbai told over the following the story he'd heard about the Rav's charitable activities at this time: "I once went to the Vizhnitz *beis medrash*, and this Jew came over to me and asked me if I was a student of Rav Berland. I told him I was.

"This man told me, 'Rav Berland married off my son. He paid for all the expenses! I'd promised to help buy the engaged couple an apartment, etc., but ultimately, I couldn't keep the promise I made, so the other party said that they were going to break off the match. By *Hashem's* great kindness, I happened to meet the Rav. I told him what was going on, and through his great good and kindness, he told me that he was going to try to help me. He took several loans out for me, and paid for everything! Your Rav married off my son!'"

Another student remembers this incident from the Rav's time at the Volozhin *kollel*: "Once, a man showed up there to ask for *tzedakah*, and he asked the Rav, 'Can you help me? I'm marrying off my children and I can't cover all the wedding expenses.' The Rav told him to come back the next day, and in the meantime, he ran to all the *gemachim* to collect a sum that would cover all of the man's expenses. He then gave the whole amount to the man when he came back the following day.

"A little later, another man came collecting and the Rav did the same thing—and then he started spending a lot of time at the *gemachim*. After a while, Rav Moshe Beninstock, who was devoted to the Rav, started to help the Rav with his work with the *gemachim*, as did Rav Gavriel Grossman.

"I later heard that many of the people who received such huge sums of money from the Rav started insulting him afterwards.[XII] Maybe that happened because when someone helps a person out, the beneficiary can feel like a failure, and then he can turn on his benefactor and start insulting him.

"Only a person who is completely attached to *Hashem* could do the things that the Rav did without getting confused by it all. The Rav sacrificed himself enormously for every matter connected to holiness," he concludes.

THE MIRACLES BEGIN

Although the Steipler tried to curtail the Rav's loans, he still happily sent people to the Rav to receive a blessing instead. Rav Shlomo Tzaddok recalls that: "The Steipler would regularly send people to the Rav for blessings and word started to get out in all of Bnei Brak that this was happening. The Rav's house became the address for people who needed some sort of salvation or miracle."

Rabbi Nachman Rosenthal, a former *Mashgiach* at the Breslov Yeshivah in Bnei Brak, tells how one day, someone came to the Steipler with a request that the Steipler should bless his wife, who was in desperate need of a specific salvation. The Steipler answered him, "Go to my neighbor Rav Eliezer Berland and request a blessing from him."

The person went the Rav's house but the Rav was in the field doing *hisbodedus* at the time, so Rebbetzin Berland told her visitor to leave a note with his name and details, and she'd deliver it to the Rav when he returned.

A couple of days later, this same man returned to the Rav's house with an envelope containing a very large sum of money, which he tried to give Rav Berland as a token of thanks for helping his wife, who'd received the salvation she needed. But the Rav refused to take the money! The man spent some time trying to argue and plead with him, until eventually he simply put the envelope down on the table and left.

XII   Editor's note: it's also possible that Rav Berland made a deal with them, that in exchange for the money they would publically insult him. Many such stories have subsequently become publicized.

The Rav discussed what had happened with the Rebbetzin and told her, "This money doesn't belong to me. I'm going to go out on the street, and I'm going to give the money to the first *Rosh* Yeshivah I meet." The Rav left the house and immediately bumped into the *Rosh* Yeshivah of the Breslov Yeshivah in Bnei Brak, Rabbi Shimon Bergstein, *zt" l*. He handed the money over to him, and Rabbi Bergstein later told Rabbi Rosenthal that this money was what had kept the yeshivah alive.

RAV MORDECHAI SHARABI STARTS SENDING PEOPLE TO RAV BERLAND

During his lifetime, Rav Mordechai Sharabi, *zt" l*, (1908-1983) was the leading kabbalist of Jerusalem in the previous generation, and head of the Nahar Shalom Yeshivah. While Rav Berland was still learning in Volozhin, someone who needed a big miracle went to Rav Sharabi for advice and a blessing. Rav Sharabi told him, "Go to the Lederman synagogue in Bnei Brak, and there you'll see an *avreich* who prays with a lot of enthusiasm and different movements. Ask him to give you a *brachah* that you should get your miracle—and don't take no for an answer, even if he tells you he's nothing and speaks disparagingly about himself and tells you he's not on the level to give you a blessing."

The man went to the Lederman synagogue, as he'd been told, and there he met the young Rav Berland. Exactly as Rav Sharabi described, the Rav initially was very self-deprecating, but the man persevered and eventually persuaded him to give him the *brachah* that led to his miracle.[XIII]

At the time that this story occurred, more than 40 years ago, Rav Berland and Rav Sharabi had never met, and the Rav hadn't yet developed a reputation for being a miracle worker. Yet the people with true *ruach hakodesh* somehow still knew about him.

ONE OF THE HIDDEN *TZADDIKIM* OF THE GENERATION

Later in his career, Rav Berland began to take many people to Uman, to visit the grave of Rebbe Nachman. "In the year 5745 (1985) when we traveled to Uman, our first stop was in the city of Vienna, where we were staying in the Satmar synagogue," begins Rav Baruch Mordechai (Motta) Frank.

XIII   This story was told by the person it happened to, Rav Avraham Chajbi, who now teaches at the Shuvu Banim Yeshiva.

"As we were climbing up the stairs to the synagogue, a *chassid* appeared and blocked the Rav's path. He told the Rav, 'Now, I'd like to get a *brachah* from you!' The Rav tried to laugh this off and said, 'Who am I, to be giving you a *brachah*?'

"But the *chassid* wouldn't give up, and he replied, 'Reb Lazer, you're not going to get away from me. The Steipler told me that you are one of the hidden *tzaddikim* of the generation! Please give me your *brachah* now.'"

FAMILY LIFE IN BNEI BRAK

During their early years in Bnei Brak, the Rav and his family continued to follow the more typical path of a devoted Lithuanian *avreich*. The Rav continued to study at the Volozhin Yeshivah, while Rebbetzin Berland found a teaching position at the Ohr HaChaim seminary for women in Bnei Brak.

As the Berland family continued to expand, they had to meet the challenge of juggling small children with a full schedule of Torah and *avodas Hashem*. The Rav and his family rose to the challenge, and many visitors to the Berland home at this time witnessed the Rav cheerfully pitching in to help around the house with the same enthusiasm and energy he applied to his other *avodas Hashem*.

THE RAV'S RECIPE FOR *SHALOM BAYIS*

Over the years, Rav Berland practiced a surefire recipe for *shalom bayis*; namely, submission, appreciation, and respect. When he was already a *Rosh* Yeshivah, Rav Berland once told his students, "All of a person's *parnassah* and Torah depends on their *shalom bayis*." He then went on to describe how each day he'd spend half the time of his *hisbodedus* on the subject of his *shalom bayis*, and the other half on the subject of learning Torah.

Rav Yosef Assulin was the Rav's *gabbai* for many years. He says: "The Rav's submission to the Rebbetzin is impossible to describe. I once took the Rav someplace to meet the Rebbetzin and he was almost bent over with awe, in respect and admiration for her.

"When I was a *gabbai*, I was the only one he had, and the Rav used to tell me, 'If I ask you for something, and the Rebbetzin also asks you to do something, always do what she asks you to do first.'"

The Rav's grandson Shmuel Isaac Zucker recounts: "There was a time when the Rebbetzin used to leave the house very early in the morning and only come back at 9 p.m. after work. The Rav used to prepare supper with her to show his appreciation and respect for her, and then they'd eat together."

On many occasions, the Rav would also spend many long hours learning Torah together with the Rebbetzin. According to one of the students at Shuvu Banim, "There was a time when the Rav and the Rebbetzin used to learn together on Friday, from midday until Shabbos came in." The student continued, "One Yom Kippur, the Rav remarked that he'd been learning with the Rebbetzin b'chavrusa all night."

"YOUR HUSBAND HAS RUN OFF!"

But being married to a budding *Gadol Hador* was not always so easy. Rav Nachman Horowitz recounts: "The Rebbetzin told me that the Rav would disappear for two weeks at a time, and that she had no idea what part of the country he'd gone to," he says. "This obviously wasn't an easy thing for any wife to handle. But each time the Rav returned, he'd appease her so nicely that she'd happily agree for him to continue doing these things in the future."

In close-knit communities, other families and neighbors often pitch in to help out if one of the parents is absent or incapacitated for some reason. But Rav Abish Dickshtein, an old resident of Bnei Brak, explains that with the notable exception of Rebbetzin Batsheva Kanievsky, a"h, who would often come over to help Rebbetzin Berland with her children when the Rav went out to do *hisbodedus* in the fields around Bnei Brak at night, Rebbetzin Berland was often by herself.

"There were times when the Rav would disappear for whole weeks, or even whole fortnights," he says. "Some of the *Litvaks* who lived on Rashbam Street in Bnei Brak used to laugh at the Rebbetzin and tell her, 'You see! Your husband has run off and disappeared!'

"The Rav used to go away to do *hisbodedus*, so I used to go and talk to the Rebbetzin to give her some encouragement, so that she shouldn't be broken by the things her neighbors were saying."

The Rav once reminisced about this period of time: "I used to tell my wife that I was going away in order to bring her back a *Rosh* Yeshivah, and that was why I was leaving the house. They used to say to her, 'What, your husband thinks he's the Chazon Ish, that he's going away and leaving you like that?' I used to tell her that I was going away to bring her back a Chazon Ish. A husband who would be a Chazon Ish. A *Rosh* Yeshivah who would be a Chazon Ish."

IF YOU BACK DOWN, YOU'LL ACHIEVE FAR MORE

Rav Meir Dovid Isaac, Rav Berland's son-in-law, explains that the Rav frequently returned to the subject of *shalom bayis* during his *shiurim* at the yeshivah. "There was barely a week that went by without the Rav talking about *shalom bayis*," he says. "The Rav always used to say that if a person wanted to go out to the field, or to visit *kivrei tzaddikim*, etc., and his wife didn't want him to, then he should back down and appease her. One should never just leave the house anyway, and leave his wife hurting or upset at him. If he backs down, he'll always achieve far, far more."

When the Rav used to go out for his fortnight-long *hisbodedus* sessions, everything was done only with the full agreement of the Rebbetzin. "You could really say about the Rebbetzin what Rabbi Akiva said about his wife Rachel, that everything I have and everything you have [referring to his students] is all from her, who supported the Rav throughout the years," continues Rav Isaac.

"But even so, the Rav's two-week absence from the house was still difficult for the Rebbetzin. Every day, something else would be going on at home, and there was no way of getting in touch with the Rav. One of the family members told me that each time the Rav would return to the house, the Rav and the Rebbetzin used to go and shut themselves up in a room alone and talk for between four and six hours. Every single time after their conversations, the Rebbetzin would come out of the room all smiles, happy for the Rav to continue going out again in the future.

"The Rebbetzin once told me that the Rav used to give her the feeling that he was always with the home, even when he was away, and that his mind was always on the home. She would tell him that a child had fallen down, and he'd ask her what day that happened. 'Was it last Monday?' he'd say. 'Because I had the feeling that something had happened at home, so I spent a long time praying about you.' That's how the Rav gave his wife the reassurance that she wasn't alone."

In later years, Rav Berland shared his unique approach to *shalom bayis* with his students, telling them: "Even when you are out of the house serving *Hashem* for hours on end, your wife and family should never leave you. They must always be at the forefront of your mind, in everything that you do."

THE MIRACULOUS RECOVERY OF THE RAV'S YOUNG SON

The Rebbetzin also acquiesced to the Rav's lengthy *hisbodedus* sessions because she'd seen for herself the miracles that this could accomplish.

At the beginning of the Rav's connection with Breslov, the Berlands' young son suffered a very serious stroke when he was four months old, which left him paralyzed for almost six weeks.

The distraught parents rushed their little boy straight to the hospital, where the doctors examined him and then told the Rav and Rebbetzin that their son had some sort of severe brain hemorrhage that was probably terminal. In shock, the parents asked the doctors, "So, there's no hope?"

The doctors responded that there was a very small chance that the little boy would make it, literally one in a thousand. They recommended that the boy should have complicated brain surgery, but warned his parents that there was a high risk that their son would die on the operating table.

The Rav responded that his son was going to live, because doing a *pidyon nefesh*[XIV] cancels all the decrees. Good as his word, the Rav immediately left the hospital to go and arrange one.

The Rav knew that his son needed an open miracle in order to recover, so he didn't hesitate to sell his apartment in order to recover. He didn't hesitate to sell his apartment in order to do the *pidyon Nefesh* that would save his son's life. At that time, the Rav's apartment in Bnei Brak sold for 10,000 Israeli liras, roughly equivalent to 500,000 NIS. Rav Berland then gave all the proceeds from his house sale to a Breslov elder, Rav Shmuel Shapira, and asked him to make the *pidyon nefesh*.

Next, the Rav quickly traveled up to Meron, to the grave of Rabbi Shimon bar Yochai, to pray for his son's recovery—and he didn't move from that spot for a week. Throughout this time, he barely ate or drank. He just cried out to Hashem to have mercy on his son.

When the week was over, he returned back to Bnei Brak, and as he was walking home he met Rav Aharon Gottlieb, who could see that the Rav was about to faint from not drinking enough. He immediately gave the Rav something to drink, and the Rav recounted many years later that the drink Rav Gottlieb gave him literally saved his life.

XIV   In *Likutei Moharan* Part II: 3, Rebbe Nachman explains that doing a pidyon nefesh can heal any illness.

By Hashem's mercies, all of the Rav's self-sacrifice and heartfelt prayers paid off and his son was released from the hospital and allowed to go home. Remarkably, the Rav's son incurred no lasting damage from the stroke, and grew up to be a healthy young man who went on to have children and grandchildren of his own.

THE RAV'S CONNECTION TO RAV CHAIM KANIEVSKY

As the Rav's family continued to grow, so did his connection to the Steipler's family, particularly, Rav Chaim Kanievsky, and his wife, Rebbetzin Batsheva. After the Steipler moved, the Rav bought his old house, because he wanted to live in a home that had been sanctified by the Steipler's holiness, and also because the apartment had its own *mikvah*. This meant that the Berlands and the Kanievskys were very close neighbors.

But they were connected in other ways, too. "Rav Chaim's Rebbetzin was a teacher at the Ohr HaChaim high school in Bnei Brak, and my Rebbetzin also taught there," recalls the Rav.

One of the Rav's acquaintances from that time remembers: "I was studying at the Ponevezh Yeshivah, and during the afternoon break I used to come and learn the *Ketzos HaChoshen*[XV] with the Rav, at his house on Rashbam Street. Every time we got into a debate, or we felt we hadn't fully understood what we were learning, the Rav would go upstairs to Rav Chaim Kanievsky's apartment to discuss the matter with him, then come down again and tell me what Rav Chaim had said."

The true depth of the connection between the two families was only revealed publicly when the late Rebbetzin Batsheva Kanievsky passed away on October 15, 2011. Rav Berland had been out of the country, so he missed the traditional seven-day mourning period, or *shiva*. However, as soon as he returned to the Holy Land, he was informed of the sad news, and that Rav Chaim Kanievsky was waiting for him to come and perform the *mitzvah* of comforting the bereaved, even though the seven days of mourning had actually already been completed.

A car was waiting to take the Rav directly from the airport to Rav Chaim Kanievsky's home in Bnei Brak. He arrived at a time when Rav Kanievsky was usually learning and didn't normally accept any visitors. (Even the most important visitors to Rav Kanievsky usually have an appointment that is limited to just 10 minutes.)

XV   A difficult commentary on the *Shulchan Aruch's Choshen Mishpat*.

However, when Rav Kanievsky heard that Rav Berland had come, he went and sat with him for a full hour and 40 minutes, during which the Rav told him about the greatness of Rebbetzin Batsheva, *a"h*, and how much merit she had for helping the Rav and his family.

During that visit, Rav Chaim had tears streaming down his face, and he commented afterwards that no one else had managed to console him over his loss the way that Rav Berland had.[XVI]

ALL THE DOORS WERE OPEN TO HIM

Already by his early 20s, the young Torah prodigy from Haifa had managed to make a big impression in Bnei Brak, and could count the spiritual leaders of the generation among his learning partners and admirers. Members of the public were already coming to him for blessings and advice, and to an outsider it appeared as though every door was open for the young Rav Eliezer Berland to blossom into a leading light in the Lithuanian Torah community.

But that didn't happen. A different path was beckoning to Rav Eliezer Berland, one that would take him from the lofty heights of the Steipler's Bnei Brak to the relative anonymity of an obscure branch of *Chassidus* with its roots in the Ukrainian town of Uman.

XVI   As told by Rav Benny Machliv, who was present at the meeting.

THE LITVAK TORAH GENIUS
BECOMES A BRESLOVER CHASSID

THE STEIPLER'S ADVICE TO "PRAY WITH THE *CHASSIDIM*"

Although Rav Berland's Torah learning was continuing to blossom in the rarefied atmosphere of the Volozhin Yeshivah in Bnei Brak, he felt something was missing.

The Rav said of this time: "One day, I was learning with the Steipler, *zt"l*, when I said to him, 'When it comes to learning Torah, I feel that I'm exerting myself and getting somewhere. But what's going to be with my *avodas hatefillah?*' The Steipler, *zt"l*, responded, 'For *avodas hatefillah*, you need to go to the *Chassidim*.'

"From that point on, I started visiting different *Chassidic* courts, until finally I merited to draw close to the path of the Master of Prayer himself, *Rabbeinu Hakadosh*, Rebbe Nachman of Breslov, *zt"l*."

Over the next few weeks and months, Rav Berland visited one different *chassidishe shteibel* after another, trying to find the place where they really understood the inner dimension of prayer. Before the Rav came closer to Breslov, he spent lengthy periods of time with two other *chassidishe* courts, that of Rav Moshe Mordechai of Lelov, *zt"l*, and also of the Vizhnitzer *Chassidim*.

(As a side note, the Rav once described himself as being a good friend of the late *Admor* of Lelov, Rabbi Shimon Biderman, *zt"l*. "He had a soft spot for Breslov," explains the Rav. "I also learned *b'chavrusa* with Rabbi Alter and was a good friend of Rabbi Avraham, too."[XVII])

Yet despite the fact that the Breslov Yeshivah in Bnei Brak was located very close to the Volozhin Yeshivah, it didn't cross his mind that *this* could be the place he was looking for.

XVII   Rav Berland was close to the following four Rebbes of Lelov: Rav Moshe Mordechai, zt'l, who passed away in 1987 and was survived by his three sons: Rebbe Shimon Biderman, zt'l, who passed away in 2010; Rebbe Alter Biderman, zt'l, who died in 2001, and Rebbe Avraham Biderman, who died in 2000.

HOW THE RAV DREW CLOSE TO BRESLOV, IN HIS OWN WORDS

The Rav once explained to his grandchildren how he'd finally come closer to Breslov, and why it had taken him so many years to discover Rebbe Nachman's path for himself.

"When the Rebbetzin was 15, she started learning some Breslov books that her brother had been given for his *bar mitzvah*," explains the Rav. "Before we got married, she asked me if I knew what Breslov was. I told her, 'It doesn't even interest me.' But she was adamant that I should begin learning the *sefarim*.

"We got married on 28 Adar, and for an entire year I pretended that I was learning the Breslov *sefarim* in order to appease her. It was only a year later, on Chol Hamoed Pesach, as we were traveling back to Haifa on a train, that she discovered my ruse. She started to ask me questions about Rebbe Nachman's *sefer Sipurei Maasios* ("Rebbe Nachman's Tales"), and she was shocked when I told her I wasn't familiar with it. So then, I had no choice.

"Afterwards, I read them a little in order to help the Rebbetzin prepare a class on Rebbe Nachman that she used to teach at the Or HaChaim seminary. We used to learn together for a whole hour, every day, and we were deeply engrossed in *Rabbeinu's* Torah. But I didn't come closer to the Breslover community (often referred to as: '*AN"SH*[XVIII]') at that point. In the Breslov shul in Jerusalem they had the Rabbi and the Gaon Rav Shmuel Shapira, *zt"l*, but you didn't really see him much except a trace of him at Meron.

"There were also a couple of other *ovdim* there who would lay down on the benches in the shul and sleep there at night. It took Rabbi Levi Yitzchak[XIX] quite a few years until he managed to get the shul in Jerusalem organized, and I liked things to be organized and orderly.

"In Bnei Brak, most of the Breslov *chassidim* were *baalei batim* (i.e., people who worked as well as learned Torah), and there weren't a lot of full-time Torah learners. So, there wasn't really any way for me to get closer to Breslov *Chassidus*.

"[Once,] they were holding a celebration for laying the foundation stone of the Breslov Yeshivah in Bnei Brak, and I said to myself that I should go and participate in the event. I watched it from my place at the Volozhin Yeshivah, but I still didn't come closer to Breslov.

XVIII   AN"SH is the short form of 'Anshei shlomeinu', a term used within Breslov chassidus to refer to other Breslovers, or 'our people'.

XIX   The leader of the previous generation of Breslov chassidus.

"I HAVE TO FIND THE TRUTH!"

Rav Berland continues: "On Purim 5722 (1961) I was crying out to *Hashem Yisbarach*, 'I have to find the truth!' I went to Lelov.

"There, they used to read the *megillah* [on Purim night] at 11 p.m., with a lot of joking around and merriment. Even from my youth, even from the age of six years old, Purim used to be my most serious day. I couldn't stand that people would get drunk and go a little bit crazy on Purim.

"The *beis medrash* of the *Admor* of Lelov was in Tel Aviv. [After they finished reading the *megillah*] I left there, and got the last number 54 bus home to Bnei Brak. I got off at Rabbi Akiva Street and the corner of Chazon Ish, with the intention of going to the Vizhnitz *beis medrash*. I started to walk toward Vizhnitz, and suddenly I found the walk really difficult—which was very strange and unusual for me.

"I wanted to sit down and relax a little, so I went into the Breslov Yeshivah in Bnei Brak, which was located on Am Haderech Street, between Chazon Ish and Vizhnitz. I went up to the first floor, to the dining room, so I could sit down a little. I opened up a *Likutei Moharan*, and I learned Torah *Alef*. I had no idea what it was talking about. I was used to learning Breslov *sefarim* like *Meshivas Nefesh* and *Histapchus HaNefesh*, which were easy to understand, with my wife. I still wasn't used to learning much deeper things.

"Just then, Rabbi Nachman Rosenthal came into the room and I asked him why it was so quiet. Where was everyone? He explained to me that on Purim night everyone went to sleep early because they would wake up the *bachurim* later, at midnight, so they could go out to the field and cry out to *Hashem Yisbarach* to save them from the *klipah* of Haman the Amalekite, and to help them merit to achieve the holiness of Mordechai and Esther.[XX] So right now, everyone was asleep.

"I said, 'What?! There are other people who go out to the field [to pray]?! That's what I've been looking for! I'm staying here!'

"From the age of 16, I used to go out and talk to God in the fields in Haifa, opposite Givat Vizhnitz. I was ecstatic. Who would have believed that there were other people who went out to the field and cried out to *Hashem Yisbarach*?

"I stayed there in the yeshivah until 5 a.m. When I came back after *Shacharis*, I saw *bachurim* drinking and messing around, and I couldn't stand all the larking about.

XX   Breslov chassidim have a tradition that for the 40 days before Purim, they should pray: "Save me from the klipa of Haman/Amalek and let me merit to be given the kedusha of Mordechai and Esther."

55

I needed things to be serious. So once more, I didn't come closer to Breslov. I went back to Vizhnitz."

THE *TZADDIK* TELLS YOU EVERYTHING YOU NEED TO KNOW

Rav Nachman Rosenthal, the former *Mashgiach* of the Breslov Yeshivah in Bnei Brak, takes up the story: "One Friday, I encountered Reb Lazer Berland by the last bus stop in Bnei Brak, and I went over to talk to him.

"I told him that there was a *sefer* that whichever page you open it to, the *Tzaddik* is telling you exactly what you need to hear, and what you need to know. Reb Lazer was interested, and asked me what *sefer* I was referring to — so I told him a list of 12 or 13 Breslover works, including *Likutei Moharan* and *Histapchus HaNefesh*. Reb Lazer heard me, but he didn't write anything down," continues Rav Rosenthal.

"That same Friday at night, all the lights went out in the dorms of the Breslov Yeshivah, so I went down to the dining room of the yeshivah, and who did I see there? Reb Lazer! He was sitting there with every book I'd mentioned opened in front of him on the table."

Rav Berland describes that fateful Friday a little differently: "Two weeks later, on Friday afternoon just before Shabbos came in, I bumped into Rabbi Nachman Rosenthal, and he told me that he was sure that I'd come to the Breslov Yeshivah [after the conversation on Purim]. I told him that now, I was going home, but that evening I would come and visit him at the yeshivah.

"I got there that evening, and they were in the middle of reciting *Kabbalas Shabbos* and *Maariv* with all the strength and crying out that you find by *Rabbeinu's* people. The Rabbi and Gaon, Rabbi Noson Libermensch was leading the *davening*, and he was praying with literally every drop of his strength — he was repeating the same word for a quarter of an hour.

"That was the last straw," exclaims the Rav. "After that, I came closer to *Rabbeinu.*

"[Rav Noson Libermensch] was a normal person and an accomplished Torah scholar, and that's what brought me closer. I went over and stood very close to Rabbi Noson — I could feel the fire in his prayers and I was rooted to the spot. So, I stood there for a couple of hours, praying the evening prayers."

THE RAV IS CALLED *"THE MESHUGGANER"*

"The other *bachurim* came to try to pull me away, but I didn't let them budge me. Afterwards, for a whole year, they called me the *meshugganer*, the crazy person, and I had no idea why. A long time afterwards, one of the *bachurim* came up to me and asked me why I hadn't moved, as they were trying to get me out of the building because it was on fire!

"He told me that on that same Friday night, there'd been a fire at the top of the building and everyone had gone outside — except for me and Rabbi Libermensch, who stayed in the building. So finally, I understood why they were calling me the *meshugganer*."

The Rav concluded with a smile: "From that time on, there's always been someone who's been careful to maintain the tradition of calling me a *meshugganer*."

WALKING THE WALK

Rav Yehoshua Dov Rubinstein was a student at the Breslov Yeshivah in Bnei Brak at this time. He recalls: "Soon after that, Rav Berland started coming to the Breslov Yeshivah to learn. He would sit there for hours and hours, learning all the Breslov *sefarim*. Whatever he learned, he'd internalize right away. For example, once he learned how one is meant to *daven* with *kavanah*, he started *davening Shacharis* for six to eight hours every day. Every day, he'd be up on the roof, going back and forth, singing.

"Later, when he heard Rav Nachman Rosenthal talking about *kiruv rechokim*, Rav Berland would go out on the street and start talking to people about God and Judaism, in any language they understood, English or Hebrew. People would shout at him for doing that. They'd get upset with him and ask him why he was talking to them about God. Why was he doing that? The same people that cursed him then, the Rav never gave up on them. Many of them are now the top people in Breslov."

HE DID EVERYTHING THE REBBE WROTE ABOUT

Rav Yitzchak Weisshandler was also a student at the Breslov Yeshivah in Bnei Brak, and clearly remembers his first encounters with Rav Berland.

"When I came into the yeshivah hall to learn, I saw one of the students clapping his hands and dancing, and saying the *korbanos* prayers while dancing and jumping," he says. "I'd never seen anything like it before, so I asked the students who it was, and they told me it was Rav Lazer Berland.

"Over time, I saw him fulfill all of the words of *Rabbeinu*. Everyone talks the talk, and gives over very nice, correct and true *shiurim*, but here I saw a person who was actually doing the work and delivering the goods. He'd go into the field to pray with all his strength, he'd dance, he'd guard his eyes, everything! Everything that *Rabbeinu* wrote about, he did.

"Others also do, but not with the same wholehearted commitment to do it to the very best of their abilities. *Davening* for hours, screaming out to God for hours, crying in his prayers, dancing for hours, being up at *chatzos*, not needing to eat, not needing to sleep — I saw it all, every single day."

Rav Weisshandler continues: "The Rav would dip in a cold *mikvah* every morning, without toweling off afterwards, and would then *daven Shacharis* for four hours afterwards. He'd stand on the roof crying out, and a neighbor once said to him, 'Hashem isn't deaf! Why are you screaming so loud?!' The Rav answered him, 'I'm deaf!'

"The Rav was a powerful figure in the yeshivah. His service of Hashem influenced all the students. The *Rosh* Yeshivah, Rav Shimon Bergstein, loved the Rav's long prayers and the way he cried out," concludes Rav Weisshandler.

THE STEIPLER GIVES PERMISSION FOR THE RAV TO GET CLOSER TO BRESLOV

With his customary thoroughness, the Rav continued to double-check everything he was starting to learn in Breslov with his mentor, the Steipler Gaon. The Rav describes the process in his own words:

"When I started to be involved with *Rabbeinu's* Torah, and I started to grasp the idea of the "*Tzaddik*," I clarified every detail with the Steipler. When I got up to *Rabbeinu's* comments where he said that the *Tzaddik* could get his students out of *Gehinnom*, I met with the Steipler and asked him if he'd be able to get me out of *Gehinnom*.

"The Steipler laughed, and responded with his customary humility that it was only with great difficulty that he could get *himself* out of *Gehinnom*. To get other people out of *Gehinnom* — who ever heard of such a thing?!

"I asked him, 'But, what if you found a *tzaddik* who could get you out of *Gehinnom?*' The Steipler responded, 'If that's the case — run after him!'

"So," the Rav concluded, "the Steipler gave me permission to draw closer to *Rabbeinu*."[XXI]

REBBE NACHMAN'S PROMISE

Rav Berland showed the Steipler the passage in *Chayei Moharan* where Rebbe Nachman took two kosher witnesses, his student Rav Naftali of Nemirov and Rav Aharon, the Rav of Breslov, and made the following promise:

"Whoever comes to my grave and says there the 10 chapters of *Tehillim* [i.e., the *Tikkun Haklali*] and gives a *prutah* to charity, then even if he sinned tremendously, I swear that I will span the breadth and the length [of the universe] to save him and give him his *tikkun*. I'm very sure about everything I say, but I'm the surest about this, because every sin has its spiritual rectification, and this rectification is the *Tikkun Haklali*.

THE RAV'S *HISBODEDUS* GOES UP A LEVEL

Rav Yehoshua Dov Rubinstein recalls that the Rav's practice of *hisbodedus* at the Breslov Yeshivah was one of the things that really started to set him apart.

"When he started to learn about *hisbodedus*, he immediately started doing *hisbodedus* all night, from evening to morning, in the forests and the fields," recalls Rav Rubinstein. "People in the yeshivah knew that if you wanted to go to a field or a forest to do *hisbodedus*, but you were scared to go by yourself, you could just go and ask Rav Lazer, and he'd come with you. The boys in the yeshivah would ask him to take him to the field, and he'd go for two hours, come back — and then another boy would ask him to take him to the field, and he'd go out and take that boy to the field, too."

XXI   The Steipler Gaon himself was also known to be very attracted to Breslov works. On Erev Yom Kippur the Steipler would be heard crying over a copy of *Likutei Tefillos* by Rav Nosson of Nemirov, Rebbe Nachman's principal student. It is told that a copy of *Likutei Moharan* and *Likutei Tefillos* would always be seen on the Steipler's table. The Steipler once told Rav Nosson Tzvi Kennig about *Likutei Moharan* "I feel that it inspires within me tremendous yiras shomayim and if a day goes by that I don't learn from this *sefer* I feel lacking in *yiras shomayim*. (B'shivcho shel Tzaddik)

DRAGGING PEOPLE TO THE FIELDS

"The Rav used to drag people to the fields," says Rav Weisshandler. "As soon as he'd bring someone closer to *Yiddishkeit*, he'd take them to the field, and tell them that they were going to be all by themselves now, and that they should look to *Hashem*.

"The Rav also used to take a lot of *bachurim* to the fields, and you can't even count the amount of his own money he spent doing that. At the beginning, we'd ride our bikes to the field, but then the Rav started taking taxis every midnight out to the field, and he'd pay for everything out of his own pocket.

"We used to go to the place that's now the campus of Bar Ilan University. Other people used to go to the Berman orchards, at the end of Nechemia Street where it meets Chazon Ish, or to Ramat Aharon. At that point, everything [around Bnei Brak] was still countryside and orchards.

"So, the Rav would arrange for taxis to take the *bachurim*. The taxis were owned by two brothers, whom the Rav would pay to go upstairs to the boys' dorms and wake up anyone who wanted to go to the field. The Rav paid for everything, and he used to settle accounts with them every month.

"An hour of *hisbodedus* for the Rav was nothing, but he wanted to encourage other people, so he'd come along for the hour with the *bachurim*, bring them back to the yeshivah, and then go back again himself[XXII]."

Another old friend of the Rav's from his time in Bnei Brak, Rav Aaron Lebel (son of the late Rav Feival Lebel), also used to meet up with him at night to go and do *hisbodedus* together in the local fields next to Bnei Brak. (As a sign of just how much things have changed, the field where Rav Berland and his friends used to do *hisbodedus* is today the location of the Coca Cola factory.)

Rav Lebel recounts that he often saw many different people going to the field to do *hisbodedus* with Rav Berland, including the present Rebbe of Gur, Rav Yaakov Aryeh Alter, who used to live close by. Rav Berland also once mentioned to his grandchildren that he used to regularly learn with the Rebbe of Gur.

As Rav Berland progressed along the Breslov path, he started to spend more and more time engaged in personal prayer. Some evenings, he'd start walking along the

---

XXII   At the time, *hisbodedus* was not something that regular people did, but was considered to be something that only the most pious people in the generation engaged in. Rav Berland wanted to bring *hisbodedus* to the masses, and these are some of the ways he made *hisbodedus* a mainstream practice in modern Breslov circles.

old train tracks that led out of Bnei Brak at 8pm, by a sign that said "5 km." He'd continue walking and talking to God for five hours until he reached the sign that said "21 km," and then he'd turn around and walk another five hours back to Bnei Brak, reaching the Breslov Yeshivah just in time to join the *vasikin minyan* for the morning prayers.

HE ONLY SLEEPS FOR ONE HOUR A NIGHT

Rav Weisshandler remembers: "There was a time when the taxi driver would take us to do *hisbodedus* at the beginning of the night. After an hour, I'd come back [to the yeshivah], but the Rav would stay in the field all night. On many occasions, he'd only come back to the yeshivah just before daybreak, soaked through from all the dew. There was a long time when Reb Lazer only slept for an hour a night. I saw this happening with my own eyes, over a long period of time. And I never once heard him say that he was hungry, or thirsty, or tired."

Rav Yaakov Reicher, another student at the Breslov Yeshivah in Bnei Brak, adds: "We'd go out to the field, and the Rav would stay there for seven or eight straight hours, and he used to cry out so enthusiastically. It's something that's really impossible to find by anyone else in our generation.

"And then, after he'd done that each night, every day he'd be enthusiastically praying and teaching, and waking other people up spiritually. The little bit of sleep he'd managed to grab was enough for him. The things that they say about the biggest *tzaddikim*, we saw all those things by the Rav."

DAVENING **ON THE ROOF OF THE** YESHIVAH

Even though he was regularly doing many long hours of *hisbodedus* every night, that doesn't mean he was neglecting his regular prayers. Rav Nachman Rosenthal remembers: "The Rav would always *daven* with the same tune, the tune he still *davens* with today. Then, as now, the Rav could go on for hours and hours, singing his *Shacharis*, *Minchah* and *Maariv* prayers with this same tune. People [in the Breslov Yeshivah] came over to him at one point and told him that he was bothering them with his loud *davening*," he says.

"Rav Berland replied that if that was the case, he'd go and *daven* on the roof! That way, he could carry on praying the way he wanted to, without disturbing anyone else."

Rav Moshe Levinson, another student at the Breslov Yeshivah in Bnei Brak also vividly remembers the way the Rav would *daven* the morning prayers.

"The Rav used to sing *Shira Chadashah* a few times with the wedding tune, before we'd say *Shemoneh Esrei*," he says. "He'd often do that for at least an hour! He'd start *Shacharis* around 4 a.m., and he'd get up to *Shemoneh Esrei* around 8 or even 9 a.m.

"The Rav didn't always pray with us. Sometimes, he'd go and pray by himself in the room that he had at the yeshivah. One time, I listened in behind the door and I heard him praying so slowly and beautifully, word by word, with wondrous melodies."

HELPING HIS FELLOW STUDENTS

As well as encouraging students to come out to the field to do *hisbodedus*, the Rav also took it upon himself to help anyone who wanted to wake up to recite the Midnight Lamentation, or *Tikkun Chatzos* prayer, which was another Breslov practice.

One of the Rav's contemporaries at the Breslov Yeshivah recalls: "There were a few of us *bachurim* who wanted to regularly get up for *chatzos*. The Rav, in his great kindness, used to come to the yeshivah each night before *chatzos* to wake us up. He did this night after night, for a very long time, like a loving father.

"And how did he used to wake us up? He used to sing such a sweet melody to wake us up; everything was done in such a refined, compassionate way. We still remember that tune today. Helping others to get up for *chatzos* with compassion and refinement—that's the Rav!"

Fifty years later, the Rav continued to offer his thousands of students a personal wake-up call. One of the Rav's drivers related that, when he would take the Rav out to the fields to pray at midnight, the Rav would be busy calling one person after another to wake them up for *chatzos*.

Then, on the way back, the Rav would make another bunch of calls to students who needed to be woken up before dawn. And later, when he'd finished his own prayers, he'd make yet another round of phone calls to other students, to encourage them to get to *shul* on time to pray—and he'd remember all these phone numbers by heart.

Even though the Rav was a *rebbei* to thousands of students by this time, he still acted like a father to each of them.

HOW THE RAV HID HIS GREATNESS

When Rav Berland was still a young child, he made a vow to never say no when other Jews asked him to do something for them. Later on, some people took advantage of this, and asked the Rav to do some crazy things for them. The Rav was only too happy to comply, as he viewed it as a way of continuing to nullify his ego. He also valued the insults and mockery that he knew would come his way as a result of acting "weird"[XXIII].

Rav Weisshandler recalls that the Rav used to nullify himself to the other students totally. "All the students would do whatever they wanted with the Rav", he says. "One time, a group of jokers told the Rav to come into the yeshivah through the window—so he did. Another time, they told him to jump into the *mikvah* fully clothed—and he did!

"The Rav's whole attitude was: 'If that's what you want, I'll do it for you.' That's the way he used to hide his greatness, by nullifying himself completely to the people around him.

"There was a student in the yeshivah who'd been a little lax, and he wanted to start learning properly, but he didn't really have a head for the *Gemara*. He wanted to understand the *Tosafos* commentaries right to the end, so who did he ask to become his *chavrusa*? The Rav, of course.

"The Rav, with his brilliant mind and his awesome abilities, sat with this boy for hours, explaining each detail over and over again until he finally understood it. He learned with him like that for 10 hours a day. Today, that student is one of the most important learned elders in Breslov."

NO ONE KNEW HE WAS A TORAH GENIUS

Despite his tremendous achievements in Torah, Rav Berland still managed to keep a very low profile when he moved over to the Breslov Yeshivah in Bnei Brak. "When he first came to Breslov at the beginning, people didn't think he was a genius or anything; they thought he was just serving *Hashem*," recalls Rav Yehoshua Dov Rubinstein.

XXIII   This was a common practice among some Orthodox groups, particularly the "*baalei mussar*" of the *Novardok* Yeshivah, who were known for encouraging others to insult them.

"He was *davening* for hours and hours, doing *hisbodedus*, serving *Hashem*. But to know that he was also a genius in learning?! They only figured that out when it came time to learn. Whatever *sefarim* were being taught by the *Rosh* Yeshivah when he was giving over a *shiur*, the Rav knew all of them by heart, as if the book was open in front of him."

Given his obvious erudition, the Rav had to resort to some unusual tactics to prevent people from honoring him for his Torah learning and knowledge.

"On one occasion, the Rav had given a *shiur* at the Breslov Yeshivah in Bnei Brak, and afterwards people started jostling to accompany him, like you do with important Rabbis," explains Rav Yosef Assulin. "When the Rav saw this, he tried to jump down the stairs—and ended up fracturing a bone and spending some time laid up in bed. When people heard this, some of them started saying, 'He's a *meshugga*! What's all this?!'

"Someone asked him why he'd acted the way he had, and the Rav replied that even one arrogant thought could destroy a person's whole life. 'I was worried I might start to feel a little proud,' he explained."

Another tactic the Rav adopted was to spend time with the people everyone else was doing their best to avoid. "The Rav didn't hang out with the most honored or respectable figures," continues Rav Assulin. "He spent a lot of time with people who'd been broken by their troubles, people who no one else would even look twice at, people who were regularly jeered at and avoided by other people. The Rav found these people and hung out with them. He learned Torah with them, and even gave them money, and a ton of encouragement."

But the Rav wasn't just spending time with the down-and-outs as a ruse; he genuinely cared deeply for every Jew he came in contact with. Let's go back to Rav Assulin:

"On one of the later trips to Uman, there was a fellow there whom the Rav addressed by his first name and his mother's Hebrew name. This fellow asked the Rav, 'How do you still remember my name and my mother's name, when so many years have passed [since we last met]?' The Rav told him, 'I pray for you every single day.'"

"BEFORE BECOMING A BRESLOVER, YOU MUST BE A *LITVAK*"

Despite his leap over to the world of Breslov *Chassidus*, Rav Berland continued to remember his years in the *Litvak* world very fondly, even many decades later. In one of his more recent lectures to his students, the Rav commented, "It's only because I studied by the *Litvaks* for 25 years that you have today in Breslov Rav Eliezer Berland!"

Rav Berland continued to put a very strong emphasis on learning Torah, *halachah,* and *Gemara* at the highest levels when he became a Breslov *chassid*. Just as he himself spent 18 or even 20 hours a day learning the *Shulchan Aruch* plus other works in his youth, he continued to encourage his students at Shuvu Banim and elsewhere to do the same, whenever possible.

On many, many occasions, the Rav told his students that "prior to becoming a Breslover, you must be like a *Litvak* and learn 18 hours a day! Only then you can channel all that energy into your *avodas Hashem*." As *Rabbeinu* said in *Siach Sarfei Kodesh*, "I want my words to spread to *Litvish* hearts."

"Everyone in Breslov, in the Breslov Yeshivah of Bnei Brak, greatly respected him," says Rav Rubinstein. "One of the Breslov *Gedolim* of previous generations once remarked that Rav Berland, who at that point was still just ripening into a true Breslov *chassid*, would end up surpassing Rav Shmuel Shapira, one of the leading lights of Breslov from the previous generation."

For their part, the Lithuanian Torah world continued to miss the young Torah genius who'd been the Steipler's study partner. Even many years later, when a couple of Lithuanian *Roshei* Yeshivah from Bnei Brak happened to meet some of the students of Shuvu Banim, they told them, "Your Rabbi used to learn with us in Bnei Brak. When he started to get close to Breslov, our Rabbis told us that the world of Lithuanian Torah had just lost a future *Gadol*."

BRESLOV, THE "DEAD" CHASSIDUS

Although the Rav had seemingly been preparing to become a Breslov *chassid* for most of his life, his transformation from a *Litvak Gadol*-in-waiting to a Breslover *chassid* was neither fast nor easy.

At the time that Rav Berland first joined the ranks of Rebbe Nachman's students, Breslov *Chassidus* was generally stagnating, and had earned itself the nickname of being "the dead *Chassidus*."

Partially, this was a reference to the fact that, unlike the other branches of *Chassidus*, the Breslovers had a dead Rebbe, Rebbe Nachman of Breslov, who'd never formally handed over his crown to another live Rebbe to replace him. But the nickname was also a reference to a far more disturbing phenomenon, namely, that Breslov *Chassidus* appeared to be on its last legs.

After being decimated by the twin evils of Communist Russia and Nazi Germany, by the 1960s the total number of Breslov *chassidim* in the world barely numbered 500 souls. There was a tiny handful of old-school Breslov *chassidim* trapped behind the Iron Curtain in Communist Russia, and another small handful of new-style Breslov *chassidim* in America, who were primarily the students of Rabbi Aryeh Tzvi Rosenfeld, *zt"l*.

The remaining Breslovers, who barely numbered 500 all together, were nearly all concentrated in small, isolated communities in Meah Shearim, Tzfas and Bnei Brak—a far cry from the hundreds of Breslov communities that can be found all over the world today.

WHAT DOES BRESLOV HAVE TO OFFER?

At that time, there appeared to be very little about Breslov *Chassidus* that would appeal to an outsider. Rebbe Nachman's grave in Uman was located deep behind the Iron Curtain, and dangerously impossible to visit. The annual Rosh Hashanah *kibbutz* (gathering) had been replaced by meetings at Rabbi Shimon bar Yochai's grave in Meron, or with a communal gathering in Meah Shearim. And apart from a few exceptionally pious individuals, most people had forgotten about doing things like getting up for *chatzos*, or spending hours in the field engaged in personal prayer.

Rebbe Nachman's true path had been stripped of its spiritual vigor and largely lost in the murk and suffering that affected all parts of the religious Jewish community after World War II. Yet even in this dark period of time, there remained a handful of visionary Breslov elders who continued to cling to the powerful Breslov ideals of the past, and who were waiting for the time when Breslov *Chassidus* would burst back into life.

SEARCHING OUT THE BRESLOV ELDERS

Rav Berland has never been a man of half-measures. Once he ascertained the awesome depth of the true Breslov path, and its ability to transform the individual and the world around him, he threw himself into the difficult job of clearing off the weeds and debris that were hiding it from view.

At the same time that he began seriously studying at the Breslov Yeshivah in Bnei Brak, Rav Berland also began seeking out the remaining Breslov elders in the Jerusalem neighborhood of Meah Shearim, to see what more he could learn from them.

RABBI ISRAEL BER ODESSER (THE SABA), *ZT" L*

One of the first senior Breslovers that Rav Berland became close to was Rabbi Israel Ber Odesser, who later became affectionately known as "the Saba."

Rav Berland once commented that, even if someone worked on himself for a thousand years, he still wouldn't come anywhere close to achieving the Saba's level of *avodas Hashem*. The Rav frequently praised the Saba's *hisbodedus*, his *dveikus* to *Hashem*, his songs and *niggunim*, and the way he served God with such happiness and enthusiasm.

Rav Berland was also very impressed by Saba Odesser's untiring efforts to bring secular Jews back to *Yiddishkeit*, including spending literally every cent he had on setting up the Keren Odesser organization, which arranged the typesetting, printing and distribution of Rebbe Nachman's books to the wider public.

IT'S FORBIDDEN TO READ BRESLOV BOOKS!

Before he became a Breslov *chassid*, Rav Odesser had been born to a family of Karliner *chassidim* in Tiveria, and continued to walk in the path of Karliner *Chassidus* for most of his youth. Once, while he was studying in yeshivah in Tiveria, he discovered a holy book in the trash whose front cover had been ripped off. Rav Odesser rescued the book and started to read it — and was stunned at the wealth of advice it contained about how to properly serve *Hashem*. (He later discovered that the book was *Hishtapchut HaNefesh*, by Rabbi Alter Tepliker.)

He started following the advice without even knowing its provenance, or the name of the book that contained it. After some time, one of his fellow yeshivah students noticed the book he was engrossed in and told him in no uncertain terms that it was forbidden for him to continue reading it, because it was "Breslov," and all the Rabbis were against it.

This was the first time that Rav Odesser had heard about Breslov *Chassidus*. He told his colleague that he didn't care if the book was forbidden by all the Rabbis and Rebbes in the world, because it had given him so much spiritual uplift and encouragement.

In later years, the Saba reminisced that, even though that yeshivah student forcibly took that first book away from him, he'd given him a priceless gift in exchange. Now, he knew that the source of his inspiration lay in Breslov *Chassidus*. From that moment on, Rav Odesser decided that he was going to sacrifice whatever was necessary in order to find a Breslov *chassid* who would teach him more about this new path he'd discovered.

Rav Odesser told Rav Berland that, after the student told him that all the Rabbis forbade anyone to read Breslov books, the student had been shocked at the Saba's *chutzpah* and asked him, "What if *Eliyahu Hanavi* would come down from heaven right now and tell you that it's forbidden to read these books; what would you say then?"

Rav Odesser answered, "If *Eliyahu Hanavi* would come down from heaven right now and tell me that it's forbidden to read these books, I would say that it's not *Eliyahu Hanavi*!"

Later on, when he'd recount this story to his students, Rav Berland would explain that this is how a person has to believe in the true *Tzaddik* who brings a person closer to *Hashem*—that even if all the Rabbis, and even Eliyahu the Prophet tell you that it's forbidden to listen to him, you shouldn't believe them, and you should tell yourself that it's clearly not the real Eliyahu the Prophet who's talking to you.

Rav Berland testified that Rav Odesser said of himself that every piece of criticism he heard about Breslov and Rebbe Nachman only made him more determined to continue.

INSPIRING THE WHOLE *AM YISRAEL* TO DO *TESHUVAH*

Despite the 50-year gap in their ages, the two men grew very close, and would frequently stay at each other's homes. Rav Berland once said: "[The Saba] spent a whole year with me at my home [in Bnei Brak]. He ate by me, he slept by me, and every night he would wake up to recite the *Tikkun Chatzos*. After that, I went to spend some time at his home [in Jerusalem], and we were like one person with one heart and one soul. He told me all of the stories, and described every detail of what had occurred to him during his life, and the story of how he came close to Breslov is a classic; the kind of story you tell to future generations. His story could inspire the whole *Am Yisrael* to do *teshuvah*."

The feeling was definitely mutual. Rabbi Aharon Berlin was a student at the Breslov Yeshivah in Bnei Brak, and one of Rav Berland's earliest followers. Rav Berlin recounted what he'd heard from the Saba about Rav Berland, when he used to accompany the Rav on his trips into Jerusalem to pray at the *Kosel* and stop over to visit the Saba at his home in Givat Shaul. "One visit of my own to the Saba really sticks out in my mind," says Rav Berlin. "We began to discuss the new *baal teshuvah* movement, which was then just beginning.

"The Saba was very enthusiastic about it all, and he told me, 'Rav Berland has a wondrous way of reaching out to *baalei teshuvah*! He has the power to inspire the entire world to *teshuvah*!'"

The Saba himself had devoted his life to trying to make Breslov *Chassidus* more accessible to the masses, and had achieved some notable successes, including the third President of Israel, Zalman Shazar. As a result of his relationship with Rav Odesser, President Shazar once agreed to come and pray at the main Breslov shul in Meah Shearim. Unfortunately, it ended in disaster.

Some of the extremists in the Meah Shearim Breslov community were outraged that a Hebrew-speaking Zionist had infiltrated their holy sanctuary—despite the fact that he'd been formally invited to come by Rav Odesser. As soon as they recognized that the man trying to pray with them was the President of Israel, they started yelling abuse and insults at him, until he was forced to leave.

Rav Berlin continues: "I also told him about Rav Berland's astounding prescience before the outbreak of the Six-Day War [in 1967]. Before anyone knew anything was happening, the Rav told everyone that there were harsh judgments in Heaven, and he danced all day to sweeten the decrees, in fulfillment of Rebbe Nachman's teaching in *Likutei Moharan* that if one wants to sweeten judgments he should dance. But Rav Odesser wasn't at all surprised by what I was telling him. 'I already told you,' he said, 'he has eyes that can see.'"

Rav Odesser passed away on October 23, 1994, at the age of 106, and was buried in the Har Hamenuchos cemetery in Jerusalem.

RAV ZVI ARYEH (HERSH LEIB) LIPPEL

Another Breslov elder whom Rav Berland got close to was Rav Zvi Aryeh (Hersh Leib) Lippel, one of the old-school Breslover *chassidim* from Uman who'd managed to make *aliyah* to Israel before the Iron Curtain came down.

Rav Berland said of Rav Hersh Leib Lippel: "He was really the founder of [today's] Breslov *Chassidus*. He gave it its momentum. There used to be just a few Breslov *minyanim* in Jerusalem, but when he arrived in Jerusalem in 5694 (1934) he immediately gave some impetus to Breslov *Chassidus*, and the *Chassidus* got back on its feet.

"After that, Rav Shmuel Shapira and Rav Shmuel Horowitz became Breslover *chassidim*, and everything was in his merit. He's the one who returned the fire back to Breslov *Chassidus*."

The Rav used to say that he learned about passion and fiery *avodas Hashem* from Rav Lippel; about guarding one's eyes from Rav Shmuel Shapira; and about simplicity from Rav Levi Yitzchak Bender.

NOT SCARED OF THE SOVIETS

For his part, Rav Lippel held the young Rav Berland in very high esteem. He believed that the Rav was the only person who'd be able to re-open the path to Rebbe Nachman's grave in Uman to the wider public.

Although the yearning for Uman burned strongly in many of the remaining Breslov *chassidim*, it was also mixed with a very strong dose of fear of the Soviet authorities. Most of the Breslov elders in the Meah Shearim community had spent many years in Uman before World War II, and had endured torture, imprisonment and banishment. In many instances, they'd also seen Breslov friends and fellow *chassidim* in Uman brutally killed by Stalin's Soviet regime, solely for the "crime" of trying to live as openly religious Jews.

Spiritually, the Breslov elders yearned for Uman and Rebbe Nachman's grave; practically, the idea of traveling back to the Soviet Union struck an unparalleled sense of terror into their collective hearts. While a very small group of American Breslov followers (connected with Rabbi Tzvi Aryeh Rosenfeld) had managed to visit the grave with official permission during Chanukah in 1963, that was the first and last time the Soviet authorities had officially issued a visa for foreign tourists to go to Uman.

Following the Six-Day War in 1967, the remote possibility of legally traveling to the USSR or to Uman diminished even further for the Breslov *chassidim* living in Israel, as the USSR abruptly cut off all diplomatic ties with the Jewish State. By the 1970s, Uman had effectively been off-limits for almost four decades.

In the intervening years, the Breslov *chassidim* in Israel had tried to adapt by holding the annual Rosh Hashanah *kibbutz* in Meron (with Rav Shmuel Shapira) or in Jerusalem (with Rav Levi Yitzchak Bender) instead. With the passage of time, many of the remaining Breslovers in Meah Shearim had effectively given up on the idea of returning to Uman.

RAV LIPPEL PUSHES THE RAV TO ACT

While most of the Breslov elders continued to wait and pray for the path to Uman to somehow be re-opened, Rav Hersh Leib Lippel stood out as being one of the very few to turn his yearning for Uman into practical action and encouragement.

When Rav Berland had first apprenticed himself to Rav Lippel as his *shamash* in the 1960s, Rav Lippel recognized that here was someone who was prepared to sacrifice himself to the very end, for any matter connected with Rebbe Nachman.

Even though it was effectively impossible to make the trip to Uman at that time, Rav Lippel took Rav Berland aside and told him that, while he'd learned everything he could about Breslov by mastering the holy books and internalizing the true Breslov path from its elders, "I can't teach you any more Breslov Torah until you've made the trip to Uman."

It was only by going to the grave of Rebbe Nachman, that Rav Berland would be able to access new levels of spiritual insight and understanding. The Rav took Rav Lippel's words to heart, and he resolved that from that point on, he was going to do everything in his power to try to get to Uman, no matter what.

Rav Lippel apparently had big plans in mind for Rav Berland. He once told his son, "Rav Lazer is the one who is continuing the fire of *Rabbeinu* in this generation."

THE ONE TRUE STUDENT OF *RABBEINU*

Rav Lippel also taught Rav Berland about the Breslov tradition of there being one "true student" of Rebbe Nachman in each generation, who had the ability to really pass on the Rebbe's teachings to his contemporaries. He encouraged Rav Berland to try to discover who it was in their generation.

THE FOUR TRUE STUDENTS OF REBBE NACHMAN

Many years later, Rav Berland taught that the four main 'true students' were:

1. Rav Noson, Rebbe Nachman's main pupil and the redactor of *Likutei Moharan*

2. Rav Nachman Tulchiner

Rav Avraham ben Rav Nachman (also known as Rav Avraham Chazan)

3. Rav Levi Yitzchak Bender

Each of these *tzaddikim* had been markedly different from the one who came before them. Rav Levi Yitzchak, for example, was nothing like his teacher Rav Avraham ben Rav Nachman. The Rav explained that each of these "true students" had been given his own way of sharing *Rabbeinu's* light, a way that was suited to his particular generation.

Rav Berland explained: "In each generation, we need to beg God to help us uncover who is the keeper of *Rabbeinu's* light in our own generation. It's only once we make the effort to do this that God will reveal to us who is the embodiment of the "true *Tzaddik*" in our own times. But it's only the people who are committed to finding out the truth who will really discover it."

Rav Lippel told Rav Eliezer that it would be worthwhile to get closer to Rav Levi Yitzchak Bender (who was related to Rav Lippel by marriage), and hinted that he'd been one of the main leaders of the Breslovers in Uman, and the man chosen as the main *shaliach tzibbur* at the Rosh Hashanah prayer services in the *Kloiz*. Rav

Levi Yitzchak would eventually become Rav Berland's most influential mentor in Breslov circles.

It's told that after Rav Lippel saw the tremendous effort Rav Berland had made to get close to Rav Levi Yitzchak, he took his hand and told him, "You will yet be the leader of the Breslov *chassidim*!"

Rav Lippel died on the 23rd Cheshvan, 5740 (November 13th, 1979).

RAV TZVI ARYEH ROSENFELD

Rav Tzvi Aryeh Rosenfeld zt'l, was a scion of Rabbi Aharon, the man Rebbe Nachman brought to Breslov to act as the town's rabbi, and the founder of the American Breslov community.

In 1923, when Rav Rosenfeld was a year old, his family moved from Gdynia, Poland, to New York City to escape the grinding poverty and violent persecution that was increasingly the lot of religious Jews who stayed behind in the 'old country'. At that time, Breslov chassidus was virtually unheard of in America.

As an adult, Rav Rosenfeld almost single-handedly built the foundation of what would become the American Breslov community, with the strong backing of Rav Avraham Sternhartz, *zt'l*, who encouraged him to stay put and do outreach in New York when Rav Rosenfeld expressed his heartfelt wish to make *aliyah*.

Rav Rosenfeld made his first trip to Israel in 1949, and from that time on made it a practice to come to Israel for ten weeks during the summer, when he participated in *shiurim* and *chaburas* in the Breslov shul.

One of the leaders of the present day English-speaking Breslov community, Rav Nosson Maimon, was a student of Rav Rosenfeld, and subsequently became his son-in-law. He recalls that Rav Rosenfeld had tremendous respect for Rav Berland.

"Rav Berland first met Rav Tzvi Aryeh in Brooklyn, New York," recalls Rav Maimon. "I was only 17 years old at the time, but Rav Berland had come to America to find a way to get to Uman. He had heard that Rav Rosenfeld was taking trips to Uman, and he came to America to see how he could help to get more Israelis to Uman via America. Rav Berland came to the US with two other prominent Breslovers, Rav Shlomo Chaim Rotenberg and Rav Moshe Beninstock. Rav Rosenfeld built a strong relationship with all of them."

When Rav Rosenfeld first met Rav Berland, he immediately decided to set up a *chabura* with him where the two men would learn the *Tikkunei Zohar* and other kabbalistic works on a daily basis whenever Rav Rosenfeld was in Israel.

Rav Rosenfeld left behind many recordings of his *shiurim* in English, and in one of those recordings you can hear him telling someone in the audience: "Do you know Reb Lazer? If you would know him you would have stood up for him three times right now. He is like the Muhammad Ali of Breslov, the greatest!"

Rav Rosenfeld passed away on the 11th of Kislev 5739 (December 11th, 1978).

RABBI BINYAMIN ZEV CHESHIN

From the time that Rav Berland started to study at the Breslov Yeshivah in Bnei Brak, he also started to come in close contact with another of the Breslov greats of that time, Rav Binyamin Zev Cheshin. Although Rav Cheshin was a Breslover *chossid* through and through, and counted as one of the Breslov Elders of his generation, he was greatly respected in the wider religious community, too.

Rav Cheshin was the *Rosh* Yeshivah of the 'Shaar Hashamayim' kabbalistic yeshivah in Jerusalem, and was considered to be one of the leading kabbalists of the last generation. He regularly studied with the great kabbalists Rav Mordechai Sharabi and Rav Tzion Bracha, who both admired him greatly.

Rav Sharabi used to stand up for him when he entered the yeshivah and would often say of him: "Rebbe Binyamin Zev Cheshin is *kadosh kadoshim* (holy of holies)." Rav Bracha once said of him, "He is the *tzaddik* foundation of the world".

Despite Rav Cheshin's exalted level of holiness and erudition, he conducted himself day-to-day as a simple *yid*. Long before anyone even dreamed of what came to be known as the Israeli *teshuva* movement, Rav Cheshin could often be found traveling around the country, giving Torah classes to non-religious people from every background.

Rav Cheshin would come to the yeshivah in Bnei Brak once a week to give a *shiur*, and he had a room in the yeshivah where he used to sleep overnight before traveling back to Jerusalem. He was known as the first person in the Meah Shearim Breslov community who was willing to teach *baalei teshuvah* and other people who were interested in coming back to *Yiddishkeit*.

Rav Cheshin also took the *mitzvah* of guarding his eyes very seriously, to the point where he would deliberately smear mud on the inside of his sunglasses so he wouldn't be able to see any forbidden sights when he walked through the city streets.

RAV CHESHIN AND URI ZOHAR

Rav Cheshin's great passion was outreach, and to that end he resisted the prevailing custom of the Breslov community in Meah Shearim, to teach Torah only in Yiddish, and began to give *shiurim* in Hebrew, as well. Of the many people Rav Cheshin drew closer to *Yiddishkeit*, the best known is probably the famous Israeli actor-turned-Rabbi, Uri Zohar.

RAV CHESHIN STANDS UP FOR RAV BERLAND

One of Rav Berland's contemporaries at the Breslov Yeshiva in Bnei Brak, Rav Aaron Lebel, recalls: "On the days when he was speaking in the yeshivah in Bnei Brak, Rav Zev would give a *shiur* on *Likutei Moharan*. Some days he would sleep in the yeshivah and other days he'd go back to his home. Usually he would sleep in the yeshivah on the days he was giving his class, and sometimes he'd also stay the next day, talk with the students and discuss Torah with them. Once when Rav Zev was learning in his room, Rav Berland walked in and Rav Zev stood up in his honor — despite his own greatness!"

Rav Lebel recounts that he'd seen Rav Cheshin stand up for Rav Berland on many different occasions, despite Rav Cheshin's advanced age and senior status. "Rav Berland was still very young then, and he didn't yet have his own yeshivah," says Rav Lebel. "But he would pray for six hours a day—he would *daven Shacharis* for six hours a day! — and that was enough for others to see that he was a very special person."

Rav Cheshin passed away on the 17th Cheshvan, 5749 (October 28, 1988).

RAV SHMUEL SHAPIRA

Rav Shmuel Shapira was born in Jerusalem in 1913, and quickly gained a reputation as one of the most outstanding students at the Etz Chaim Yeshiva, under the auspices of the world-famous *Rosh* Yeshivah, Rabbi Isser Zalman Meltzer.

In 1934 at the age of 21, Rav Shapira met Rabbi Shmuel Horowitz, who enticed him over to the path of Breslov *chassidus*. When Rav Meltzer was told the news, he reportedly said: "Whoever made him a Breslover will never leave *Gehinnom*." When Rabbi Shmuel Shapiro heard this, he replied: "That's correct. Because he'll never be sent there!"

Rabbi Shmuel frequently spent his nights in the fields around Jerusalem doing *hisbodedus*, and would then spend his daylight hours learning Torah quietly in some out-of-the-way *shul* where he was careful to avoid any public recognition.

As part of his spiritual preparations for Rosh Hashanah, Rav Shapira normally spent the whole of Elul up in Meron, where he once commented: "Here I have everything I need—a synagogue, a *mikvah*, and mountains for *hisbodedus*. It's *Gan Eden* on earth."

Rav Shmuel Shapira--who came to be known as 'the *Tzaddik* of Jerusalem--was also renowned for his tremendous personal holiness, and particularly his practice of never raising his eyes in public. Together with Rav Cheshin and Rav Levi Yitzchak Bender, Rav Shapira was responsible for building the main Breslover shul in Meah Shearim.

Shortly after the new Breslov *shul* was built, it's told that there wasn't always a *minyan* for the daily prayers. These three Torah giants would laugh and ask each other why they'd gone to all the trouble and expense of building such a large synagogue But the truth is, they had a vision for Breslov *Chassidus* that went far beyond its current, limited horizons. They believed the day would come when even the massive new Breslov synagogue they'd just built wouldn't be able to contain all the people who would come to pray there.

Rav Berland once explained it wasn't for nothing that the Breslov synagogue they'd built was affectionately called "the *shul*," because the letters of "shul" spelled out Shmuel (Shapira), Velvel (Rav Cheshin's Yiddish name—the u and the v are represented by the same letter *vav* in Hebrew), and Levi (Yitzchak Bender).

"THIS IS NOT A PERSON, IT'S AN ANGEL!"

"There was no Uman for Rosh Hashanah in those days," recalls Rav Yehoshua Dov Rubinstein. "Breslov would be divided, with some people staying in the shul with Rav Levi Yitzchak Bender in Jerusalem, while others would go to Meron with Rav Shmuel Shapira. Rav Berland was always in the group that would stay with Rav Bender, while I would go with my father to Meron. One year, I decided to stay on in

Meron for Yom Kippur too. And *davka* that year, Rav Berland also came to Meron for Yom Kippur.

"So, I was there in Meron, and I saw the Rav standing in the corner on *Erev* Yom Kippur *davening Shemoneh Esrei*, standing in the same spot, *davening* to *Hashem* with such *dveikus*, without moving, from before Yom Kippur until after Yom Kippur had ended, for more than 24 hours straight! We made *havdalah* at 8 p.m., and the buses were waiting to take everyone back to Jerusalem, and the Rav was still standing there, *davening*. We didn't know what to do," continues Rav Rubinstein.

"Rav Moshe Beninstock[XXIV] was also there, and he told everyone to get their stuff together and to get on the bus, and he promised them that when everyone was ready to go, the Rav would join them at the last minute. In those days, if you missed that bus out of Meron, you had no other way of getting home, so the Rav would be stuck there. But they listened to Rav Beninstock, got everything together and went out to where the bus was waiting.

"Everyone sat down, and Rav Beninstock was going back and forth between the bus and Rav Berland to check what was going on. As soon as he saw that the last person had taken his seat, he went up to Rav Berland—who was still *davening*—and whispered something in his ear. The Rav ran straight to the bus. They gave him a cup of grape juice, so he could make *havdalah*, and they also gave him something to break his fast with, but he only took a small bite.

"Then, Rav Beninstock asked him if he'd like to say something to the *kehilla*, so the Rav took the microphone and gave over a four-hour *dvar Torah* while the bus was driving home [The old buses and old roads of those days made the trip to Meron much longer than it is nowadays]. He didn't eat anything else, he didn't speak to anyone; he just gave over Torah throughout the entire bus ride.

"As we were approaching Jerusalem, the Rav said on the microphone, 'We've just been in such a holy place, how can we go to sleep?' By that point, it was already 3 a.m. So, someone asked him, 'So what should we do?' The Rav replied, 'Let's do *hisbodedus*! Let's go to the field!' So, a few people joined him in the field.

"After spending the rest of the night in the field, he appeared for *Shacharis* in the Breslov *shul* in Meah Shearim the following morning, and again he just stood there *davening* for hours and hours. When the *minyan* had finished, he went up to the roof to continue his prayers with song and great enthusiasm. Some people went over

---

XXIV   Today, Rav Moshe Beninstock is the main *baal tefillah* on Rosh Hashana in the main *kloiz shul* in Uman.

to Rav Shmuel Shapira and asked him, 'What do you say about this Rav Lazer Berland?' Rav Shmuel replied, 'It's already known to us that this is not a person, it's an angel!'" concludes Rav Rubinstein.

THE RAV ENCOURAGES PEOPLE TO HUMILIATE HIM

For his part, Rav Berland did his best to damp down the rumors of his holiness and erudition, by following his tried and trusted method of playing the fool in public.

"Throughout all the years we've known the Rav, we've seen that one of his spiritual devotions is to bring shame upon himself," begins Rav Ben Zion Grossman. "It's not just that he doesn't go after honor; he literally encourages people to insult him and humiliate him.

"Once, when he was beginning to come close to Breslov, the Rav met Rav Shmuel Shapira in Meron. The Rav opened up a copy of the *Kitzur Shulchan Aruch* and started to ask Rav Shapira to explain to him some of the very simple *halachos* it contained. Rav Shapira obliged, and started to answer him as simply and straightforwardly as he could. But the Rav wasn't satisfied with this, and asked him the question again, as though he hadn't understood the answer.

"People started to notice that something was going on, and before long a small group of Breslov chassidim were gathered around Rav Shapira and the Rav. They were all wondering why the Rav was asking Rav Shapira such simple questions about the *Kitzur Shulchan Aruch*. Once the Rav was sure everyone had seen how little Torah he seemed to know, he accepted Rav Shapira's explanation and left.

"Of course, the Rav already knew the whole *Mishnah Berurah* by heart when he was still a child, and he knew the *halachah* clearly. He also had learned *b'chavrusa* with the Steipler, *zt"l*, every single day for a number of years, where he used to reveal nuances in all the aspects of the *halachos* contained in the *Shulchan Aruch*."

Rav Grossman concludes, "The amazing thing is that despite all this, he still managed to convince everyone that he'd turned into a complete *am ha'aretz*."

The connection with Rav Shapira continued down the generations, with Rav Shmuel's sons Rav Shimon Shapira and Rav Nachman Shapira accompanying the Rav on some of his clandestine trips to Uman. The two brothers continued to be in close contact with Rav Berland and his Shuvu Banim Yeshivah for many years, until Rav Nachman's recent passing in March 2013.

For example, when Rav Berland first became embroiled in the controversy caused by the extremists within Breslov in 1989, Reb Nachman Shapira wrote a note to the Rav's students in Shuvu Banim which said the following: *"Rabbeinu* is proud of you! [I hope] that my lot should be with yours!" Rav Nachman continued to be a strong supporter of the Rav and Shuvu Banim, and stood up for them against the Breslov extremists until the very end of his life.

THE MIND AND THE SPIRIT OF *RABBEINU*

As mentioned previously, while a person can and must do everything in his power to draw close to the "true *Tzaddik,"* i.e., Rebbe Nachman, by learning his teachings and doing his best to follow his advice, this is only half the equation.

The other, and just as necessary, half of the equation is to also find the *Tzaddik* of *this generation*[XXV] who embodies Rebbe Nachman's light in our times. If a person has one without the other, he will not be able to follow the path of the true *Tzaddik* in its entirety, the way Rebbe Nachman intended.

Rav Berland understood this, and went to great pains to try to find the one "true student" of Rebbe Nachman in his generation who was able to fully shine Rebbe Nachman's light into the world.

After a strong hint by Rav Lippel that he should concentrate his efforts on Rav Levi Yitzchak Bender, the Rav turned his attention to get close enough to Rav Bender to learn what was really going on beneath his apparently simple exterior.

RAV BENDER'S BRUSH WITH THE KGB

While Rav Bender kept a very low profile in Meah Shearim, before World War II he'd famously risked his life to attend the last Rosh Hashanah gathering in Uman in 1938, where he'd only narrowly escaped being caught and executed by the murderous Soviet authorities. After World War II, in 1949, Rav Bender made *aliyah* to Israel and devoted the last 40 years of his life to ensuring that Breslov *Chassidus* in the Meah Shearim section of Jerusalem had a strong foundation from which to grow.

While he undoubtedly had many public achievements under his belt, up close he still seemed to be an unlikely candidate for the "true student of the generation".

XXV   Sometimes also referred to as "the true student of the generation." See *Chayei Moharan* 230.

Rav Bender kept to himself and ran away from any hint of status, honor, or public recognition, to the point that it was often difficult to see his true spiritual greatness because of the great lengths he went to in order to hide himself.

Only people who steeled themselves to successfully break through all these disguises and mysteries would be able to subsequently find this hidden light, and be able to learn from the deep wisdom of Rebbe Nachman that had been passed down from generation to generation.

Rav Berland spent many years trying to discover the bearer of this light before discovering Rav Levi Yitzhak Bender. But even then things were so straightforward, as Rav Levi Yitzhak hated any hint of being honored by others, so even if someone just tried to escort him on the street, he would yell at him to go away. Whenever he saw Rav Berland coming toward him, he would run away from him as fast as his legs could carry him.

The Rav once said that each of the Breslov elders had taken a different element from *Rabbeinu*. Rav Hersh Leib Lippel was renowned for his service of Hashem, Rav Shmuel Shapira had taken upon himself guarding his eyes from unholy sights, Rav Velvel Cheshin had taken on drawing other people closer, and Rav Levi Yitzchak had taken the essence of *Rabbeinu* himself.

Rav Berland also stated: "I was by all of them, I slept by all of them over a long period of time, until *Hakadosh Baruch Hu* had mercy on me and revealed Rav Levi Yitzchak, who possessed the light of *Rabbeinu* himself."

RAV BENDER POURS A JUG OF WATER OVER THE RAV

From the beginning when the Rav started to draw close to Breslov, he used to occasionally come up to Jerusalem from Bnei Brak, where he'd visit Rav Levi Yitzchak Bender and ask him if he could learn *Mishnayos* with him. (Learning *Mishnayos* is generally considered to be one of the simpler forms of Torah learning.)

Rav Levi Yitzchak thought that the Rav must be a *baal teshuvah* who didn't know how to learn, so in his humility he started learning *Mishnayos* with the Rav, and taught him the way one would teach someone completely ignorant of Torah, very slowly and with a lot of explanation on every subject.

One day, Rav Levi Yitzchak asked one of the other Breslov elders if he could take over his *chavrusa* with this new *baal teshuvah*, as his time was very precious and he felt he could use it better in other ways. The Breslov elder had no idea whom Rav

Levi Yitzchak was talking about. When he finally understood that he was referring to Rav Berland, he started laughing out loud.

"He's a *baal teshuvah*?!" he asked incredulously. "He knows the whole of *Shas* by heart!"

When Rav Levi Yitzchak heard this, he was stunned and also hurt. Had the Rav been making fun of him? The next time the Rav came to see him, Rav Levi Yitzchak poured a jug of water over him. "You came to ask me about more *Mishnayos*?!" he challenged him, still upset.

The Rav replied calmly, "Of course I know how to learn *Mishnayos* by myself, but I wanted to experience with you how Breslover *chassidim* used to learn *Mishnayos* in the old days, back in Uman." Rav Levi Yitzchak was amazed by this answer, and decided to suspend judgment about the Rav.

But that wasn't the end of the story.

PLAYING THE FOOL IN *SHUL*

Rav Aharon Lebel takes up the tale. "My father, Rav Feivel Lebel, *zt"l*, brought the Rav to the [Breslov] *shul* [in Meah Shearim] at the beginning of his drawing closer [to Breslov *Chassidus*]. The Rav would ridicule himself completely and everyone thought he was just a *meshugganer* crazy person.

"In the *shul* there was another of the big *ovdei Hashem*. He was a recognized *talmid chacham* and also very knowledgeable in all the *Gemara* and *poskim*—and he enjoyed seeing the Rav bringing insults and humiliation upon himself, as he also engaged in the same sort of spiritual devotion of lowering himself. So this man and the Rav, climbed on some tables and started dancing in the *shul*, before the morning prayers began.

"The Rav came down before the prayers started, so the other man asked him why he'd stopped, but the Rav didn't respond. So, this other man also started to believe that the Rav was crazy, and started talking to him as though he was a fool, and gave him a slap.

"After *Shacharis*, this man was walking down the stairs out of *shul* when he fell and broke his leg. He had to stay in bed for many weeks. He later said to my father, *zt"l*, 'For 30 years already I've been going down these stairs, and I've never fallen even once. Why was today different? It seems as though it's connected to the *meshugganer* you brought here today..."'

THE SHABBOS CHANUKAH *DRASHAH* IN MERON

Good as he was at playing the fool, anyone who spent any real time around Rav Berland, or watched him learning Torah, praying and engaging in his other spiritual devotions, couldn't be fooled for long. It was only a matter of time before the Rav's true abilities started to shine through to the Breslov elders of Meah Shearim.

Rav Aharon Lebel recounts: "On Shabbos Chanukah 5726 (1962) in Meron, Rav Levi Yitzchak Bender honored my father, Rav Feivel Lebel, *zt"l*, by asking him to teach some *Likutei Moharan* in front of the community during the third Shabbos meal.

"My father told Rav Levi Yitzchak that there was another *avreich* there who knew how to learn even better than he did, and that his name was Reb Lazer Berland. Rav Levi Yitzchak asked my father, 'What?! The same person who comes to ask me what you should do if you forgot to say a *brachah* on something?! [This is a very simple question more fitting for a young child than a big Torah scholar.] Or who asks me what the Rebbe says about sticking a child in a cupboard?!'

"My father told him, 'Yes, that's the one.'

"Rav Shmuel Shapira, *zt"l*, then joined in and told them that Rav Berland had also asked him what to do if you forget to say the blessing after going to the bathroom, and all sorts of similar questions like that. But my father managed to convince them that despite all this, he really did know how to learn Torah, and persuaded them to ask the Rav to speak.

"So Rav Berland spoke, and the audience was amazed. (The Rav was just 27 years old at this time.) After the learning session, the Rav saw that people had been really impressed by him, so he started to do headstands and to throw his *shtreimel* around. So, then people started to say to each other, 'He knows how to study, but he's still a *meshugganer*!'"

Rav Aaron Berlin fills in the missing part of the story: "As that Shabbos Chanukah gathering in Meron drew to a close, Rav Levi Yitzchak invited me to his room, and together with Rav Shmuel Shapira, they asked me a number of questions about Rav Berland for a full hour, to find out what he's all about, where he comes from and how I know him," he discloses.

Apparently, Rav Berland had passed the test, because after that Shabbos, Rav Berland started traveling from Bnei Brak to Jerusalem every week to be with Rav Levi Yitzchak. Despite the fact that Rav Levi Yitzchak was 40 years older than Rav Berland, the two men forged a very strong relationship.

Later on, when members of the community continued to approach Rav Bender with negative comments about his young protégé, he told them, "What can I tell you? What I see in Rav Lazer, I don't see in any other person."

THE RAV RAN AWAY FROM RESPECT

Rav Yehoshua Dov Rubinstein explains why even then, the Rav often went to such lengths to provoke negative comments about himself: "At the point when people started to greatly respect him and give him a lot of honor, the Rav started to do things that looked very foolish, and to deliberately make a fool of himself, in order to stop other people from showing him respect," he says.

"He'd particularly act like that in front of Rav Levi Yitzchak Bender, to ensure that Rav Bender wouldn't show him any particular respect or honor. But Rav Bender was a very astute person, and he knew the truth. He once said, 'Reb Lazer, he knows everything! I don't know how, but he knows everything!'"

RAV LEVI YITZCHAK WARMS UP TO THE RAV

Over time, Rav Levi Yitzchak came to understand that he was dealing with an extraordinary individual in Rav Berland, one who was sincerely committed to learning and living by Rebbe Nachman's teachings, no matter how much effort he had to exert. Slowly, slowly, Rav Levi Yitzchak's attitude started to soften toward his unwanted follower and he gradually started to draw him closer and share with him more and more of his deep knowledge of Breslov Torah.

For his part, Rav Berland redoubled his efforts to squeeze every last piece of information and insight out of him.

Every day, he would be waiting by Rav Levi Yitzchak's door, ready to accompany him to *shul*, and would patiently wait for him for hours, simply in the hopes of hearing some more pearls of wisdom about how best to serve God, and how to follow the path laid out by Rebbe Nachman. Rav Berland knew that this was one of the times when a person had no choice but to display some of the "holy brazenness" described in *Likutei Moharan*.

TORAH FOR BREAKFAST

"The Rav was very close to Rav Levi Yitzchak Bender, and served him for many years," explains Rav Gavriel Grossman. "Apart from the times when he would talk to him at the *Kosel* and when he was on his way home, there were also times when the Rav would arrive at his house at breakfast time.

Rav Berland escorting Rav Levi Yitzchak from the Kosel, together with a number of Rav Berland's students

"The Rav would come with a lot of questions, to encourage him to share all of his knowledge about *Rabbeinu*, and because he did this, he merited to reveal and continue the Breslov traditions.

"Rav Levi Yitzchak wasn't always comfortable with this, and often participated against his will. I remember once that Rav Levi Yitzchak wanted to stop these discussions, and he said to the Rav, 'The law is that you don't speak during a meal.'

"The Rav immediately got up and took a volume of the *Shulchan Aruch, Orach Chaim* from the bookshelf. He opened it to chapter 170, and began reading a commentary called the *Shaarei Teshuvah* on this law, that a person shouldn't speak during a meal, where it says in the name of the *Prisha* [a commentator] that the concern we have in regard to this law was only for those who ate while reclining.

"When Rav Levi Yitzchak heard this, he was amazed at the Rav's erudition, and he warmed up to the Rav tremendously."

"RAV LAZER IS SOMETHING ELSE!"

Another student from that time explains: "Rav Levi Yitzchak hated any hint of notoriety, and wouldn't let anyone make a big deal out of him, under any circumstances. One time, a few of the Breslover *avreichim* wanted to escort him home. Rav Levi Yitzchak sent them packing, and asked them why they were trying to honor him.

"The students asked him, 'But you let Rav Lazer escort you, even with a big group of people!' Rav Levi Yitzchak said to them, 'Rav Lazer is something else! He's got his path, and I've got mine.'"

BUNDLES OF MONEY IN THE *SHUL*

Rav Yehuda Frank, *zt'l*, told the the following story to Rav Avraham Elbaz:

"Rav Levi Yitzchak Bender called me over and told me that every Thursday night, someone was leaving a big bundle of money in the Breslov shul in Meah Shearim, together with a note to Rav Bender that it should be distributed amongst the Breslover *chassidim* in honor of the holy Shabbos. It was enough money to give everyone a handsome amount.

"Rav Levi Yitzchak told me to hide out in the *shul* that Thursday night, to see who was leaving him the money. I hid out all night, until at 3 a.m. I saw the Rav come in, leave the money, then run away again.

"The following morning, I told Rav Levi Yitzchak that it was Rav Berland, and he told me, 'I knew it! Only he could do something like that!' This continued for quite a long period of time, until the Rav held a gathering in Bnei Brak and brought Rav Levi Yitzchak over from Jerusalem to speak.

"Rav Levi Yitzchak said that he knew about the Rav's wondrous activities, and how every week he was giving *tzedakah* to needy families. As soon as the Rav heard that his cover was blown, he stopped," concludes Rav Frank.

THE THURSDAY EVENING *SHIUR*

If there's one thing that really started to put Rav Levi Yitzchak Bender on the map as the Breslov spiritual leader of his generation, it was his Thursday night *shiur*. Rav Bender had been giving his *shiur* for years to a very small group of people, perhaps no more than a handful.

Before Rav Berland appeared on the scene, Rav Bender had actually stopped giving over Torah classes, as so few people were turning up to hear them. But once Rav Berland discovered Rav Bender all that started to change, and the Thursday night *shiur* became one of the major highlights of the week for the burgeoning Breslov community.

"In the first years when Rav Levi Yitzchak arrived in Israel, the Breslover *chassidim* didn't grasp who Rav Levi Yitzchak really was, because he behaved in a very simple way," says Rav Shalom Arush. "The person who really uncovered his greatness, and who started to reveal it to the public, was the Rav. The Rav discovered his *shiurim* and re-energized them. He acted as Rav Levi Yitzchak's attendant and he learned a great deal from him.

"Everything that Rav Levi Yitzchak did to lead Breslov, the Rav was a big part of it all."

SEVEN TAXIS FROM BNEI BRAK

Rav Shlomo Gabbai, one of Rav Berland's earlier followers, recalls that every Thursday evening "seven taxis would leave from Bnei Brak to Jerusalem, whatever the weather. The Rav used to say that whoever didn't come to the *shiur* was missing out on something so huge, it was impossible to explain."

Rav Aharon Berlin explained that the Rav had instituted a rule in the yeshivah that everyone *had* to come hear Rav Levi Yitzchak's *shiur* on Thursday night — and tens of young men were answering the call every week.

Rav Yitzchak Weisshandler adds: "We used to take taxis[XXVI] every Thursday from Bnei Brak to go and hear Rav Levi Yitzchak's *shiur*. Rav Velvel[XXVII] Cheshin also used to travel with us from Bnei Brak to Jerusalem, and the drivers knew that they had to

---

XXVI   Rav Berland would pay for everyone's taxi fare out of his own pocket.
XXVII   Rav Binyamin Zev's Yiddish name.

87

keep a place for him next to the driver, so he wouldn't have any risk of sitting next to, or behind, a strange woman[XXVIII].

"But when Rav Berland even so much as saw that there was a woman in the taxi, he'd wait for a different one. There were many occasions when the Rav would pay for the empty seats out of his own pocket if the taxi hadn't filled up."

Rav Weisshandler continues: "It's impossible to describe how much the Rav valued every word of Rav Levi Yitzchak's *shiurim*. The Rav would leave the taxi as soon as it got close and start running toward Rav Levi Yitzchak's home. And after the *shiur*, the Rav was lit up like a burning flame!"

It quickly became known in Breslov circles that the Rav would often spend all night after the Thursday *shiur* doing *hisbodedus* in one of the forests surrounding Jerusalem, begging God to help him be worthy of fully understanding, and fully internalizing, Rav Bender's words.

RAV BENDER FALLS FOUL OF THE BRESLOV EXTREMISTS

As the Rav started bringing more and more of his students and followers with him to Meah Shearim to drink from the wellsprings of the Breslov elders, some of the more extreme members of the Breslov community in Meah Shearim started to get increasingly disgruntled about this flood of outsiders whom they viewed as trying to take over "their" *shul* and "their" *Chassidus*.

Their main complaint was that all matters to do with Breslov *Chassidus* and the Rebbe's Torah should be given over in the lingua franca of Meah Shearim: Yiddish. They lived in a society that was still openly hostile to Torah Judaism and religious Jews, and one of the ways they believed they could block out the deleterious impact of the modern, secular world on their doorstep was by maintaining a different language from their Hebrew-speaking, and often anti-religious neighbors.

So, when Rav Levi Yitzchak began his *shiurim* again at the behest of Rav Berland and his followers, he initially continued to give it over in Yiddish, but agreed to have a translator present to translate it into Hebrew for the *baalei teshuva* who didn't know Yiddish.

XXVIII   In those days, taxis in Israel would pick up other passengers on the way, in order to fill up all the seats.

Over time, the number of people sitting at the Yiddish table at Rav Bender's *shiur* continued to be no more than a handful, while the numbers of people sitting at the back close to the Hebrew translator grew very rapidly. One day, Rav Levi Yitzchak decided that it was time to take the next step toward making Breslov teachings more accessible to the public. He announced that from that point on, he would be giving over his Thursday night *shiur* in Hebrew.

BREAK DOWN THE DOOR

When they heard this unwelcome piece of news, the Breslov extremists were very upset. Rav Yehoshua Dov Rubinstein explains how they tried to retaliate, by blocking the entrance to the *shul* where Rav Bender used to speak: "Someone who was really against Rav Levi Yitzchak locked the door by affixing a huge padlock to the outside, in order to stop people from coming to the *shiur*," he says.

"When we got there, Rav Levi Yitzchak said to us, 'Why are you just standing there? Bring some crowbars and break down the door!' So, we smashed down the door and everyone came in for the *shiur*. Rav Levi Yitzchak told us afterwards, 'You have no idea what this *shiur* is doing in *Shamayim*! How precious it is in *Shamayim*![XXIX]"

But the seeds of *machlokes* had been sown, and Rav Berland and his community would continue to reap the bitter fruit for many decades to come.

XXIX   Rebbe Nachman teaches that the more obstacles a person encounters on the path of holiness, the more precious it is to Hashem.

THE NEXT GENERATION OF BRESLOV CHASSIDUS

LEARNING THE ROPES FROM RAV LEVI YITZCHAK

Part of the reason that Rav Berland was so attracted to Rav Levi Yitzchak Bender was because he wanted to find someone who was really *living* the Breslov traditions. In Rav Bender he found the repository of some of the deepest secrets contained within Breslov *Chassidus*[XXX], plus a living example of how a true Breslover *chassid* should actually behave, think and learn.

For example, Rav Bender had a very rigorous learning schedule, which saw him complete many of the principal Jewish works each year, including the whole Talmud, the *Shulchan Aruch*, and the mystical works of the *Zohar*[XXXI].

He was also a firm adherent of Rebbe Nachman's advice to his followers that they should seclude themselves with God and talk their heart out to Him for at least an hour a day (a practice that's known as *hisbodedus*). But perhaps the thing that Rav Levi Yitzchak was best known for within Breslov circles was his unwavering commitment to reciting the *Tikkun Chatzos* at midnight over the destruction of the Temple. Indeed, Rav Bender rarely gave a lesson where he didn't stress the importance of *hisbodedus*, and getting up for *Chatzos*.

This last practice was so important to Rav Bender that he very rarely attended any weddings or other events scheduled in the evening that could prevent him from getting to bed early enough to wake up at midnight to recite the *Tikkun Chatzos*. The midnight lament marked the start of Rav Bender's day, and for 75 years, his whole routine and learning schedule was built around it.

"In his last years of life, Rav Levi Yitzchak Bender used to learn *Likutei Moharan* with the Rav after *chatzos*," explains one of the Rav's students. "One time, the Rav

---

XXX   Rav Bender knew many of the traditions that had been passed down by word of mouth directly from Rebbe Nachman, but never written down in the Breslov books. He passed this information on to Rav Berland, who later used this knowledge to help compile the five-volume work known as the *Siach Sarfei Kodesh* teachings.

XXXI   Rebbe Nachman advised his followers to complete all the major works of Torah every single year, and to repeat this practice every year—advice that Rav Bender, and Rav Berland both followed.

and Rebbetzin went away to a different city, to have a bit of a break. At night, the Rav would wait for the Rebbetzin to fall asleep, and then he'd leave immediately and travel to Jerusalem as fast as he could, in order to arrive for his regular learning session with Rabbi Levi Yitzchak, after midnight."

THE TRUE BRESLOV PATH

Rav Berland was a very adept student. Slowly but surely, by drawing on the insights, encouragement, and spiritual strengths of each of these giants of Breslov *Chassidus*, he managed to uncover the true Breslov path that had been all but forgotten for decades.

This renewed path had Rebbe Nachman's grave in Uman at its heart, but was also framed by a strong commitment to regular *hisbodedus;* serious, in-depth Torah learning; getting up at midnight; making outreach a priority; and putting a very strong emphasis on personal holiness and guarding the eyes.

BRESLOVERS NEED TO LEARN TORAH!

Whenever the Rav gave a Torah class, he'd include literally hundreds of explicit Torah references, ranging from basic *Chumash* to some of the most obscure, esoteric sources. When he was in his home in Jerusalem, he had three identical, huge wooden tables in three rooms of his house that would often be strewn with many tens of holy books, all opened at a particular page that the Rav was learning, and that he wanted to cross-check with the other books on the table.

Over the years, he made a number of pleas to other groups within Breslov *Chassidus* to put more emphasis on learning Torah.

"People make a mistake and think Breslov is dancing in the streets," he said. "That's not true. A person who does not learn *Gemara b'iyun*, Rebbe Nachman says, is called a *fessel kishkes*, a barrel of innards. It says in *Siach Sarfei Kodesh* (volume 2:257) that Rebbe Nachman said, '*Ich vil mein zach zohl gein oif litvishe hertzen*[XXXII],' or in other words, *Chassidus* is really for *Litvaks*."

The Rav continued: "If a person wants to mitigate his negative thoughts, he must learn *Gemara*. People think that it's enough to just go to Uman, but the bad thoughts don't go away if one doesn't learn *Gemara*.

"The Maggid of Mezritch was first a *Litvak* and then a *chassid*. Everyone was," he continued. "Rebbe Nachman said after you are *Litvish*, then come to me...When I traveled to Uman on forged passports, in the years before the Iron Curtain fell, I met the heads of the [Soviet] government in Kiev who told me, 'We know why you Jews are the smartest nation in the world. It's because you have the Talmud. That's why you are so strong.'"

On another occasion, the Rav told his students: "*Rabbeinu Hakadosh* says that in order to gain *seichel*, a man must learn *Shas*; he must learn Torah. A person must realize that Breslov and *Gemara* are one! The essence of Breslov *Chassidus* is that you do everything that is written in the Torah! You don't just go according to your own feelings and opinions or whatever's comfortable.

"You must know that Breslov *Chassidus* does not nullify even the tiniest little detail [in the Torah], *chas v'shalom*! No *minhag* of *Am Yisrael*! It only comes to add! It comes to add more *yiras Shamayim*, more *tefillah* with *kavanah* and more *shmiras einayim*, etc.

"The Rebbe said, 'I want my ideas to spread into Litvish hearts' (*Siach Sarfei Kodesh* 2:257). The Rebbe said, 'Be *Litvaks*!' Start to learn! With the Rebbe there is nothing new! The Rebbe says, 'I go in the old way which is completely new.' In Lesson 101 of *Likutei Moharan*, the Rebbe explains: 'Whoever accepts upon himself the yoke of Torah'—that is, the study of Torah in depth, *b'iyun*. The 'yoke of Torah' is in-depth study—Torah *b'iyun*, *Gemara*, and *poskim*.

"We have nothing other than what the Rebbe tells us. If a person wants something new let him compose a new *Likutei Moharan*! Let him create a new Breslov! We go, however, according to the original Breslov—what is written! The original Breslov is to learn Torah in depth, to learn *Gemara* and *poskim*.

"Look at how the Chazon Ish studied Torah! Look at how the Steipler studied Torah! Be a Breslover! There is nothing new here!"

SCREAMING ABUSE AT NEWCOMERS

Rav Berland's emphasis on outreach enraged some of the regulars at the Breslov shul, and many of his followers and students experienced a rough reception when they first tried to visit 'Rebbe Nachman's *shul*' in Meah Shearim.

One of the Rav's senior students, Rav Eliyahu Succot, recalls what happened the first time he came to the Meah Shearim *shul*, to try to see Rebbe Nachman's chair, that's on display there.

"While I was there, someone started screaming at me in Yiddish," he remembers. "I didn't know what he was saying, but I knew he wanted me to leave. Afterwards I understood that in his eyes, he thought I wasn't dressed properly." Heartbroken and in tears, Rav Succot started walking down to the Kosel, when he noticed that a young boy from the *shul* appeared to be following him.

"The main teachings of Reb Shlomo Carlebach had all been about Rebbe Nachman and here I was, in the place of Rebbe Nachman and everyone was screaming at me. So I was walking and crying, and there was a young boy about 12 years old walking beside me. We didn't speak to each other because he didn't know English and I didn't know Yiddish."

"Some 15 years later, he came to my house," Rav Succot continues. "He asked me if I remembered that someone had screamed at me in the Breslev Shul. I said 'yes, I remember'. Then he asked me if I also remembered that someone had followed me all the way to the Kosel afterwards. I said 'yes' again, and told me that it was him.

"I became very emotional, because he told me that he was a direct descendent of Rabbenu. Then I understood that despite the hurt I'd received, the Rebbe was with me. Afterwards, he told me that he'd spoken to his father, who knew the person who'd screamed at me. When the father heard what had happened, he spoke to this *chassid* and told him: 'Listen, I see that there is going to be a very great light of Rebbenu shining in the world, and all the people who will be drawn to this light aren't going to look like they came from Meah Shearim. We have to open our hearts to be able to speak with them, and to know how to receive them, because this is what the Rebbi wants. You mustn't go screaming at people because of the way they're dressed.' It was told that this Chassid did *teshuva*."

Other people who experienced a less than friendly welcome from the extremists at the Meah Shearim shul included Rav Shalom Arush, Rav Gedalya Koenig, zt'l and also Rav Eliezer Schick, zt'l.

THERE IS NO "TRUE TZADDIK"

But perhaps the biggest controversy of all revolved around the idea that there was a "true *tzaddik*" in every generation, who, while not replacing Rebbe Nachman in any way, shape or form, had been given the unique ability of passing the Rebbe's teachings on to the next generation.

Some of the people within Breslov disagreed with this notion in principle. There was only the Rebbe, and no one else was needed or required![XXXIII] Others accepted the basic idea of a "true *tzaddik*" in every generation, but balked at the idea that this person could be anyone other than one of their own. In their minds, it was simply ludicrous that an upstart national-religious pseudo-*Litvak* could even be considered as a candidate for Rebbe Nachman's "true student," however impressive his talents, commitment and achievements might be.

As time went on, this group became increasingly disturbed by the large following of "outsiders" Rav Berland was attracting to Breslov *Chassidus*—a group that was many times larger than their own group of "original" Yiddish-speaking Breslovers — and they were also very upset that so many people were streaming to Rav Berland to receive a blessing, as his reputation as a miracle worker became more widely known.

For as long as the three main Breslov elders were alive, the Breslov extremists could do nothing against Rav Berland and the hundreds and thousands of people he was introducing to Breslov teachings.

But in their own minds they were clear: When the time came to decide who would lead the next generation of Breslov *Chassidus*, the gloves would come off, and they'd deal Rav Berland and his hippie, *baal teshuvah* followers a blow they'd never recover from.

XXXIII   Some Breslov factions subsequently coined the phrase: "There are no *gedolim* and no *ketanim*" - i.e. they don't recognize the authority of any Rabbis and *Gedolim* at all.

THE PROPHETIC LETTER OF RAV SHMUEL HOROWITZ

Rav Shmuel Horowitz (1903-1973) was a very well-respected Breslov elder who authored the multi-volume autobiographical work *Yimei Shmuel*.

Rav Horowitz was a native of Poland who had become a Breslover *chassid* at a very young age, and who yearned to make the trip to visit Rebbe Nachman's gravesite in the Ukrainian town of Uman. Sadly, after the Communist revolution in 1917, the way to Uman was sealed, and it would take Rav Horowitz many long years before he finally achieved his goal. In 1930, at the age of 27, he risked his life to illegally cross the border between Poland and the USSR, to get to Uman.

Rav Horowitz stayed in Uman for three years, collecting a number of the important writings, stories, and teachings of the earlier generation of Breslov greats, including those of Rav Avraham Chazan (1849-1917), also known as "Reb Avraham ben Reb Nachman." Rav Horowitz eventually got back to Israel in 1933[XXXIV], where he published some of the material he'd collected.

RAV AVRAHAM CHAZAN APPEARS IN A DREAM

The late Rav Eliezer Shlomo Schick, *zt"l*, once said: "It's only due to Rav Shmuel Horowitz's efforts that we still have the works of Rav Avraham ben Rav Nachman. Rav Shmuel once told me that after he'd printed Rav Avraham's *Biur Halikutim*, Rav Avraham came to him in a dream, kissed him on the forehead and thanked him for printing his book with such great self-sacrifice."[XXXV]

Although Rav Horowitz made every effort to publish as many of the manuscripts, letters, and works as he could, there were still many letters from that time which have never been made available to the public[XXXVI]. One of them contains the account of Rav Getzel, a close student of Rav Avraham Chazan.

XXXIV   Although Rav Shmuel Horowitz's autobiography became a Breslov classic, and he's very well-known in all Breslov circles today, he confided to Rav Eliezer Schick before he died that during his lifetime, he was subject to tremendous persecution from the Breslov community in Meah Shearim, which is why he didn't pray with the other Breslovers in the Breslov *shul*.
XXXV   Rav Shmuel Horowitz had never met Rav Avraham, nor seen a picture of him. While Rav Horowitz was in Uman, he asked some of the people who'd known Rav Avraham in his lifetime to describe his appearance, and realized that it was the same man he'd seen in his dream.
XXXVI   Some of these manuscripts are available in microfilm in Jerusalem's Hebrew University.

RAV AVRAHAM'S PROPHECY

In that letter, Rav Getzel wrote the following:

"Midday, Friday, 8 Tammuz, 5632 [1872]. Rav Avraham emerged from the *mikvah* and dressed in his Shabbos finery. Filled with holy enthusiasm and powerful *dveikus*, he said, 'After about 50 years[12], a young and charismatic man will renew Rebbe Nachman's pathway in a wondrous manner, never before seen in the world. This will create a great revolution with regard to the redemption and will bring much good to the entire world. [May it come] speedily in our days, *amen*."

In his lifetime, Rav Avraham Chazan had been renowned for having an almost prophetic level of insight. He was also the only Breslov elder who'd been entrusted with Rebbe Nachman's *Megillas Sesarim*, or "hidden scroll," that included information about events that would unfold prior to the final redemption.

When Rebbe Nachman first revealed the teachings contained in the hidden scroll, he made it clear that they should be kept secret until the proper time. The Rebbe's principal student, Rav Noson Sternhartz, encoded this chronicle to ensure that it would remain hidden, and the key to deciphering the code was transmitted to only one person in each generation. It seems as though Rav Avraham was hinting to something he'd seen in the hidden scroll when he made these statements.

WHO WAS THIS NEW BRESLOV LEADER?

When this letter recently came into the hands of Rabbi Avraham Ben Chaim, a well-known elderly lecturer and the head of a Breslov synagogue in the Tel Aviv area, he said that from the moment he saw it, he immediately thought of Rav Berland. "Rav Berland was the charismatic and dynamic person that Rav Avraham ben Rav Nachman must have been referring to, and he has certainly breathed much new life into Rebbe Nachman's path," stated Rav Ben Chaim.

Of course, as the person who'd actually collected all of this material from Uman, and who'd risked his life to smuggle it out to the Breslov community in Israel, Rav Shmuel Horowitz clearly also knew about the contents of this letter, and perhaps also some of the deeper secrets it was hinting to. That perhaps explains something about the following encounter between Rav Horowitz and Rav Berland.

RAV BERLAND MEETS RAV HOROWITZ IN MERON

Rav Aharon Berlin takes up the story: "When I was a young man, nearly every Shabbos I would travel up to Meron with Rav Berland. During one of our trips, I noticed that while the Rav was praying a lengthy *Amidah* with his usual intensity, the saintly Rav Shmuel Horowitz was watching him with great interest. Since Rav Shmuel seemed so engrossed, I waited for a good opportunity to ask him what he was thinking about Rav Berland.

"When I was finally able to ask him, Rav Shmuel's voice filled with awe and he said, 'You should know that I have seen many people pray, but I have never seen anything like him. His prayers are so fiery, with so much *mo'ach* [intellectual force].'

"I was astounded," admits Rav Berlin. "I asked him, 'What do you mean, that you haven't seen anything like this? You were among the circle of the greatest *ovdim* in Breslov from the previous generation! How can it be that you did not see the like of Rav Berland before?'

"Rav Shmuel explained, 'You are correct that I saw many lofty *ovdim* in Poland and Uman. They were *tzaddikim*, but they were men. Here we are talking about a Godly angel. There is no comparison!' He added, 'I have also never seen anyone with such a mind.'"

Rav Berlin continues: "Those who knew Rav Shmuel are aware that he never exaggerated. He was careful to say exactly what he meant. Clearly, this was the truth as he saw it."

On another occasion, Rav Horowitz told someone else: "I've seen men who reached the level of angels, but literally an angel like Rav Eliezer Berland, I have yet to see. And who knows what lofty levels he still has ahead of him?"

AN AUTHENTIC BRESLOVER *CHASSID*

Rabbi Michael Goll is the *Rosh* Yeshivah of *Maginei Eretz*, and one of the first students of Rav Eliezer Berland. A few years ago, he traveled up to Meron and happened to meet a Lelover *chassid* whom he described as being a true servant of *Hashem*.

"We started talking about Breslov *Chassidus*, and I could tell that this Lelover *chassid* truly grasped the greatness of Breslov *Chassidus*," says Rav Goll. "He told me that he believed Breslov was very special — but with one caveat: He opined that today's Breslov *Chassidus* wasn't the same, authentic Breslov of years past.

"When I heard this, I asked him, 'Do you know Rav Eliezer Berland?' The Lelover replied, 'Yes! He truly remains authentic, and is something very special.' Then he started telling me how the late *Admor* of Lelov, Rav Moshe Mordechai (1903-1987), had said that Rav Berland is the greatest servant of *Hashem* in this generation.

"So, then I asked him, 'Did you hear [the *Admor*] say this with your own ears?' And he told me that he had, and then he went on to tell over other great things he'd heard with his own ears from the Lelover *Admor* about Rav Berland."

The two men parted company, and Rav Goll didn't think about the conversation again until he happened to meet up with the Lelover *chassid* again, a while later. It was only then that Rav Goll discovered that his new friend happened to be Rebbe Alter Biderman, the son of the late *Admor* of Lelov, who was actually the *Admor* of Lelov himself at the time.

WHO COMES AFTER RABBI LEVI YITZCHAK?

The three men who built the Breslov *shul* in Meah Shearim—and who'd laid the foundations for the burgeoning growth of Breslov *Chassidus*—all passed away in the same year: 1989. Rav Berland later explained that as long as these three Torah giants were alive, there hadn't been any hint of an intifada, or any Arab uprising against the Jewish nation, because their merit had shielded *Am Yisrael* from Arab violence. It was only when the three of them died in the same year that the Arab uprising erupted across the whole country.

That same year, the route to Uman was also finally thrown open, as the USSR quietly imploded and the fearful Soviet empire vanished, only to be found in the history books.

Things were changing fast all over the world. What was going to happen next? Who was going to guide everyone through the enormous changes occurring? That question reverberated around every community and every country, including the still relatively small community of Breslov *chassidim* in Meah Shearim.

RAV LEVI YITZCHAK'S LAST WORDS

Barely a day would pass without someone attempting to slander Rav Berland and his followers to Rav Bender, in an attempt to get the Rav and Shuvu Banim excommunicated and cast asunder from the Breslov community in Meah Shearim. This constant *machlokes* and slander bothered Rav Bender tremendously, and in private conversations he would speak about how disturbed he was by the actions of these "troublemakers" in the Breslov community.

Rav Bender's path was always to try and strengthen and uplift others, and he stayed away from any hint of *machlokes* or communal politics. But after Rav Shmuel Horowitz and Rav Velvel Cheshin passed away, Rav Bender became increasingly concerned about what the Breslov zealots would attempt to do to harm Rav Berland and his community after his own passing.

As his physical strength started to wane toward the end of his life, Rav Bender departed from his usual circumspection to make a very unusual and powerful plea for unity. The following comes from the last recorded lecture that Rav Bender gave on Thursday, 19 Sivan, 5749 (June 22, 1989), just a month before he died from cancer on July 25, 1989:

"LOVE AND UNITY BETWEEN US IS LACKING!"

Rav Bender began: "It says about the *meraglim*: 'All of them were leaders of the Children of Israel.' However, when they realized that they wouldn't be the leaders in *Eretz Yisrael*, they made such a terrible storm with their evil speech that they caused the entire nation to remain in the desert.

"It's impossible to even imagine how much Rebbe Nachman could reveal to us and influence us, if only all the Breslov *chassidim* would be united as one... By us this is missing! I see it, and others see it as well; love and unity between us is lacking!"

Rav Bender continued: "When I begin to speak about the topic of love, people don't understand what I'm referring to, they have no idea what I'm talking about, but we need to know that this is what's lacking, this is what's lacking by us!!! ... Even if I don't agree with the other person I still need to love him!

"We have to be very careful not to lose or even lessen the love between all the Breslov *chassidim*. When I'm talking about how we need to hold ourselves together in unity, people have no idea what I'm talking about! It seems to them that I'm talking in a different language!

"I cannot speak about the specifics, because our way is not to interfere in another person's life... So, I speak in a general manner, but from my words one must take specific meanings... the power of *Rabbeinu* is so strong, but it could be so much more awesome, 'so much more beautiful and even more beautiful'[XXXVII] — and it all depends 'if we are holding ourselves together in unity!!!'

"Rebbe Nachman said: 'I judge everyone to the side of mercy, apart from people who instigate strife and communal discord.'

"We see in the Torah that Aharon *HaKohen* and Miriam the prophetess spoke disparagingly about Moshe *Rabbeinu* (*Bamidbar* 12:1) ... They spoke *lashon hara*, they argued against Moshe *Rabbeinu*, and *Hashem* immediately punished them... Both of them were great people and certainly had pure intentions; nevertheless, they caused *machlokes* and they were punished!

"And Moshe *Rabbeinu* himself wasn't so bothered by their speaking against him... [but] for the sin of speaking *lashon hara* there is always a punishment. Whether the punishment will occur immediately or be delayed—this is a decision made Above, but certainly a punishment will come!

"*Hashem* has mercy on us. We have Rebbe Nachman, a merciful Rebbe, and a true merciful leader! *Rabbeinu* judges everyone favorably. Nevertheless, WATCH YOURSELVES! Watch yourselves with this one point, because about this he is not silent. You will get punished for this [the sin of speaking *lashon hara*] no matter how great you are!

"We have no idea about the secrets of the arguments between the *tzaddikim*; therefore, DON'T GET INVOLVED! It seems like they are arguing, but in reality, they are working together in a way that's deeper than we can imagine...All of a sudden, a third person gets involved and gives his opinion—'this one is good, that one is bad...' He's messing up the whole thing!"

XXXVII   A direct quote from Rebbe Nachman.

"ARE YOU TALKING ABOUT THE *MACHLOKES* HAPPENING TODAY IN BRESLOV?"

At this point in the lecture, someone in the audience asked Rav Bender, "Are you talking about the *machlokes* that is happening today in Breslov?" referring to what was occurring with Rav Berland and his followers.

Rav Bender replied, "We cannot be specific, so we are speaking in general terms... Even during the times of the *machlokes* about whether Rosh Hashanah should be in Meron or in Jerusalem, Rav Shmuel Shapira, *zt"l*, never opened his mouth against another person. He did what he thought was right and went to Meron, but before he would leave he would come and depart from me with love and friendship.

"He would give me his *pidyon* and I would give him mine. We were one soul! He would go to Meron and I would stay in Jerusalem; we separated but we constantly prayed for each other... And he returned from Meron with love and friendship.

"This is the true way! Because with argumentative words each person hurts the other and it can lead to forbidden speech...May *Hashem* help us that we live long and begin to listen to *Rabbeinu*...He wants from us only one thing: Stick together! Each of you must be filled with love for the other and go in the way of truth."

PASSING THE BATON ON TO RAV BERLAND

The import of Rav Bender's words was clear: Even holy people, even *tzaddikim* in their own right, even leading Rabbis could fall into the sin of speaking evilly about other *tzaddikim*. And if they did that, they would be sorely punished for it. No matter who took over the leadership role from Rav Bender, Breslov *Chassidus* should pull together and unite behind him.

Rav Berland was out of the country in the U.S.A. to arrange a large upcoming trip to Uman when the doctors told Rav Bender that he only had a few days left to live, shortly afterwards. When Rav Bender received his grim prognosis, his first thought was to call Rav Berland from his hospital bed. The two men—Rabbi and student—had much to discuss, and Rav Bender spoke about many things. But amongst his last words, Rav Bender gave over to the Rav his "will" about how to manage the community in his absence.

It seemed clear that Rav Bender was passing the baton of the leadership of Breslov *Chassidus* on to Rav Berland. Two weeks after that last phone call, on July 25, 1989, Rav Levi Yitzchak passed away.

THE *MACHLOKES* EXPLODES

Even after he'd established the Shuvu Banim Yeshivah in the Old City in 1982, Rav Berland still made a point of *davening* at the Breslov *shul* in Meah Shearim on Friday night and also going there every year for the Yom Kippur services.

On more than one occasion, Rav Berland wrote prayers for a few of his students to recite that included the request that they should merit to live near the *shul,* and to *daven* there every day. The Rav explained that the very walls of the shul were imbued with *yiras Shamayim* in the merit of its three founding fathers, and that praying in the *shul* that they'd built was a huge privilege.

The Rav always explained to his students that the Shuvu Banim Yeshivah in the Old City should be considered as though it was just another branch of the main Breslov *shul* in Meah Shearim, and certainly not as any type of replacement. As always, the Rav was for peace. But his detractors in the Breslov *shul* were for war, and when Rav Levi Yitzchak Bender, the last Breslov elder of the previous generation, passed away in 1989, they launched their first open attack.

THE $100 MILLION HOTEL IN UMAN

Ostensibly, the argument that erupted was over Uman, or more specifically, the Rav's plans to open a huge hotel in Uman, in order to make Rebbe Nachman's grave as accessible to the masses as possible[XXXVIII].

Rav Shmuel Stern, *Rosh* Yeshivah of Nachalei Netzach, was part of the group of people who accompanied Rav Berland out to Moscow, to conduct the official negotiations to build the hotel.

"In 5749 [1989], when the path to Uman had already been opened and diplomatic ties had resumed between Russia and Israel, the Rav wanted to broaden the appeal of traveling to Uman for the public," he begins.

"He put forth a proposal to the Russian government to build a multistoried hotel in Uman in partnership with Breslov *Chassidus* and the Russians. A group of us flew out with the Rav to conduct the negotiations in Moscow with the government officials, including Rav Gavriel Grossman, Avi Katz, Beni Ze'evi, and a few others.

XXXVIII   At this stage, Rav Berland was also exploring options to privatize the local army air base near Uman, in order to create cheap flights that would enable as many people as possible to visit Uman, affordably.

"We came prepared with very specific, detailed plans of where and how to build, including professional architectural plans, maps and blueprints that the people at Shuvu Banim had spent a lot of time and money on.

"The Rav told Rav Gavriel Grossman to offer them a deal where we'd put up $50 million toward the project, and the Russians should put up another $50 million. The officials discussed our offer between themselves, then decided it was too much money, and that we should build a hotel for $50 million instead, with the costs split 50-50.

"At that time, the Rav had a number of different ideas and plans [to open Uman up for the masses], and had already secured backing from a number of wealthy donors. But for a number of different reasons, nothing came of it."

Someone asked the Rav why he wanted to build a hotel for the extraordinary sum of $100 million, and he replied, "It's forbidden to minimize miracles!"

THE RAV IS ABUSED IN THE *SHUL*

The main reason why the project came to naught was due to the extremists in the Breslov *shul*. When they heard what the Rav was up to, they immediately objected to his plans to bring more outsiders to Uman, and demanded that the Rav turn over control of this project to them.

Over the following months, the antagonism of this original group of Breslov zealots only intensified. As time went on, a small group of them made such a concerted effort to whip up a storm of controversy and hatred around the Rav that people even started yelling at him and throwing things at him when he came to the Breslov *shul* to pray during *selichos* in 5751 (1990).

Rav Yosef Assulin was Rav Berland's gabbai at this time. He recalls:

"In 1989, the Rav brought a lot of the Breslov elders to Uman and he was tremendously respected as a result, literally given honor fit for a king. However, the Rav did not like that he was being honored so much, and he made every effort to turn things around.

"It's impossible to describe what went on (in 5751) at the Breslov shul in Meah Shearim. Torah scholars were standing on tables and yelling at the Rav in front of thousands of people. It's impossible to describe the kind of disgrace the Rav received there.

"The wonder is that before he entered the Breslov shul for selichos on that motzaei Shabbos, the Rav told two of his students that they should leave and do selichos somewhere else, and that they shouldn't step foot inside the shul under any circumstances. He said this to them because these two people would have been completely broken if they'd witnessed the unbelievable disgrace and insults that were directed at the Rav.

"I remember standing there next to the Rav and they were yelling and screaming in such a stormy way. I wanted to yell back, but the Rav turned to me and said: 'let them, let them'. So that's how it was for a full 20 minutes. Breslover *chassidim* were yelling at him in a way that simply can't be described. To my great surprise, when we left the shul I looked at the Rav and he seemed to be in a state of total bliss and contentment. Anyone who didn't see this with their own eyes cannot understand what I'm saying.

"The Rav walked away from the biggest disgrace imaginable in a state of utter bliss and contentment, as though he'd just won the lottery! The Rav met the *Rabbanit* downstairs [outside the shul] and he said to her in disappointment: 'Only 20 minutes?! I was hoping they would continue for at least two hours! I've been waiting for that shower of insults for many, many years. It's a shame that it only lasted a few minutes.' We simply cannot grasp what material this Jew is made of," concludes Rav Yosef Asulin.

RAV YEHUDA SEGAL INTERCEDES

Rav Yehuda Zerachia Halevi Segal, *zt'l*, was a leading kabbalist of the previous generation, and a man who was known to have *ruach hakodesh*. After Rav Levi Yitzhak's passing, Rav Segal decided to intercede, to try to end them *machlokes* between Rav Berland and his detractors.

Rav Segal decided to intercede, to try to end the *machlokes*. On one occasion on 4 Kislev, 5752 (November 11, 1991), he wrote a letter to Rav Yaakov Meir Shecter, the official head of the community in the Breslov *shul*, where he emphasized how important it was to have peaceful relations within the Breslov community, and that the rectification of the world (*tikkun olam*) depended on this.

Rav Segal wrote: "The very high level of piousness and *avodas Hashem* of the *gaon* and *tzaddik* Rav Eliezer Berland, *shlita*, is well known to me. It's forbidden to harm an angel of God...and *Rabbeinu Hakadosh* (Rebbe Nachman) is extremely upset about recent events...The honor of *Rabbeinu Hakadosh* forces me to intercede and protest about what is going on."

Rav Yehuda Zerachia Segal once told Rav Michael Goll the following:

"You should know, wherever I go, the demonic forces run 200 meters away from me. But wherever Rav Berland goes, the demonic forces run many thousands of meters away from him. That is the enormous power of his holiness!"

RAV SHECTER'S SCRIBE

While Rav Yaakov Meir Shecter himself stayed out of the *machlokes* against the Rav as much as possible some of the people in his circle at the Breslov *shul* weren't as discerning, and frequently tried to stoke the controversy against the Rav.

In recent years, one of these close acquaintances of Rav Shecter sent a messenger to Rav Berland while he was in Morocco, to request forgiveness for himself. He said that all the *machlokes* there had been in earlier years between Rav Shecter and Rav Berland had been all his fault, because he'd spoken against Rav Berland and tried to cause trouble between these two Torah scholars.

Rav Berland was surprised when he received this message and said, "What *machlokes*?! There never was any *machlokes* between us! Rav Yaakov Meir is my best friend. Many decades ago, when I incurred debts of more than $40,000, he set up a special appeal to help me. There was never any *machlokes* between us at all."

This same person said that whenever he spoke negatively about Rav Berland to Rav Shecter, Rav Shecter was affected and hurt by his words, to the point of literally falling ill.

Rav Yaakov Meir went through a lot of suffering in his life, and on a number of occasions he said, "It's a shame Rav Lazer [Rav Berland] is not here, because if he was here he would strengthen me."

Rabbi Ephraim Nachman Anshin, the *Rosh Kollel* of Orot HaNachal in the Breslov *shul* in Meah Shearim, said that one time, he'd met the Rebbe of Gur while he was on the way to visit Rav Yaakov Meir Shecter, and the Rebbe told him, "Today there are two *tzaddikim* of the generation, Rav Eliezer Berland and Rav Yaakov Meir Shecter."

RAV BERLAND PUTS BRESLOV ON THE MAP

Despite the controversy, Rav Berland continued to toil tirelessly to bring more and more people back to *Yiddishkeit*, and to expose them to the teachings of Rebbe Nachman and the true, authentic path of Breslov *Chassidus*.

According to Rav Shalom Arush: "The Rav really began the ascent of Breslov in our generation. He literally established the glory of Breslov. There was nothing in Breslov without the Rav! I know for a fact what he did, and he did it all!"

On another occasion, Rav Arush commented:

"Today, *baruch Hashem*, there are already many *kollelim* that encourage their students to recite the *Tikkun Chatzos* prayers, and lots of *chassidim* get up for *chatzos*. There were always some individuals who'd get up for *chatzos*, but whole communities that would get up at midnight? That simply didn't exist.

"The Rav started it off, with his self-sacrifice," continued Rav Arush. "The Rav expected us to get up for *chatzos*, and he didn't just expect it, he made it happen. At that time, I was the Rav's driver. I used to drive him around all night, and he'd go from one student's house to another, waking them up for *chatzos*. The Rav truly sacrificed himself for the community, in a way that's impossible to describe.

"How would Breslov look today, without the Rav? We have so much to be grateful to him for."

THE RAV'S PATH

"The wise man who despises worldly matters is one among many and is only found one in a generation of generations"

-- The Rambam, writing in his Introduction to *Mishnayos*

Rav Berland's apprenticeship at the knee of the Breslov greats of the previous generations helped him develop a very clear spiritual path that a true Breslov *chassid* should follow.

This path included:

» In-depth Torah learning

» Lengthy, heartfelt prayers

» *Chatzos* (i.e. being awake from midnight onwards) and *Tikkun Chatzos*

» *Hisbodedus*

» Personal holiness

» Visits to *kivrei tzaddikim*

» Outreach work, to bring Jews back to their religious roots

» Performing acts of kindness and giving *tzedakah*

» Accepting criticism and humiliation with love

» Self-sacrifice and nullifying the "self" to God's will

These ten areas really exemplified the Rav's approach to becoming a true Breslover *chassid*. The Rav put every word of Rebbe Nachman's teachings and advice into practice in his own life, and he encouraged his followers to do so, as well.

In this chapter, his students, colleagues, and family members describe the Rav's spiritual path, as they saw him live it day by day.

WHO CAN EVEN SPEAK HIS PRAISES?

Rav Yosef Palvani authored the works *Chemdas Yosef* and *Darchei Iyun*, and he has known Rav Berland for more than 40 years.

"I had the *zechus* to know the Rav from the time he left Bnei Brak to move to Jerusalem, over 40 years ago. I saw his greatness, and his amazing separation from materialistic things. 'Who can even speak his praises?'

"Who doesn't know the greatness of Rav Berland in *limmud Torah*? Every single part of the Torah is clearly in his hands. Whenever someone has a conversation with him, or mentions something about the *Shas*, *Yerushalmi* or any holy *sefer* and they'd quote something, he completes the quotation as though the book is open in front of him. And his *shmiras einayim*, guarding his eyes—no one can compare to him!

"In *avodas Hashem*, he would go to fields and deserts for three days to do *hisbodedus*, going to one place for 12 hours and praying, standing there without moving. We're just scratching the surface; if we spoke about all the things we know about him, about all of his greatness, we'd never finish.

"We don't need proof of his greatness. His greatness is known to anyone who has any connection to him."

Rav Palvani was very close to the Sephardi Torah giants Rav Abba Shaul and Rav Ovadia Yosef, as well as many other of the nation's holiest leaders. But he still says, "By any of them, we didn't see the *avodas Hashem* that we see by Rav Berland. The *kedushah*, the *shmiras einayim*, the *tefillah* and the *gemilus chassadim* he does for people."

Rav Palvani continues: "He's an angel of God! I was raised by all of the great leaders of the past generation, and they were great *tzaddikim*, including people who had *ruach hakodesh*. But I never saw things like this."

IN-DEPTH TORAH LEARNING

Rav Meir Dovid Isaac recalls that:

"The Rav possesses a wonderful ability to concentrate. Sometimes he would sit there with the *Tosafos*, studying it so deeply with complete concentration that he had no idea who was coming in or who was going out. I saw him like that a few times, sitting there in deep contemplation of that same *Tosafos*, with his small *Shas* next to him, for many hours. In the middle of his learning, he'd get up, bring over another volume of the *Gemara*, and so forth, but the whole time he was concentrating on that same *Tosafos*.

"I have no idea what goes on in the Rav's head that he could be so absorbed in a single *Tosafos* for so many hours, but I can tell you that he's not from this world."

Rav Moshe Yosef Pass remembers that:

"On the last night before the Rav left to go to Miami, the *mekubal* Rabbi Yitzchak Meir Morgenstern was with the Rav all night, until daybreak. Several times his *gabbaim* tried to get him to leave, but the Rav wouldn't let them enter.

"In the morning, Rav Morgenstern commented that he'd never found a person who was as knowledgeable in the words of the *Arizal* as the Rav, and he recounted that he and the Rav had gone through all of *chassidus* and the principles of the *Etz Chaim* during the night. And the Rav was extremely familiar with all these works, to a unique degree."

Rav Shmuel Stern, *Rosh* Yeshivah of Nachalei Netzach, gave over the following story:

"When the Rav lived in Har Nof, I lived in the same building, and since I'd heard that anyone could ask the Rav whatever he wanted, I approached him and asked him if it would be possible to learn *Etz Chaim* and the *Shaar Hakavanos* with him.

"I told him that there was a bomb shelter downstairs in the building, and at night at *chatzos*, we could learn there. The Rav told me, 'On *Motzoei* Shabbos, at 4 a.m., we'll meet there.' I cleaned out the bomb shelter, and I brought the books there. At 4 a.m. I came downstairs, and after a minute or two the Rav appeared. We went to the bomb shelter and started to learn.

"We learned like that night after night for two years, and we would learn until daybreak.

"It was the Rav's way that every time the *Etz Chaim* brought a source, he would open it up and go into it, and continue in that way as one book led to another book. At the beginning of our learning, that was difficult for me, because we'd set aside the time to learn *Etz Chaim*, but I kept finding myself in the middle of other books.

"Also, the Rav grasped the subjects with such speed; who could keep up with him? But afterwards, I saw that my learning with the Rav opened up new understandings in Torah for me."

Rav Yosef Asulin was the Rav's *gabbai* for many years. He recalls that:

"Once, I came to pick up the Rav from the *Kosel*. He was so exhausted, he fell asleep in the car. I took him back to his home (which was then in Har Nof), and the Rav told me to come back again an hour or two later, after *chatzos*. He asked me to find him a copy of the *Etz Chaim* in the meantime, to take with him.

"I got there at 2 a.m.—and the bed was exactly how I'd left it two hours earlier. He hadn't slept in the bed at all; he was still engrossed in his *Etz Chaim*."

THE RAV'S BOOKS

From his youth, the Rav has always been an avid reader. In his Jerusalem home in Hachomah Hashlishit the Rav actually has three entire rooms full of books, and he has a very in-depth and unique method of learning.

As he learns through a particular sefer, Rav Berland will open every sefer that is referenced in that work, or otherwise connected to the topic that he's learning, and he will read everything connected to the topic. This method leads him from the *Chumash*, to the Talmud, to the *Midrash*, and then over to the early commentators and the later commentators, before delving into the works of *Kabbalah*, *halachah*, and the *poskim*.

Visitors to the Rav's home would see hundreds of books piled up on every table in the house, testimony to the Rav's insatiable thirst for Torah. The Rav would literally run from bookcase to bookcase, comparing sources from the hidden Torah with those from the revealed, delving into a *midrash* here, a tractate of *Gemara* there, his fingers racing to keep up with the pace of his thoughts.

As part of his collection of books, the Rav also has a number of unique, handwritten works that he'd collected, authored by various *tzaddikim* over the generations. Whenever the Rav would teach publicly, his *gabbaim* would have the difficult task of wheeling in a few bookshelves full of *sefarim*, including an entire *Shas*, plus a long list of the other books the Rav had told them he'd need to refer to, throughout the course of his Torah lecture.

Rav Yitzchak Dovid Grossman, the Rabbi of Migdal Ha'emek, once commented that the only way the Rav could possibly be familiar with all the sources he quoted was if he literally sat studying his books every second of the day or night.

"The love the Rav has for the Torah and for the holy books is impossible to describe," says Rav Yosef Asulin. "When we went to a hotel for a week, I had to take along between 400 and 500 books—without any exaggeration, and that was just for one week.

"I saw that the Rav simply can't be parted from his books. He would tell me exactly what he needed, and I'd take a van and go fill it up with all the books he wanted.

"The Rav really lives for his books. He values his books more than the air he breathes. The books of the Rav have already gone on many journeys. Every place where the Rav was exiled to, the books were exiled with him. The first time he went abroad, they sent a shipment of two and a half tons of books—and that happened every place he journeyed to, whether it was Holland, South Africa, Zimbabwe—wherever he went, truckloads of books went with him."

THE RAV'S BOOKS OPEN TO THE RIGHT PLACE

Many onlookers have frequently witnessed the Rav opening his books to exactly the place required. One of his *gabbaim* explains: "This didn't just happen with one or two books; it happened with tens of books in every *shiur* he gave. They all opened up at exactly the right place."

Rav Yosef Shor agrees: "I saw many times that the Rav would open a book and place his finger on the place he'd opened it up to, and then immediately start flicking through the book a few pages, as though he was looking for the place. Afterwards, he'd come back to the page where he'd put his finger, which is where he first opened the book. He hid the fact that he'd opened it at exactly the place he was looking for."

According to Rav Yehoshua Dov Rubinstein:

"The Rav had the practice that whenever he mentioned a *sefer*, he would open it up 'inside' [i.e. he would open the *sefer* to the passage he was discussing]. Once, the Rav told my son that if he didn't open the book immediately at the right place, he understood that he needed to do *teshuvah* for something."

DON'T CLOSE THE BOOKS!

Rav Naftali Biton, one of the Rav's *gabbaim*, recalls: "The Rav really didn't like it when people used to close his books. The Rav used to say, 'I'm here in the middle of learning the *sugya*, and you closed the books?!' On Friday, for the sake of *Shabbos Kodesh*, the Rav would invariably open up even more books, and then afterwards return each one to the bookshelf, each to its own place. The love and connection the Rav had to each book is unique."

The Rav used to say that a person should learn his *sefarim* with the exact original layout of the pages. That way, after studying the book a few times, his mind would visually remember each page and he would be able to recall where on the page a specific point was mentioned. The Rav followed the same method with the thousands of books that lined the walls of his home library: Not only did he know on exactly which page each point was mentioned; he also knew exactly where the book was kept in his own personal library.

Once, someone mentioned to the Rav that they could get the *Otzar Hachachmah* computer program, which lets the user access tens of thousands of Torah books at the touch of a button. The Rav quickly brushed off the offer and replied, "Sitting in front of a computer is not learning; a person must bend over a book; a person must feel and smell the pages."

Another time, the Rav commented, "Each *sefer* you open delights the *tzaddik* who wrote it. 'His lips are muttering in the grave,'[13] and he is revealing secrets to your *neshamah* far beyond what is actually written in the *sefer*."

THE TRIP UP TO MERON

"Rav Levi Yitzchak had a tradition to travel up to Meron every Erev Rosh Chodesh," explains Rav Yehoshua Dov Rubinstein. "On one of his trips he traveled together with Rav Nachman Berstein, Rav Moshe Beninstock, Rav Gavriel Grossman, the Rav and the driver whose name was Sinai. They were driving along the Bikah highway (Route 90) when the car suddenly flipped over a couple of times, until it came to rest on its roof.

"Miraculously, everyone came out of the car completely unscathed. The driver told me that at first, when everyone got out of the car, they started checking and saw that no one was injured, *baruch Hashem*. They were so preoccupied with what had just happened, they didn't pay attention to the fact that the Rav wasn't with them—until they suddenly realized that he was missing.

"They went back to the car to check what had happened to him, and they found him sitting on the roof of the upside-down car (while still inside), learning from the *sefer* in his hand like nothing unusual had just happened."

The Rav didn't want to waste any time outside fussing over what had just happened; rather, he used the extra time as an opportunity to grab some more peaceful learning.

AT THE DENTIST WITHOUT ANESTHETIC

The Rav's dentist shared the following anecdote: "When the Rav came to me, and I saw the state of his teeth, I told him that he'd need to have a long and complicated treatment which required heavy anesthetic. The Rav told me, 'You can treat me without giving me any anesthetic; I won't feel anything.' I told the Rav that it simply wouldn't be possible to treat him without giving him anesthetic. The Rav replied, 'Believe me, every free moment I have, I'm learning, and I really don't need any anesthetic.'

"And so it was. I gave him a long treatment of more than an hour, and every time I turned around to take another instrument from the tray, or to find something, I'd see that the Rav was completely engrossed in his book. It seemed to me that because he was so engrossed in his learning, he had the strength to disconnect from his present reality, and so he didn't feel a thing."

LEARNING WITH THE ADMOR OF BELZ

Rav Aaron Boyamil is a communal activist in the religious community, and has been a welcome guest in all the courts of the great *tzaddikim* of the generation, including Rav Berland. He described how a number of years ago, he accompanied Rav Berland on a visit to the *Admor* of Belz.

The *Admor* had arranged the meeting for 8 p.m., and told them that he only had 10 minutes to see them, because at 8:10 he had to officiate at the wedding of the son of one of his *gabbaim*.

Rav Boyamil recounted that the Rebbe of Belz was enjoying Rav Berland's company so much—a holy Jew who knew the entire Torah by heart—that he ended up sitting with him for two and a half hours. Every time the Rav showed the *Admor*

Rav Berland learning with the Admor of Belz.
You can see the gabbai in the background

something in one of the holy books he had there in his office, the *Admor* would take a pen and write next to it, so that he'd be able to go back and review it later.

He recalls: "They opened the *Rambam*, the *Zohar*, the books on *halachah*, the *Gemara*, and so forth. Every few minutes the Belzer Rebbe's *gabbai* would come into the room and tell the Rebbe that he had a *chuppah* and everyone was waiting for him. After a few interruptions, the Rebbe told them to send his son instead, to be the *mesader kiddushin* in his place. The *Admor* of Belz explained, 'I have now discovered a Jew who's such a *tzaddik*, that I want to stay with him a little longer.'"

LENGTHY, HEARTFELT PRAYERS

Another area of *avodas Hashem* that has always been key for Rav Berland is *tefillah*, praying. It's a rare moment indeed when the Rav is not studying Torah, or engaged in lengthy, heartfelt prayers.

HASHEM IS RIGHT IN FRONT OF YOU

In one of his many talks on the subject of prayer, Rav Berland told his students:

"Man has *apikorsus* in his heart[14]; he doesn't believe that *Hashem* is right in front of him every second. When a person does not have *kavanah* in *tefillah* and when he doesn't sense that *Hashem* is right in front of him it is because he has *apikorsus* in his heart. He doesn't believe that *Hashem* is here.

"When a person speaks to his friends he is very careful about every word that leaves his mouth. If he speaks to a king he's much more careful! He is constantly on guard, making sure not to say the wrong thing or something that makes no sense. When he talks with a friend he doesn't talk pointlessly.

"He can talk for 10 hours straight because he sees the person in front of him; he sees a person with a face, hands and feet. *Hashem* is *chai v'kayam*. He exists! He's right in front of us! Yet we don't feel that He is here. That shows that we have no *seichel*! When a person does not sense *Hashem's* presence and does not *daven* with *kavanah* it is only because he has no *seichel*!"

Rav Shmuel Stern recalls:

"One time, the Rav said to me: 'There's no reason to speed through the prayers.' He continued that when a person prays slowly, saying each word with *kavanah*, the *yetzer hara* doesn't have the patience to wait for the person to finish, so he goes to find another victim. By the time a person finishes praying at 10 a.m., or at 11 a.m., the *yetzer hara* has already found someone else to bother. For the rest of the day, the person will be free of the *yetzer hara*. All of a sudden, things will start going his way: his *parnassah*, his learning—everything will sort itself out by itself."

Rav Shmuel Stern continued:

"The son-in-law of the Rav once told me that he'd seen the Rav *bentch Birkas Hamazon* for six hours straight. One time, I got to the yeshivah during *seudah shlishis* and I saw the Rav reciting the blessing after meals. I've never seen a *Birkas Hamazon* like it, with so much *dveikus*. Everyone else had finished already, but he continued and continued. I understood that this person really wasn't a part of this world."

CHATZOS AND TIKKUN CHATZOS, THE MIDNIGHT LAMENTATION

According to Rav Shmuel Isaac Zucker, one of the Rav's grandchildren:

"The Rav's daily schedule started every night before midnight. It would never happen that the Rav would be in bed, or even grabbing a nap at the yeshivah, between *chatzos* until after the morning prayers. Everyone who was with the Rav knew this, from the year 5726 (1965), when he first started following *Rabbeinu's* path, up until our days.

"It was simply impossible that the Rav would sleep between *chatzos* and *Shacharis*. The Rav himself always used to say, '*Rabbeinu Hakadosh* used to say, from *chatzos*, we're awake—so we're awake!'

"The Rav would usually try to sleep an hour or two before midnight, but this was usually the exception to the rule. But even in those rare times when he went to sleep late, after 11 p.m., he would still always be back in the study room before *chatzos*.

"The Rav used to say: 'We have to fulfill *Rabbeinu's* words with *mesirus nefesh*. If you're tired, so then after *Tachanun* take your *tefillin* off and go to bed. Then come back later and make up whatever you missed. But from midnight until *Shacharis*, we need to be awake.'"

HISBODEDUS

Rebbe Nachman of Breslov famously taught that all of the *tzaddikim* throughout the generations only reached the spiritual level they did because they engaged in the practice of *hisbodedus*, or personal prayer.

Despite the fact that *hisbodedus* has come to be viewed in our times as an exclusively Breslov practice, in earlier years every great Torah personality set aside a certain amount of time each day to talk things through with his Creator. It's known that the Steipler engaged in *hisbodedus*, and that the Chofetz Chaim also regularly did *hisbodedus* for a couple of hours a day, when he'd account for what he'd spent his time doing every single second of the previous day.

Far from being a "fringe" practice, *hisbodedus* was held in the highest esteem by all of the nation's *tzaddikim* throughout the ages, as *the* single best way to work on oneself and draw closer to *Hashem*.

OVERCOMING THE DOGS OF THE WORLD TO COME

Rav Yisrael Meir Brenner, a leading figure in modern Breslov, knew the Rav from his Bnei Brak days. Before he drew closer to Breslov *Chassidus*, Rav Brenner was one of the foremost students of Rav Elazar Menachem Mann Shach, *zt"l*. He recounts that more than 45 years ago, he accompanied Rav Berland to a field next to Bnei Brak, where the pair of young *avreichim* wanted to spend some time in *hisbodedus*.

Rav Brenner recalls that as they were walking, they encountered a pack of ferocious wild dogs, and he was pretty scared. Rav Berland took him by the hand and told him to continue walking with him, and not to be afraid. The Rav told him, "When you overcome the dogs in this world, you'll also overcome them in the World to Come." This is a lesson that's brought down in *Likutei Moharan*, Lesson 50.

The Rav continued to take him to the same field with the dogs on a regular basis, each time holding his hand until he overcame his fear. Rav Brenner relates: "Until this day, it's only in the Rav's merit that I regularly do hisbodedus."

HISBODEDUS AS A ROSH YESHIVAH

Even after Rav Berland opened the doors of the Shuvu Banim Yeshivah, he still made *hisbodedus* one of his main priorities. Many of his earliest students recount that during the first days of the yeshivah, the *Rosh* Yeshivah would sometimes disappear for many weeks at a time. When he returned, he would be lit up with a tremendous radiance and holy fire! The Rav would walk into the yeshivah, stand by the *bimah* with a copy of the *Likutei Halachos* in his hand, and give over a fiery Torah lecture that would last for many long hours. His students would just stand there awed, drinking in every word.

Rav Berland giving over a shiur in the Old City, before
the walls of the Shuvu Banim yeshiva were plastered.

"One time, a guy came to see the Rav and asked him to make a schedule of *avodas
Hashem* for him," says Rav Yosef Asulin. "The Rav gave him a complete routine for
all 24 hours of the day, but then he told the Rav that he'd meant that he wanted to
follow the same schedule as the Rav himself. At that point, the Rav told him, 'If you
want to do things like me, that's only spending time in the field.'

"There was a stage when the Rav would regularly go out to do a two-week *hisbodedus* session. He had a cave in the vicinity of Yericho, and he had a lot of *sefarim*
there, so he'd frequently go and spend two solid weeks praying, doing *hisbodedus,*
and learning in that cave. The Rav would even spend Shabbos in that cave.
"The Rav had an Arab driver to whom he used to pay a lot of money, and he used to
take the Rav to all these places so that no one else would be able to discover where
he was doing his *hisbodedus*. The Rav once said, 'Whoever hasn't tasted a two-week
hisbodedus has never really tasted *hisbodedus* in their life!'

Rav Moshe Levinson remembers that:

"There were times when the Rav would go to the fields on *Motzoei Shabbos* just with
his *tallis, tefillin,* and a few holy books, and nothing else. He would return on Friday,
and we used to ask him, 'What did you sustain yourself with the whole week?' He
said, 'I found a few almonds on the ground, and also the owner of the orchard gave
me permission to eat some of his oranges.'"

Rav Nachman Horowitz adds: "We also asked him once what he ate when he went
to the field, and he told us that he got by on a few pecan nuts." He continues: "The
Rav went around the whole country. He once reflected that there wasn't a single
forest or desert that he hadn't done *hisbodedus* in. Once, I was in a field near Bnei

Brak and I found a *siddur* there. The Rav later told me that it was his *siddur* which he'd used to pray from for many years when he was in that field."

PERSONAL HOLINESS

GOING TO THE *MIKVAH*

On one of the Rav's early trips to Uman, it was snowing heavily in the Ukraine, and the weather was extremely cold. Even so, the Rav decided that he was still going to dip in the lake (as there were no *mikvaos* at that time)—but when he got there, he saw that the lake was completely covered with ice. But he didn't give up; he just broke through the ice and dipped in the freezing cold lake anyway.

"I was by the Rav in Johannesburg on *Shabbos Kodesh*," recalls Rav Shmuel Isaac Zucker. "At around 9 p.m. they finished the meal, but I'd noticed that the Rav was very tired and completely exhausted already from the beginning of Shabbos.

"I was sure that right after the meal, the Rav would go straight to bed. Once we finished, the Rav said to us, 'Nu, now you need to go to sleep, and I—I'm going to the *mikvah*!' (At that point the pool outside was being used as a *mikvah*, and the weather was so cold it was minus three degrees that night.) The Rav went to dip, came back—and he was completely animated and alert.

"He sat down and studied the whole night, from 9 p.m. until the next morning. In the middle of the night, I asked him, 'How is it possible that the Rav has energy?' The Rav told me, 'It's forbidden for a Breslover to give in to himself, even once.'

"The Rav regularly used to dip in the *mikvah* that was in his home. On many occasions when he was tired and hadn't slept much, instead of trying to go to sleep, he'd go to the *mikvah* instead. When he returned he'd always be full of vigor and completely rejuvenated, as though he'd just woken up from an eight-hour sleep. What we could only achieve after a few hours of sleeping, the Rav could do in a couple of minutes of going to the *mikvah*."

"THAT'S NOT A *MIKVAH*; IT'S A JACUZZI!"

These days there are heated *mikvaos* in almost every Jewish town, but the Rav would often tell his students, "A heated *mikvah* is not a real *mikvah*; it's a Jacuzzi! *Mikvaos* are meant to be cold! Rebbe Nachman promised that nothing will happen to you if you go to a cold *mikvah*. No one ever died from dipping in a cold *mikvah*. As long as the water isn't frozen, it's above zero and it can't kill you. And if it *is* frozen, just break the top layer, because underneath it's not frozen."

The Rav would also remind his students to dip whenever they passed a body of water, be it a spring, lake or the Kinneret, and encouraged his students by reminding them that heated *mikvaos* are a very recent innovation. "The *Arizal* said that he only reached his high spiritual level by dipping a lot in the *mikvah*," he'd tell them. "And this definitely wasn't attained by going to a heated Jacuzzi!"

GUARDING THE EYES

Rav Moshe Levinson recounts:

"The Rav used to talk about closing our eyes a lot in his *shiurim*. He would always say: 'A man comes to this world to be blind [i.e., in regard to seeing unholy sights).'"

Rav Abish Dickstein, who has known the Rav from his early years in Bnei Brak, remembers that:

"The wife of one of the families in Bnei Brak used to cook the food for the Rosh Hashanah gathering [*kibbutz*] in Jerusalem. Her family requested that she should come back in the van with us, so she wouldn't have to travel back on the Egged bus.

"We, the *bachurim*, didn't agree to have a woman with us in our van, but we didn't really have the energy to fight with them about it. In the middle of the trip, when we were already on the highway, Reb Lazer suddenly requested that he should be let off by the side of the road, and ran off to the forest.

"As a *bachur*, even though I was also really upset that we had a woman in the van[XXXIX] with us, I didn't have the strength to go with him. Afterwards, I was full of regret that I didn't leave with him, and that I let him go by himself. There was no way for him to get back to Bnei Brak from there, especially not in the middle of the night.

"The following morning, I asked Rabbi Avraham Rosenthal to take me to Reb Lazer so I could calm down and check that he'd arrived safely. I got to him in the afternoon, and he was wearing his *tallis* and was in the middle of saying *Tehillim*. I asked for his forgiveness that I hadn't accompanied him when he'd jumped out of the van. He smiled and nodded, and then continued with his *Tehillim*."

XXXIX   This was because of *tznius* issues.

"Everyone was guarding their eyes. No one wanted to travel with a woman in the van, but when it really came down to it, we didn't do anything to stop it from happening. But with the Rav, he really practices what he preaches to the ultimate degree, even if it requires extreme self-sacrifice. That's the uniqueness of the Rav."

VISITS TO *KIVREI TZADDIKIM*

Rav Berland's extensive visits to the graves of holy *tzaddikim* deserve a chapter of their own, and will be covered in much greater detail later on.

PERFORMING ACTS OF KINDNESS AND GIVING *TZEDAKAH*

Rav Moshe Shavili was also one of the Rav's attendants. He recalls:

"One time I was driving with the Rav and I ran out of gas. I told the Rav that I didn't have any gas, so Rav Berland took out a massive bundle of money—literally tens of thousands of shekels—and told me to take it and go fill up the car. I protested that it was just gas and I didn't need so much money, but Rav Berland told me, 'Take, take! Whatever you need, just take it!' Money really wasn't an issue for the Rav; he didn't really think about it."

THE RAV WOULD GIVE WHATEVER HE HAD

Whenever someone would ask the Rav for money, he would literally give him whatever he had. The Rav would say in his *shiurim* that the Baal Shem Tov had a custom to never finish a day with money. The Rav seemed to practice this custom himself, too.

"The Rav's daughter once recounted that, when she was a girl, she saw a banknote peeking out from her father's spare jacket pocket," says Rav Nachman Rubinstein. "She was so used to the fact that in their house they never kept any money around, but immediately distributed it to others, that she asked her father, '*Abba*, why do you have money in your pocket?' The Rav responded, 'Oh, you're right!' and he immediately went to give it to charity."

At one point, the Rav's family tried to prevent people who were asking for money from coming to the Rav's house, as the Rav would never say no. The Rav got around this restriction by throwing money down to people from his balcony.

Rav Benny Ze'evi used to live underneath the Rav's apartment. People used to knock on his door in the mornings and ask him if he'd found any envelopes containing money lying around his porch. The Rav used to arrange for people to come at night, and then he'd throw envelopes full of money down to them.

Rav Ze'evi recalls: "The Rav arranged with me that I should check if any of those envelopes accidentally found their way onto my balcony, and if they did, I should return them to him."

'HE'S RICH. JUST ALLOT HIM ONE MINUTE.'

"The Rav is completely unique when it comes to money," explains Rav Yosef Asulin. "He's completely uprooted every connection to money. Whenever he'd meet the public, or go out to a public event like a *bris*, the Rav's pockets would always fill up really fast with money for charity. People would literally stick money in his pockets in order to get a *pidyon*. But then a beggar would come along and the Rav would give him everything.

"It made no difference to him whether it was a well-known person from one of the yeshivos, an official charity collector or a simple beggar. The Rav distributed everything he was given and didn't keep anything for himself.

"Rich people used to come and see the Rav, and because they were giving huge *pidyonos* of tens of thousands of dollars, and sometimes even more, I used to think that I should try to arrange a longer audience for them with the Rav, which is how it usually works in other *Chassidic* courts.

"But the Rav said to me, 'He's rich, you can allot him just a minute. Everything's fine by him, why are you giving him so much time with me?' But when we were talking about a poor man, or an unfortunate person, the Rav would tell me, 'This one needs a lot of time. After all, he's poor, and he surely has a lot of difficult tests to endure. He needs time to pour out his heart, he needs to do that. It will do him good.'"

A MAN OF ACTION

According to Rav Naftali Biton:

"The Rav is also a man of action, and doesn't just pray for people. He also tries to help them in practical ways, too. When people weren't having their children accepted at the local *cheder*, for example, the Rav would phone the *cheder*. He wouldn't just pray for them and give them a blessing, he'd also try to take action."

Once, when the Rav was still living in Bnei Brak, a non-religious person brought his son to the Rav to get a blessing before the boy turned 13. The father stood him next to the Rav and told his son, "You can ask this Rabbi for whatever you want." The boy turned to the Rav and told him that he wanted a new bike. Without any hesitation, Rav Berland took out a few hundred shekels and gave it to the bar mitzvah boy to buy a bike."

On another occasion, Rav Moshe Levinson recalls that:

"A few years ago, the Rav sent me to Miami to learn Torah and do some outreach work with the people there. One of the donors there told me that the Rav had requested him to give a *pidyon* of $100,000. Initially, he wanted to try to avoid giving it, but eventually he got a grip on himself and he gave the Rav the full amount.

"Five minutes after he made the payment, the head of a Sephardi *kollel* came to see the Rav, and started crying that the *kollel* had run out of money and was about to close down. The Rav immediately gave the full $100,000 over to this man — and all this happened right in front of the donor who'd just given the money.

"The donor said that the whole thing had been a really big spiritual test for him, but as a result of giving the money, he'd seen huge blessings in every area of his business."

Rav Moshe Levinson continued:

"The suffering of *Am Yisrael* really pains the Rav. It's known that the Rav prayed for half a year to really feel the sorrow of *Am Yisrael*. Rav Yitzchak Weisshandler once spoke with the Rav, and the Rav asked him what had happened to all the students at the Breslov Yeshivah in Bnei Brak who had ended up leaving.

"Rav Weisshandler wanted to know why the Rav was so interested, especially after all these years had passed, and he replied, 'I'm still praying for them all today, that they'll return to the right path.'"

DERECH ERETZ PRECEDES THE TORAH!

Rav Shlomo Gabbai reminisces that:

"One of the sights that I'll never forget occurred on one of the trips to Uman. We all got off the plane after we landed, but the Rav and the Rebbetzin stayed behind and cleaned up the whole cabin. The Rav told us, '*Derech eretz* precedes the Torah!'

"And he meant it literally. They took a big bag, and they collected all the garbage and stuff that people had left behind on the plane. The Rav and Rebbetzin literally turned themselves into the attendants for the group, and they cleaned up the whole plane."

ACCEPTING CRITICISM AND HUMILIATION WITH LOVE

While every "great" person in the Torah world learns Torah, and every notable *tzaddik* does *hisbodedus*, this next pillar of Rav Berland's path, accepting criticism with love, is by far the most difficult to grasp, or to really understand. Yet this facet of his *avodas Hashem*, more than any other, is what really defines Rav Eliezer Berland and the dramatic direction his path has often taken, especially in more recent years.

Rebbe Nachman famously stated in *Likutei Moharan* 228 that every *tzaddik* who is involved with bringing people closer to *Hashem* will inevitably face a lot of opposition. In Rebbe Nachman's words: "By necessity, there has to be *machlokes* around someone who is causing people to do *teshuvah* in order that this person shouldn't have any peace whatsoever. Then, whoever still comes close to him, you can be sure that they're genuine."

Rebbe Nachman explains that *Hashem* Himself makes sure that there will be *machlokes* around these types of *tzaddikim*, and if we look back through the generations, we can see this idea in practice.

No one has embodied this phenomenon more than Rav Berland, who from the very beginning literally sought out criticism and embarrassment because he took to heart Rebbe Nachman's teaching that accepting criticism and shame with love can enable a person to reach the loftiest spiritual heights.[15]

The Rav once told his students in Morocco: "If a person truly has humility, and truly holds himself at a very low level, and if he accepts all the criticism and shame that's heaped on him with love, then he will live a long life, possibly even longer than 120 years."[16]

When he saw one of his followers being disgraced by someone else and refusing to answer back, the Rav told him, "In the merit of holding your tongue and accepting these insults with love, all your sins are forgiven!"

GOD ALWAYS GIVES DOUBLE

Rav Yosef Asulin recalls that:

"Some people swindled me out of a lot of money, so I went to pour my heart out to the Rav about it. The Rav said to me, 'They swindled *you* out of tens of thousands of shekels. They've swindled *me* out of hundreds and thousands of dollars—and I forgave them. Do you know what gifts I got from *Hakadosh Baruch Hu* as a result of what they did? It's impossible to describe!'"

"The Rav continued, 'We say in *parashas hamann-- dvar yom b'yomo*--that *Hashem* would provide enough *mann* for each day-- of his day-- and we know that each day of *Hakadosh Baruch Hu* is like a thousand years. Every day, enough *shefa* appears to last for a thousand years. Even if someone steals from you, robs you, instead of running after the robbers and all the money they swindled you out of, turn to *Hashem*. Go the field; do an hour of *hisbodedus* about the fact that they stole a billion dollars from you. [If you do that,] you'll get two billion dollars in its place, because every second, a new two billion dollars is being sent down for you. If they stole four billion, then you'll receive eight billion.

"'God always gives double, however much they steal from you, if you go to the field instead of going to the police or working on plans to catch the thieves. What are you going to do when you catch them? Take revenge? Go to the field; cry to *Hashem*. Now, you've got a broken heart; it's the time when your prayers will be accepted, because prayers aren't accepted without a broken heart.

"'Now they stole your money; it's only to give you a broken heart, in order for your prayers to be accepted. Whoever has a broken spirit, it's as though he offered all the sacrifices in the world. That's why God arranges for you to have some damage to your property, or for your child to fall over and have to go to the emergency room; it's all just so that you'll have a little bit of a broken heart, and then you can rescue the whole of *Am Yisrael.*'"

SEEKING OUT INSULTS

"I realized that the Rav made a big effort to embarrass himself, and that he would constantly try to find different ways of causing himself to be humiliated," says Rav Yaakov Gerwirtz. "You could see he was actually seeking insults, and he was so completely disinterested in people showing him any honor or *kavod*. So as much as possible, he was seeking insults and humiliation. This was a big wonder to me.

"When the *Admor* of Kretchnif came for a visit to the United States, I asked the Rav to come and visit him with me, and, as is the Rav's way, he immediately agreed to whatever I asked him. It seems as though the *Admor* suspected and understood that the Rav was not an ordinary *avreich* when he came to visit him. The *Admor* asked him, 'Who are you?' and the Rav answered simply, 'A *baal teshuvah*.'

"If someone had asked us the same question, we'd tell them we belong to this *Chassidus*, or that we're a student of such-and-such a Rabbi or Rebbe, etc. But the Rav, in his complete humility, simply answered that he was 'a *baal teshuvah*.'"

Rav Moshe Teplinsky adds:

"The Rav only has one desire left, from all the lusts that he broke—and that's the desire to be insulted!"

LOVE YOUR DETRACTORS AS THOUGH THEY ARE YOUR DEAREST FRIENDS

Rav Berland once remarked that if a person would truly know how much good his detractors and enemies are doing for him, he'd love them as though they were his dearest friends—and he has lived by this statement for many decades. Whenever someone spoke badly about him, or sought out ways to harm him, the Rav continued to treat him with great respect and kindness, and even 'helped' them to fight against him!

Speaking in Zimbabwe, the Rav once explained: "Only that which a person does from the depths of wretchedness and lowliness endures forever. When a person reaches the peak of lowliness and wretchedness, only that endures. When a person wants to consecrate himself, it's only possible via humility. It's impossible to attain any true holiness or *kedushah* without humility. Only that which a person does with a broken heart is eternal."

The Rav continued: "On Chanukah, we go down to within 10 *tefachim* of the ground [to light our *menoros*], but on Purim, we descend to the 50th gate of *tumah*, because everything is for a purpose. If it means that we'll merit lowliness and humility, then it's worth it because, thanks to the lowliness, we'll get to build the *Beis Hamikdash*."

Rav Dovid Rubinstein (the Rav's grandson) shared that:

"In Uman I met a Satmar *chassid* who told me that around 15 years ago, the Rav somehow got a reputation for being a 'Zionist'. The extremists on the Satmar papers started writing things against the Rav for being a Zionist and so forth. Around this same time, the Rav went to *chutz la'aretz* for a visit, and came back to Israel on a plane that was nearly full with Satmar *chassidim*.

"Two hundred people were on that plane, all followers of Satmar, plus the Rav. The Satmar *chassid* in Uman told me, 'I saw with my own eyes how someone started to yell all sorts of horrible things at the Rav, and when he finished, the Rav moved on to someone else, and soon the whole plane was yelling insults at him.

"The Rav just moved from one person to the next, *mamash* as though he was inviting them to argue with him, and honestly, he had the whole plane yelling insults at him. This continued for around eight hours. He really knows how to do these things properly, because everyone on the plane got an opportunity to insult him."

THE TZADDIK IS LIKE A TREE

In *Chayei Moharan* 401-402 Rebbe Nachman said:

"All of the great *tzaddikim* reached their specific exalted level but remained there. I, however, become a new person every minute, thank God, every minute." [Rebbe Nachman] then gave a reason why people are against him: "For the *tzaddik* is comparable to a tree (as in the verse, "A *tzaddik* blossoms like a palm tree"[7]), and before every *tzaddik* reaches his level there must be some kind of controversy surrounding him, people who are against him. For our Sages say (*Sanhedrin* 7), *machlokes* is comparable to water, and water is what is needed to make the tree grow. So each *tzaddik* needs some kind of persecution in order to reach his level.

"I, however, need to have controversy surrounding me constantly and have people always against me, because I constantly need to grow higher and higher and cannot remain on the same level. For if I would know that I am standing now on the same level that I was an hour ago, I would feel as if there is no reason for me to be in this world."

Another time, when Rebbe Nachman's students were complaining how hard it was for them to bear the suffering from all the *machlokes* and persecution, he answered them, "Believe me, I have the power to put an end to all the *machlokes* and make peace so that there would not be one person against me, but what can I do? There are exalted levels and spiritual worlds that it is impossible to reach without this kind of persecution.

"We see proof of this from Moshe *Rabbeinu*, who certainly had the magnetism and ability to draw all the Jewish people toward him, as it says, 'And Moshe gathered all the people.'[18] Nevertheless, we see that when it says 'They looked after Moshe,'[19] our Sages say what they said [i.e., that they called him a glutton and accused him of adultery.][20]

"And all this because there are certain levels a person cannot reach without having some controversy against him, without having people against him, etc. Like a tree, the more water you pour around it, the higher it grows."

SELF-SACRIFICE AND NULLIFICATION TO GOD'S WILL

THE RAV DOESN'T SLEEP

According to Rav Yehoshua Dov Rubinstein:

"The Rebbetzin told us that one time the Rav hadn't slept for three days straight and he was pinching himself to keep himself awake. The Rebbetzin said to him, 'Why are you making yourself suffer like that? Go to sleep!' But the Rav replied, '*Rabbeinu* said that from *chatzos* until the morning we have to be awake—so I'm staying awake! With *mesirus nefesh!*'"

Rav Shalom Arush used to accompany the Rav as his *shamash* for a couple of years. Rav Arush recalls: "I never once saw the Rav pouring himself a drink or asking for something to eat, and I was with him for years, day and night. I couldn't grasp the magnitude of his spiritual *avodah*.

"I had the privilege of being his driver and attendant, and I was with him 24 hours a day. We used to go on the road, and the Rav would give *shiurim* from one end of the country to the other. In Beer Sheva, he'd give a *shiur* from the night until the morning. In the morning, we'd pray *Shacharis* with enthusiasm, then return home. And so it was in every other part of the country, too.

"The Rav would get home close to Shabbos, after not sleeping the whole night. He'd tell me to come back to him after the Shabbos meal. I'd come back and the Rav would tell me, 'Let's go to the field!' I'd fall asleep in the field, and the Rav would be there doing *hisbodedus* the whole night."

After Rav Shalom relinquished the post of *shamash* to others, the yeshivah administrators realized that they'd have to provide Rav Berland with two attendants, so they could keep up with his pace without burning out—one for his daytime activities, and another for the nighttime.

"The Rav barely slept, and he barely drank or ate," says Rav Moshe Shavili, one of his first students. "Pretty much the only time I saw the Rav really eat was on Shabbos. The Rav was very special like that—he could sit with you for hours without eating or drinking. Also guarding his eyes—he was really like an angel," he says.

Rav Nachman Berland, his son, concurs:

"My father used to push his body to the limit. He would learn and pray without going to sleep, sometimes even for two days in a row. And he didn't let himself relax, to the point that he'd be on the verge of collapsing from exhaustion. Only then, would he go to sleep."

BITUL TO OTHER PEOPLE

"One of the most notable things about the Rav is the way he completely nullifies himself to other people," explains Rav Meir Dovid Isaac. "He has a schedule for what he wants to do in a given day, and where he wants to go, but then someone will show up and ask him to come with him to Meron, for example, to give some Jew there chizzuk and encouragement—and the Rav will cancel all his plans to accommodate the other person.

"In his earlier years this happened all the time, often without limits. He would end up traveling out of his way for many long hours, just because someone had asked him for a favor. Later on, when he started to have his own attendants and gabbaim, things eased up a little. The gabbaim would prevent this from happening, and the Rav would nullify himself and do what the gabbaim wanted.

"If you actually think about this, it's an amazing thing. We've seen tzaddikim who were also giants in Torah, or giants in tefillah, for example, but when it comes to the Rav's trait of nullifying himself to his fellow Jew, I've never heard about anything like this, anywhere else in the Jewish world.

"And the most amazing thing of all is that despite all his tremendous self-nullification, the Rav still adheres to his schedule of avodas Hashem. According to the laws of nature, if someone would accede to every request from another Jew, his schedule and all his avodas Hashem would get messed up. But the Rav always manages to do what he needs to do—his Torah learning, his praying, and his other spiritual devotions.

'YOU WOKE UP JUST IN TIME!'

Rav Nachman Rubinstein, one of the Rav's grandsons, recalls that:

"I was by the Rav in Johannesburg (in 5774) with other members of his family. I got up early and prayed together with the Rav, at 5 a.m., and we finished around 8 a.m. When we finished, the Rav went downstairs to his room, and then another member of the family woke up. The Rav said to him, 'Oh, you woke up just in time! Let's pray *Shacharis* together. (He said *'Hashem'* instead of the full name, during the blessings, without his relative noticing.) He was sure the Rav had just gotten up too, and that they were praying together for the first time that day.

"When they finished, around 11 a.m., another relative woke up. The Rav went over to him, his face shining, and said to him, 'Oh, you woke up just in time! I also need to pray *Shacharis* now!' And he started to pray with him again.

"The Rav didn't take his own honor into consideration at all. All he was concerned about was that the other person should have this kindness done for him, and should leave Johannesburg with a good feeling, that he prayed with the Rav."

A DAY IN THE LIFE OF RAV BERLAND

Forty years ago, in 5733 (1972), the Rav went to America for six months in order to get the Green Card[XL] that would enable him to travel to Uman, ostensibly as an American citizen.

When the Rav arrived in New York, he started looking for a place to pray the morning service with a *netz minyan*. Forty years ago, in Brooklyn, there was only one *shul* that *davened netz*, the *shul* of Rav Yaakov Gerwirtz, located in Boro Park on 51st Street between 12th and 13th Avenues.

Since it was so rare at that time to *daven netz*, they called the *shul* the *"Vasikin Shul,"* which it's still called today. The *shul's* Rabbi, Rav Yaakov Gerwirtz, is in his 80s now, but he recounted that the first time he met Rav Berland was on Shabbos *parashas Vayeira*, when they decided to try and extend the *netz minyan* to Shabbos, as well.

XL   Many other Breslovers from Israel subsequently used this strategy, as at that time it was the only way they could legally try to get to Uman with a foreign passport. They would find a community that would ostensibly "hire" them as their Rabbi, and after being in the U.S. for a minimum of six months, they would be granted the Green Card that would enable them to travel on a U.S. passport.

"We were missing three more people to complete the *minyan* that Shabbos—until suddenly Rav Berland entered with two other people (Rav Moshe Beninstock and Rav Shmuel Varhaftig). Everyone there felt like we'd been sent messengers from Heaven, in line with that week's *parashah* where it's written, 'And behold, three men appeared to him²¹.'"

From that day on, there has always been a sunrise *minyan* in that *shul*, even on Shabbos. Rav Gerwirtz understood immediately that the Rav was a very holy Jew, and he gave him a lot of honor and invited him to his house for *Kiddush*. Afterwards, when he saw that the Rav didn't even have a place to sleep, he gave him an entire floor of his house, and asked him to stay as his guest for the entire six months.

During the time he was staying with Rav Gerwirtz, the two men became very friendly. Many years later, when Rav Gerwirtz was asked to describe a little of Rav Berland's legendary *avodas Hashem*, he replied, "I saw the Rav here [in New York] for half a year, and he would serve *Hashem* in ways that were above and beyond nature. Sometimes, he would stand up to say *Shemoneh Esrei* for 12 hours continuously. I saw him sit and learn for hours, without even sleeping or eating, and I can testify that the whole time he stayed with me he never slept on his bed during the week. He barely slept two hours a night, sitting on a chair.

"On Friday night, he would pray so profusely that he would end up making *Kiddush* when it was 3 a.m."

Rav Gerwirtz added that the Rav had a special grace that, whenever he would start dancing, the people had such respect for him that no one would leave the circle of dancers, even after they'd been dancing for more than an hour. Rav Gerwirtz concluded: "The Rav is not a servant of *Hashem*; he's an angel!"

THE MIRACLE WORKER

Know: There are 24 types of spiritual ransoms [pidyonot], corresponding to the 24 Heavenly courts of justice. For each and every court there is a unique corresponding ransom to ameliorate its judgments. Therefore a ransom is not always effective, since not everyone knows all 24 ransoms...

But know: There is a certain ransom that includes all the 24 courts of justice and is able to ameliorate [the judgments of] all the 24 courts... But among the tzaddikim, not everyone knows of this ransom. Only one in a generation knows of it...

Likutei Moharan I: 215

AN OPEN SECRET

The Rav's reputation as a miracle worker began even before he left the yeshivah at Kfar Chassidim, where the other students would ask him to pray for them when they were unwell.

By the time Rav Berland moved to Bnei Brak, his ability to miraculously help people with his prayers and blessings had already become an open secret among the generation's leading *tzaddikim*. Leading rabbis like Rav Mordechai Sharabi, Rav Yaakov Yisrael Kanievsky, and Rav Yitzchak Kaduri would send people to Rav Berland for a blessing.

Rav Berland had begun corresponding with Rav Yitzchak Kaduri in his younger years, and sent him many letters containing a number of questions he had about *Kabbalah*. After their correspondence had continued for some time, Rav Kaduri started occasionally telling some of the people who came to him for help that Rav Berland was the one *tzaddik* in the generation who controls all 24 of the Heavenly courts, and that only he could help them.

This sentiment was echoed in more recent times by Rav Yoram Abergel, *zt" l*, as the following account shows: "A year and a half ago, around six months before his untimely death[XLI], I went to ask Rav Yoram, *zt" l*, a number of questions, and one of

XLI   Rav Yoram Abergel, *zt" l*, passed away on 27 Tishrei, 5776 (October 10, 2015) at the age of 58.

them concerned all the commotion surrounding the *tzaddik* and *gaon*, Rav Eliezer Berland," explains Dan Ben-Dovid, one of Rav Abergel's close followers.

"I didn't really know very much at all about Rav Berland, *shlita*, or his Shuvu Banim community. But there was so much commotion going on around him, the matter came to my attention. So, I asked Rav Yoram Abergel, 'Honored Rabbi, there are a lot of things being said about Rav Berland, with people saying all sorts of different things about him.'

"Rav Yoram gave me a very big smile and quietly whispered in my ear, 'Rav Berland, *shlita*, rules over the 24 Heavenly courts,'" concludes Ben-Dovid[XLII].

HIDING HIS GREATNESS

Over the years, there have literally been thousands of miracle stories involving Rav Berland's blessings and *pidyonos*. Many people have also testified that they saw Rav Berland defending them in the Heavenly courts during a clinical death, where they were later given permission to return to this world, thanks to the Rav's intervention.

With his customary humility, the Rav himself has always gone to great pains to try to play down and hide the open miracles and otherworldly situations he's been part of, but here we bring a very small selection of some of the people he's helped with his blessings and prayers.[22]

THE TERRIBLE ILLNESS DISAPPEARS: RAV BINYAMIN KNAPELMACHER

"One of the times that I merited to really see the power of the Rav's prayers was with regard to a good friend of mine, Rabbi Binyamin Knapelmacher," begins Rav Shmuel Stern. "While Rabbi Knapelmacher was on a trip to America, he suddenly started to feel ill. He came back to Israel and discovered that he had cancer. He actually lost consciousness for a couple of weeks, and the doctors gave up on him and called in his family to say their farewells to him.

"One night, the Rav showed up at the hospital with a few students, and I also had the merit of being part of the group that came to visit. He entered Reb Binyam-

---

XLII   Rav Berland only started accepting *pidyon nefesh* payments after the three Breslov elders passed away in 1989.

in's room and saw him lying there unconscious. He started to recite the *Tikkun Haklali* next to him, very loudly, together with the rest of the group.

"The nurses came from all over the ward to see what was going on. The Rav told us to say the *Tikkun Haklali* together three times, and then as he was leaving he told Reb Binyamin's children, 'In another 24 hours, your father is going to wake up.'

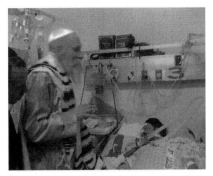

Rav Berland at Rav Knapelmacher's bedside, in the intensive care unit.

"And so it was! After 24 hours, to the utter shock of all the doctors and his relatives, Rav Binyamin woke up and started moving around. Hashem helped him to have a complete *refuah sheleimah* and return to his *avodas Hashem*."[XLIII]

THE BOY GOT UP AND WALKED

When Uziel Kalifa's youngest son was three weeks old, he started vomiting almost every hour. The parents didn't know what to do, and the doctors also didn't have a clue what was going on. They told the parents that it was hopefully just infant reflux, and that it would pass.

But as time passed, the situation only continued to get worse and started to become very serious. After several months of watching his son constantly vomiting, one day the father saw a strange growth on the child's stomach. They went for a medical checkup and the doctors told them that the child had an enlarged liver, and that he needed to undergo a whole series of tests in the hospital.

In the hospital, they told the parents that their child had a very rare, serious disease. Only 10 to 20 people in the world develop this disease, and there was no treatment available for it. The parents were completely devastated when they heard this dire prognosis; never in their wildest dreams had they thought things would get so serious and that there would be no solution to their son's health problems.

XLIII   The Rav often asked his driver to take him directly to the bedside of a seriously ill person who'd been hospitalized. While there, the Rav would recite the *Tikkun Haklali*, and on many occasions, the sick person would recover.

Over the next year and a half, the parents went through *Gehinnom*. They went to every expert in the world, tried all types of treatments and medicines and paid lots of money, all to no avail.

By this point, the child's development was very delayed, and the parents were already on the verge of despair. At age one and a half, the baby still didn't know how to crawl, was still vomiting everything he ate, and was experiencing life-threatening crises on a regular basis. The parents had to keep measuring the baby's blood sugar, even in the middle of the night, because their son's blood sugar would sometimes drop to 28 (normal is above 90), which was life-threatening. When that happened, they had to take him to the hospital immediately.

"We had a year and a half of suffering that was so harsh, it's difficult to describe what we endured," says Uziel.

A few months ago, the brother of Uziel brought him a copy of the *Knishta Chada* newsletter [put out by students at the Shuvu Banim Yeshivah], and he got a lot of *chizzuk* from the stories and *divrei Torah* it contained, so he started to read every newsletter he could lay his hands on.

In one of the more recent newsletters, he saw an advertisement for Rav Berland's miracle hotline. He immediately called up and told his story to the Rav's *gabbai*, who told Uziel that he would speak to the Rav on his behalf and get back to him.

The *gabbai* happened to call back when Uziel was with his son in the hospital in Tzfas because his son had developed a lung infection. The *gabbai* told Uziel that the Rav had advised him to do a *pidyon nefesh* for his son and then everything would be fine.

Uziel didn't think twice. From the moment they gave the *pidyon nefesh*, they were discharged from the hospital with the child, and not a week passed without some progress in his condition. The child started to walk, even though he'd never learned how to crawl and was already two.

Up to this point, the parents had been carrying their son everywhere, but suddenly he just started walking on his own two feet. Uziel reported that after the Rav performed the *pidyon* for them, the family experienced huge miracles that were impossible to understand or explain.

Today, *baruch Hashem*, Uziel's son is running around the house like a normal child. Uziel put it this way: "It's like witnessing *techiyas hameisim*, the revival of the dead." After a while, the parents went back to the doctors for another checkup, to see how their son's liver was doing. Before the *pidyon*, their son had a liver count of over 2,000; afterwards, it dropped to only 400. When the doctors saw the way the little boy was running around, they were at a complete loss to explain what had happened.

THE RAV IS NOT A PRIEST

Rav Dovid Rubinstein related that an extremely wealthy individual came to see the Rav and gave him an enormous sum of money as a *pidyon*. The wealthy man told the Rav that he was going through a lot of difficult tribulations, and the Rav told him, "Now, everything will start to improve—but from now on, take upon yourself to stop doing *aveiros*."

The man refused to accept the Rav's words and said, "That's hard for me."

The Rav replied, "Until now, everything has been atoned for, but from now on you have to be a kosher Jew." But again, the man wouldn't agree. Suddenly, the Rav said to him, "What am I, a priest?!" [i.e., that people could just come and pay some money and "confess their sins" and that would be enough to atone for them.] And with that, the Rav stood up, gave the man his money back, and left the room.

THE VANISHING CASE OF HODGKINS LYMPHOMA

Mrs. Michal H. was staying with her 12-year-old son in Europe when the boy suddenly developed breathing difficulties. They went to doctors and discovered that he had an 8-cm growth in his lungs, very close to his heart. He also had a second growth in his neck, and the doctors discovered that he had a type of cancer called Hodgkin's Lymphoma, and that it had already spread throughout most of the upper part of his body.

They immediately started chemotherapy, but the boy's situation continued to deteriorate.

The mother called Rav Berland's *gabbai* and asked to pass on her son's name to the Rav for a *brachah*, prayer and advice. The Rav had advised her to do a *pidyon nefesh* for her son.

From the Rav's words, the mother immediately understood that her son's situation was very serious. At the same time, money was so tight that the woman was struggling even to find money to buy the basics like food.

She called the *gabbai* again and requested a *brachah* from the Rav that she would be able to actually pay the *pidyon*. The Rav told her, "There will be miracles upon miracles" — and that's exactly what happened.

Shortly after she'd received the blessing from Rav Berland, the woman's niece called her up and said that she was very worried about the boy and she didn't know what to do for him. Mrs. H. replied that there was nothing to do. She told her niece, "Rav Eliezer Berland promised me that if I make a *pidyon* for him, we'll see miracles. I don't have the means to make a *pidyon*, but he said there will be miracles upon miracles, so I'm not worrying."

The niece said that she would get all the family involved. She called everyone in the family and collected all the money required for the *pidyon nefesh*.

While all this was happening, another miracle took place: The woman's former workplace contacted her and told her they were prepared to pay her the money they owed her, money she never dreamed she would ever receive. The amount they paid her was almost equal to the amount of the *pidyon nefesh*.

The first miracle was that she put the money together for the *pidyon nefesh* so easily, and the second miracle was that she then received almost the same amount again from her former employers. She wanted to give the money back to her family members but they insisted that she keep it.

After she did the *pidyon nefesh*, the Rav advised her to travel to Paris, to the hospital where her son was being treated.

When she got to Paris, the woman was put up by one of the community's prominent families who had a free *hachnasas orchim* guesthouse for people who were visiting the city. She stayed in Paris for a number of weeks, visiting her son, who was still in very grave condition, every day. He could now only speak with great difficulty, and he certainly couldn't get up or walk around, as the disease had spread throughout his body.

Slowly, slowly, the mother strengthened her son and encouraged him to get up and take a few steps, and even to walk outside a little. She saw some small improvements, but overall, his condition remained very serious.

The woman returned to Israel, and after a few days she arranged a telephone call between her son and Rav Berland. The Rav strengthened the boy a lot, and the same morning after he'd spoken with the Rav, there was a breakthrough in the boy's condition.

He told his mother, "Ima, today I *davened Shacharis*." She was in shock, because not that long ago he didn't even have the strength to say *Modeh Ani*. After a few days she spoke with her son again and asked him if he'd managed to *daven Shacharis* that morning, as well. He replied, "I *daven Shacharis* every morning!" He'd simply forgotten that he was ill, and he started to behave as though he was a healthy, normal boy. The Rav had said there would be miracles upon miracles, and a little while later, so it was.

When the doctors ran their tests on the boy, they were astonished to see that most of his illness, almost 95 percent, had disappeared. The illness had already spread throughout the upper and lower parts of his body, and also into the bones, and the doctors didn't hold out much hope for him. They were amazed to see that everything had disappeared and that the illness had vanished.

THE NEAR-DEATH EXPERIENCE OF REVITAL LEVY

Rebbetzin Revital Levy is a well-known lecturer in Israel who famously had a near-death experience. She describes how Rav Eliezer Berland intervened in the Heavenly court to ask that she be given a second chance at life.

Revital's story was first published in 2012, by the *B'Chagvei Hashela* outreach organization located in Tiveria. Since her story was widely publicized, Revital has been asked to tell her story over in many different forums and communities across Israel.

When members of Shuvu Banim contacted Revital to verify her story, she said the following:

"After I promised the Heavenly *beis din* that I would do *teshuvah*, that's what I did [when I woke up again]—except the *teshuvah* only lasted for about four months. My husband was very secular, and he found the whole idea of me doing *teshuvah* very difficult. So once again, I became a secular Jew, this time for another 11 years, until we ended up getting divorced in 2006."

Revital continues: "I really wanted to be a *tzaddekes. Hashem* gave me the privilege of buying a very modest apartment, and about two-and-a-half years after my divorce, a yeshivah student who was collecting money for his yeshivah in Jerusalem showed up at my door. I asked the young man, 'Who is your Rabbi?' He told me the name, but I'd never heard about this person before.

"Then he took a picture of his Rav out of his bag and showed it to me, and I was shocked to the core of my being: It was the Rav who had defended me in the Heavenly court! I almost fainted on the spot. I told the student that I'd been searching for the Rav who'd saved me [from a Heavenly death sentence] for 11 years already, and I had no idea who he actually was.

"But now, God had answered my prayers and helped me find that awesome *tzaddik*—Rav Eliezer Berland. Only people who have experienced what I have [i.e., a clinical death] understand how great and awesome he is considered to be in *Shamayim*. His word counts for so much there; I was there, so I know.

"Immediately after that I did real *teshuvah*, and shortly afterwards I married a real *tzaddik* of a man who does outreach at the Dvar Shmuel Yeshivah.

"Then, in the winter of 5771 (2011), I had a dream one Friday night where the Rav appeared wrapped in his white *tallis*, with his wife the Rebbetzin by his side, standing in front of a bookcase full of holy books. He said to me twice, 'I want you to go on *shlichus* for me!' [Something that Revital consequently did, publicizing her story in as many different places as possible within Israel.]

"Some months later, in *Cheshvan* 5773 (2012), I asked God to show me what was going on with the Rav. That same night I had dream. All the books containing the spiritual accounts of the whole nation of Israel were opened in front of me, and I was hovering over them. Seeing this awesome carpet made up of millions of open books was a truly amazing sight to behold.

"Standing to the right of these books was Rav Berland, and he was holding an enormous pair of scissors in his hand. I understood from the dream that he was cutting up the harsh judgments facing *Am Yisrael*."

THE DISAPPEARING JAIL TERM

A secular man described how he'd gotten mixed up in a difficult situation that had even been publicized in the media, and now, after many court appearances and lawsuits, he'd finally been sentenced to seven years in jail by the court.

This man had a *baal teshuvah* friend who told him about a big Rav in Jerusalem called Rav Berland and that it was worth trying to go to him to get a *brachah* so that he'd come out of prison healthy in body and soul.

But the man who'd been sentenced poo-poohed the idea, saying, "Are you crazy? You think I have nothing better to do right now than go to Rabbis?!" But the friend kept badgering him, until finally he agreed to go. The day before he was meant to start his prison term, he came to the Rav and told him the whole story.

Rav Berland told him to start keeping Shabbos and to lay *tefillin* every day, and if he did that then everything would be okay. He told the Rav that he didn't understand, but the Rav just repeated that he should keep Shabbos and put on *tefillin* and everything would be fine, and then he escorted him to the door. His friend was waiting outside and asked him what the Rav had said to him, but he didn't respond. Instead, he said, "Come, let's take a taxi to the jail."

When they arrived at the jail, the friend suggested to the man that he shouldn't show the court order to the guard, but just present his *teudat zehut* (identity number) instead. So he turned to the guard and told him that he had been ordered to go to jail for seven years. The guard asked him for the court order and he simply said that he had forgotten it at home. The guard then asked for his *teudat zehut*, which he gave him. The guard checked and said that he couldn't find anything about him on his computer. The man asked him to check again and the guard got angry and said, 'You think I have nothing better to do than waste public time on you?!'

But the man persisted and asked him to check the central register in Tel Aviv, providing him with the full details of the case. The guard checked there and again he didn't find anything. The case file had simply disappeared! After experiencing these miracles, the man did *teshuvah*.

SAVED FROM CERTAIN DEATH AFTER
BEING STABBED BY A TERRORIST

Rav Shlomo Elmaliach is the brother of Asher Elmaliach, the security guard who was seriously injured at Jerusalem's Central Bus Station in a terrorist attack on December 10th, 2017. In an interview that Rav Elmaliach gave to the *Breslov HaOlami* Line, he described how his brother was cruelly attacked, and then recounted the many miracles that saved his brother's life:

"The terrorist *mamash* dressed up to look like an Israeli," begins Rav Elmaliach. "It was impossible to tell that he was actually a terrorist. He'd already successfully gone through the security check at the entrance to the Central Bus Station, but for some reason my brother, Asher, grabbed his coat, and asked him to show his identity papers.

"The terrorist appeared to have gone into shock - we later found out that he's a resident of Shechem (Nablus), and the son of one of the leading extremists in the Palestinian Authority. So, my brother asked him to take off his coat, which the terrorist did without revealing that he was carrying a long, thick knife that had been sharpened on both sides.

ONE IN A MILLION COULD SURVIVE

"When the terrorist saw that my brother was busy checking his papers, he dashed at him and evilly thrust the whole knife into his heart. Every single person that this happens to usually dies on the spot. The medical experts and professors told us that one in a million people could survive from being stabbed in this way."

Rav Elmaliach continues:

"From that point on, we've witnessed miracle after miracle, and behind them all has stood the *gaon* and the *tzaddik*, Rav Eliezer Berland, shlit'a. It all started a month before the stabbing, when my brother donated a large sum of money to me, to help me print and distribute the *peirush* (Torah commentary) that I'd written on the book "Etz Chayim" (the 'Tree of Life').

"He'd persuaded me to come to the bus station to get the money from him, and there he asked me that I should give him a *bracha* that 'the *tzedaka* should save from death'. In the merit of that charity he'd given, there was a lady from Magen David Adom who was there at the time of the stabbing, and who stopped him from bleeding to death.

"When we told Rav Berland what had happened, he immediately wanted us to bring a *pidyon*, but at that stage the family didn't understand the importance of giving a *pidyon* to the *tzaddik*. My son, Nachman, saw that paying the *pidyon* had got held up, so he told the Rav that he would give the *pidyon* himself, but because my brother's condition had worsened, the Rav told him that this initial amount would no longer be enough.

ASHER ACTUALLY DIED AT 3AM

"My brother had a punctured lung, broken ribs, and other things had been damaged in his body, apart from the terrible stab wound he'd sustained to the heart. At 3am, my brother died, and it was only the external respirator that was keeping him going.

"My son immediately ran over to Rav Berland, shlit'a, who told him: "Asher is in a critical situation, and you need to immediately bring a sum of money to do the *pidyon nefesh*, within the next few minutes."

"My son and my son-in-law threw themselves into pulling the money together, gave it to the Rav, and then Asher's situation started to improve. I immediately said to them that under no circumstances would I expect them to pay off the loan they'd just taken in order to do the *pidyon*, and that I would take responsibility for all of it.

"Afterwards, I found out that the amount my brother had given to me the month before was the same amount of money needed to do the *pidyon nefesh* with Rav Berland, shlit'a. The really amazing thing is that when I gave the money for the *pidyon*, I immediately felt a sweetness that is impossible for me to describe in words.

"I immediately contacted everyone back at the hospital and told them that Asher would live, but everyone thought I'd gone mad, because they knew his situation was very bleak, and that there was almost no hope.

"The following day, the hole that the knife had made in his heart was somehow plugged, in a completely miraculous way. Another day passed, and there was another huge miracle: the hole in his lung also somehow closed up - and that's when it started to get publicized all over the country.

"The doctors were in complete shock that he'd started to reconnect to us. The head professor at the hospital told me to my face that all the healing my brother had experienced was completely unnatural.

"The *tzedaka* that my brother had given and all of his *mesirus nefesh* really stood for him, in his time of need. But without any doubt, the merit of Rav Berland is what made the most difference of all."

SICK SISTER FROM PETACH TIKVA

Avi Dahan is a student in the Shuvu Banim Yeshivah who hails from Petach Tikva. His sister was very ill, and her life was literally hanging in the balance. She was hooked up to life support, trying to overcome a disease called Pemphigus Vulgaris, which is a chronic disease that many people (estimated at around 75%) used to die from before the advent of corticosteroids in the 1950s.

The disease causes the person to develop wounds, both internally and externally, that are impossible to heal. Avi went to visit Rav Berland to ask for a blessing for his sister, and the Rav told him that within two months, she would completely recover her health — and she did.

THE SPINKA REBBE OF BORO PARK

The following story was told over by Avreimi who heard it straight from the holy mouth of the Spinka Rebbe:

"I learned many hours with Rav Berland," the *Admor* told Avreimi. "To my great sorrow, my daughter was suffering from cancer; she had a tumor in her brain. The situation became so serious that she began to fall every time she stood up, and she could no longer walk."

The *Admor* continued: "I wasted no time in coming to talk to Rav Berland about my daughter, and the Rav promised me that she would walk again. I asked the Rav, 'And if not?' The Rav answered me that if that was not the case, I would need to come back again."

The *Admor* returned home and tried to walk with his daughter — but to his great dismay, she started falling again. "She fell, and my spirit also almost fell," the *Admor* confided to Avreimi. "But I immediately did a *cheshbon hanefesh* and I realized that I'd made a mistake in questioning the Rav.

"The following day I went back to the Rav, but this time, I didn't repeat the same mistake. From that day on, we began to see great wonders: My daughter started walking again, and then, *baruch Hashem*, recovered completely. Today she is a mother with her own children."

THE SERIOUS ILLNESS AND THE MIRACULOUS BIRTH

"Our connection with the Rav began five years ago, when my wife first became ill," explains Doron Avivi (not his real name). "At that time, we began to come closer to Breslov, and to read the books and follow some of the advice of Rebbe Nachman. We even merited to visit the holy *tziyun* in Uman a number of times.

"In Nissan of 5775 (2015), just a few short months ago, my wife was in her 19th week of pregnancy when she began to feel pain in her upper body, on both sides. We went for some tests, and we were shocked when the doctor told us she had cancer." Doron explained that very soon afterwards the doctors discovered a number of additional tumors.

"The doctors believed that my wife's pregnancy was somehow speeding up the rate the illness was spreading. The surgeon came to speak to us, and he advised us to abort the baby. But my wife refused; she was determined to protect our child at all costs. So after that, we decided to consult an expert oncologist.

"In the meantime, to our dismay, the doctors discovered another growth, and they wanted to do some more tests to check how far it had spread. They told us that if the results of the tests were as they feared, then we'd be forced to abort the baby. But if not, they were prepared to wait until the 31st week, and then begin to do a much more intensive treatment.

"During this period we went to many holy gravesites, and we also visited, Rav Dovid Abuchatzeira, and Rav Yoram Abergel, zt'l, who both told us that we'd see amazing miracles. But they emphasized that we needed to follow the advice of the doctors, even if this meant losing the baby. They told us that whatever happened, we needed to accept the situation with love. Their words strengthened us a lot, but on no account did we want to lose our precious child.

"Deep in our hearts we knew that Rav Berland held the key to our salvation, and that, despite all the efforts we'd already made, eventually we'd have to turn to him for help," continues Doron.

Before the last test results arrived, the Avivi family decided to contact the Rav through his *gabbai*, Natan Soloman, and the Rav advised them to make a *pidyon*. "We weren't surprised when we were told we needed to make a *pidyon*, because we knew how serious the situation was and that we needed a huge miracle."

Rav Berland also repeated several times, and emphasized to the couple, that they should do everything in their power to protect and guard their precious baby. However, the couple was concerned about the severity of the illness and they told the Rav about their misgivings.

"When the Rav heard this, he immediately advised us to follow the doctors' recommendations, even about how to deal with the baby," says Doron. "We were brokenhearted. And we were also dreading going through the terrible treatments."

Having spoken to the Rav and having made the *pidyon*, the couple went to get the results of the tests. "It was bizarre," says Doron. "Even though the doctors told us it had spread, they decided that the pregnancy could continue until the 31st week, just like the Rav had initially told us."

A few days later, they got back in touch with Rav Berland's *gabbai*, Natan Soloman, and were told that the Rav was inviting them to Holland. "My wife and I traveled to Holland together, and initially we were concerned about all the *tumah* we were exposing ourselves to by being in a non-Jewish country. But when we were with the Rav, we felt like we were in *Gan Eden*. Even though Holland is not a simple country for a religious Jew to be in, we felt that the place was holy. I even merited to pray *Shacharis* with the Rav, and he held my hand for a long time during the service, while my wife was pouring her heart out to Rebbetzin Berland.

"After *davening*, the Rebbetzin asked the Rav if we could go in to see him, and he agreed. He told us that within 40 days, everything would pass. Then he gave us a personal prayer to say, a bottle of holistic drops to take, and a special order of learning for my wife and me to learn together.

"But strangely, as the 40 days came to an end, my wife felt the pain getting stronger. She also began to have very strong pains in her thighs, to the degree that all the doctors were concerned that the illness had spread. We spoke to the Rav again, and again he reassured us that within a week, everything would be fine.

"It didn't stop," Doron continued. "What did happen, though, is that we suddenly discovered a natural doctor who was happy to see us, though she warned us that she doubted she'd be able to do anything more than just lessen my wife's pain a little. After the treatment, my wife's condition started to improve miraculously, until it all disappeared. We merited great miracles, and we greeted our baby, *baruch Hashem*, who was born healthy and well."

THE COLUMBIAN HEART TRANSPLANT

"My father has suffered from heart disease for the last 12 years," begins Sharon Mizrachi. "The situation continued to deteriorate from year to year, until five years ago, around Pesach time, my father was admitted to Tel Hashomer Hospital for over a year. He would stay in the hospital the whole week and be released only for Shabbos. I remember that period as being very difficult. Every time he needed to leave home to return to the ward, it was very hard for my father to go back to the hospital. Of course, my family would go and visit him during the week, but whenever we got ready to leave he'd have tears in his eyes. It really broke our hearts to see the sadness and great suffering that our father went through."

Sharon continues: "Relatively speaking, my father is not an old man. But by the time he hit his 50s, his heart was functioning at only 15 percent of normal capacity." In Israel, there's a very big halachic debate surrounding organ donations, which means that it's very difficult to arrange a heart transplant in Israel.

"We prayed a lot and hoped that *Hashem* would send us a miracle," continues Sharon. "The whole time this was going on, we were visiting one country after another to explore the possibility of arranging a heart transplant for my father, but they all fell through. Then the miracle occurred, the first in a chain of miracles that we experienced.

"Suddenly, we discovered that Columbia could be a real possibility for arranging my father's heart transplant, but it was still a very risky, life-threatening operation to undertake. At the same time, we heard about a young man of 24 who'd undergone a heart transplant in Israel, and who'd died immediately afterwards as his body had rejected the new heart.

"It was clear to me that my father needed to visit the *tzaddik* of the generation before deciding to go ahead with the operation. So I did what I had to do, and I took out a loan in order to pay for a *pidyon nefesh* for my father, and then we went together to see Rav Berland.

"My father was scared of two things: After he'd waited and suffered so much, he was afraid that the Rav would tell him that he shouldn't travel to Columbia for the operation. And at the same time, he was also still very afraid of actually having the operation, because he knew the chances of it succeeding, according to the laws of nature, were not very good at all.

"Things were so bad that the hospital asked my mother to sign a document stating that, in the event that the operation was not a success, God forbid, she wouldn't make a legal claim against the surgeons, and that we fully understood the risks involved."

Sharon notably perks up when he describes the moments when he first met Rav Berland:

"When we finally got to see him, it was very emotional," he says. "The Rav had just finished doing the *chalakah* haircutting ceremony for a little three-year-old boy. After that happy event, he immediately turned to my father and said to him, 'How long I've been waiting for you! Here, I've prepared a prayer for you, for your *refuah.*'

"The Rav smothered my father with love and held his hand continually, while stroking his face. My father was speechless, so I had to help him, and I explained to the Rav about my father's difficult condition. I asked the Rav to make a decree in the Heavens that my father would come through the operation in good health, in fulfillment of the dictum, 'a *tzaddik* decrees and *Hashem* fulfills.'

"As soon as the Rav heard this, he turned to his attendant who was in the room with him and said, 'You see this man? When he gets back from Columbia, he should come straight to me.'

"These words worked like magic for my father. When he heard what the Rav said, a huge stone rolled off his heart and his fears diminished considerably. Since then, he's been very close to the Rav and loves him tremendously.

"My father had to live in the city of Mediin, in Columbia, for three months, while he was having the operation. There, they gave him the heart of a 35-year-old non-Jewish man. We merited to see great miracles in Columbia. The heart transplant was very complicated, and the days following the operation were also critical, as his body needed to accept the foreign organ that had just been transplanted. We were all very anxious about whether the heart would be accepted or not.

"While we were waiting for my father in the emergency room, post-recovery, he suddenly developed a very high fever and his body started swelling until he was in critical condition. My father was *mamash* at death's door, so much so that the non-Jewish professor who'd operated on him turned to my mother and suggested she start saying some chapters of Psalms. My mother started crying a river of tears and praying with tremendous fervor. But I knew that the Rav had already cleared the path for us, and that we would see a great miracle.

"My father could so easily have died then. Instead, the day after the operation his vital signs stabilized and his life was saved. You can perhaps understand a little more about the scope of the miracle that occurred if I tell you that before my father went into the operating room, they asked my mother if we wanted him to be sent back to Israel for burial, in the event he didn't make it. And a few days after my father returned to Israel, an American woman who underwent the same operation in the same hospital died."

But more miracles were still to come.

"The operation cost around $300,000, which by all accounts is a huge sum of money," says Sharon. "But *Shamayim* decreed that the insurance my father had taken out only months before his operation would agree to cover the hospital fees. We saw with our own eyes how much the *pidyon* proved itself; who knows what would have happened if my father had tried to go it alone, without the blessing of Rav Berland."

ESCAPE FROM AN INDIAN PRISON

Ronen Dvash's amazing story of how Rav Berland's *pidyon nefesh* helped him escape from an Indian prison has been immortalized in the book *Escape from India*.

Dvash, a formerly secular Israeli with a marijuana habit, fell afoul of the Indian authorities when he was in India on business. He was kept in a hellish Indian prison for months, where he contracted malaria and almost died.

His family couldn't get anywhere with the corrupt legal system in India, and it seemed as though Dvash would end up spending decades in an Indian prison before his case even came to court.

Dvash had a spiritual awakening in prison, and as a result he asked his family to spend the money they'd collected for his legal fees on a *pidyon nefesh* with Rav Berland instead. The Rav wrote him a personalized prayer asking *Hashem* to blind the eyes of the guards so that he could escape prison, and told him to recite it daily. Shortly after the *pidyon nefesh* was made, Dvash was miraculously able to escape from this high-security Indian prison and return to Israel without his passport, thanks to a series of unbelievable miracles.

He subsequently did *teshuvah* and began publicizing his experiences by writing *Escape from India* and releasing a video where he tells the story in his own words.[23]

THE MIRACULOUS SHIDDUCH AT 33 YEARS OLD

There was a young man who waited a long time for his marriage partner but, after he turned to Rav Eliezer Berland, *shlita*, he found his wife-to-be literally in the blink of an eye. Here's his amazing story in his own words:

"Until the age of 33, I had difficulty finding my marriage partner," explains 'Ilan'. "It seemed as though there was no chance, God forbid, of ever settling down and building a Jewish home.

"Of course, I tried to get things moving any way I could, and spent a lot of money in the process. I spoke to experts and rabbis in the hope that some miracle would occur. But nothing helped, and I felt as though I needed a miracle on the level of 'splitting the sea', *mamash*, in order to get married.

"One day, someone told me about the *Gaon* and *Tzaddik* Rav Eliezer Berland, *shlita*, who I hadn't paid attention to before. I knew he was successful in bringing people close to *Hashem*, and that people had seen miraculous salvations as a result of his blessings.

"So, at that moment, I decided I had to meet the Rav, come what may. So that's what I did," continued 'Ilan'. "I grabbed the bull by the horns, and went to see the Rav. At that time, it was difficult to see the Rav, for a lot of reasons. The outside door at that time was covered in a layer of foam, to muffle the sound of the people knocking who were trying to see him.

"After I'd been there for a while, someone from the community passed by and saw that I'd been waiting a long time. He told me that I had to register in advance, and then I had to wait until the Rav received the public. But he also told me that I should go out to the field and pray to the Creator of the world for help to see the Rav. He told me if I did that, for sure I'd succeed, and the Rav himself would open the door for me.

"I took his advice," continued 'Ilan'. "I poured my heart out to *Hashem* that I would merit to see the Rav and get his blessing. After I finished, I went back to the Rav's house. Behold, in front of my astonished eyes, the door opened and the Rav stood in the entrance.

"I started trembling and felt completely shocked by what had just happened, that he was actually standing in front of me and my prayers had really been answered. The Rav, *shlit'a*, spoke to me in a very gentle way, and said: 'Come back on Monday, and she'll be waiting for you here, downstairs, and we'll complete the *shidduch*, God willing.'

"I felt like I was in a dream," continues 'Ilan'. "I kissed the Rav's hand, and then found myself walking home, and I still couldn't believe what had just happened. Waiting for the minutes, hours, and days to pass, to see what was going to happen, was pretty stressful. That fateful Monday finally arrived, and I quickly made my way to the Rav's house.

"I went up the stairs and the bodyguards stopped me dead in my tracks. They told me: 'You can't go in! You aren't registered! There's a process you have to go through!' So I told them that the Rav had told me to come back at this time, and I started to kick up a fuss. After a quick discussion, one of the bodyguards felt sorry for me and went inside to clarify what was going on.

"After a few minutes, he came back and told me that the Rav said I should enter immediately. I flew up the stairs, and I entered, and I saw another man sitting there with the Rav, who was requesting advice and a blessing for a shidduch for his daughter, who'd reached marriageable age a long time since.

"As soon as I entered the room, the Rav immediately turned to him and said: 'Behold, the groom has arrived!' Then the Rav turned to me, and said: 'She's waiting downstairs. You can go down and meet her, and then come back to me with the details on Thursday.'

"So I went downstairs," continues 'Ilan', "and I explained that I'd prayed a lot to be blessed with a suitable marriage partner, and told everything that happened from the moment I first came to the Rav's house until now, and everything the Rav had said...

"*Baruch Hashem*, the matter progressed in a good way. On that Thursday, with the Rav's advice, we celebrated our engagement.

"During the engagement party, the situation took another twist: The Rav took a piece of paper and a pen, and told us the following: 'I'm writing the date when the marriage needs to take place. Not a day before, and not a day after!' I took the piece of paper, and we immediately started looking for a wedding hall to hire on that specific date.

"We searched high and low, but all of the suitable halls in the area weren't available on that date. We didn't have any choice, so we had to widen out the halls we were willing to consider--and still no luck! So finally, we had to go even further afield, and look for halls in Rishon LeZion, where we finally managed to find a wedding hall available on that date.

"The owner of the hall could see we were from Jerusalem, so he asked us why we coming so far out to find a wedding hall. I decided to tell him the whole story, and explained how the Rav had made our *shidduch*. The moment he understood what Rav we were actually talking about--Rav Eliezer Berland, *shlita*--he stood up and got very emotional, and started banging on the table. Everyone in the hall stopped what they were doing to look at him.

"He called everyone over to come and listen to him, and he said the following: "I have to tell you all a story that happened to me more than 10 years ago, when my daughter slipped on the tiled floor of our kitchen and fell on her head. She was in a critical situation and the best doctors in the hospital despaired of doing anything for her. They were convinced that she'd never be a fully-functioning person again.

'I was so distressed, I turned to Rav Berland, *shlit'a*. The Rav told me to make a *pidyon nefesh*, and then she would have a complete recovery, with *Hashem's* help. I immediately did what he said, and he told me: 'Come back in a week, and tell me how she's doing.' What can I say?' continued the owner of the wedding hall.

"Suddenly, he started crying before continuing his story: 'In the time it took me to come back from the house of the Rav, *shlit'a*, they'd already unhooked my daughter from the life-support... She had started to recover under the eyes of the doctors, who looked on in disbelief and kept saying how this was a medical miracle that defied explanation.

"'After a week, I went and updated the Rav about the improvement in her condition, and two months after that I took my daughter, who was now able to walk again, with me to visit the Rav.' The hall owner then turned to us and said: 'Listen. The Rav said to me: 'You own a wedding hall, don't you?' When I said yes, he said to me: 'In ten years' time, I'm going to send a couple to you, who will want to get married in your hall.' He then asked me to cover all the costs of that wedding.

"'I'm obligated to the Rav,' continued the owner of the wedding hall. 'He saved what is most dear to me, in all my life. Now I have to do what he requested of me. The circle is now complete. You are the couple being sent to me now.'"

'Ilan' concludes his amazing story: "The owner of the hall paid for all the wedding expenses, and by doing so paid off his obligation to the Rav. He told me: 'I was so happy that I promised to do this, and that I'm now able to fulfill it!"

THERE IS NO SUFFERING WITHOUT SIN

From the Rav's Torah lessons:

The Rebbe says in *Likutei Moharan* 206 that a person sins and harms his soul. At first things continue to go well for him, but then *Hashem* begins to send him slight hints. If he still doesn't get it, *Hashem* calls to him more loudly, until the person starts getting kicked and pounded with suffering.

You sinned? Do *teshuvah*! The same Torah that told you it's a sin tells you about *teshuvah*! But if you don't do *teshuvah*, then maybe after some suffering something will start to sink in and you will begin to do *teshuvah*, begin to sob over your spiritual blemishes, get shaken up a drop! If not, then God forbid, a spouse will get sick, and if not a spouse, then the children, God forbid!

The Rebbe promised that he will fix everything, but the question is, how will he fix? How much suffering must a person endure in order to receive his rectification? Sometimes it hurts to go to a doctor, and if someone is really sick the surgery can be painful.

We are Jews! Nothing is rectified for free! By the Christians nothing needs to be done; just go to the priest and confess to him once a year and he says "forgiven, forgiven" afterwards, and everyone continues as before. By Jews there is no such thing! A person must pay for his sins! He must pay for every transgression! If a person doesn't do *teshuvah* and doesn't wake up, then he starts getting hit with suffering, as it says, "There is no suffering without sin.²⁴"

UMAN, UMAN

When Rav Berland committed himself to following Rebbe Nachman's path, he hit an enormous obstacle: At the time that Rav Berland started to draw closer to Breslov *Chassidus*, the gates of Rebbe Nachman's resting place in the Ukrainian town of Uman were still slammed firmly shut. Uman was under Soviet rule, and the authorities in the USSR were openly hostile to anything and anyone connected to the practice of Judaism.

To make matters worse, the Soviet Union broke off all diplomatic ties with the State of Israel after the Six-Day War, which meant that no Israeli citizen was allowed to travel to the USSR on an Israeli passport.

Despite all these obstacles, after Rav Hersh Leib Lippel encouraged him to make the trip, the Rav threw himself into breaking through the Iron Curtain with his customary dedication and single-mindedness.

First he made a number of journeys to Greece, to see if he could enter the USSR from there, but his attempts came to naught. The next option was to try the ruse devised by Rabbi Yaakov Teplinski, *zt"l*, to spend six months in America as the "Rav" of a *kehillah* there, in order to obtain a Green Card that would enable him to travel to Soviet Russia on a U.S. passport.

At the time, it seemed like the only way of getting into the Ukraine. So in 5733 [1972], Rav Berland traveled to America and stayed there for six months, hoping for the Green Card that would unlock the gates of Uman. Getting the Green Card was relatively easy, if time-consuming. But getting to Uman still proved enormously risky, dangerous, and difficult.

THE RAV'S FIRST TRIP

All told, the Rav attempted to get to Uman *nine different times* before he actually succeeded. Each attempt required many thousands of dollars in airfare, bribes, and other expenses, plus a tremendous amount of planning, self-sacrifice, and prayer. Getting into the USSR was only the first obstacle. Once there, tourists were routinely spied on by the KGB and the Soviet's official tourist agency, Intourist, and they were given itineraries by the Soviet authorities from which it was strictly forbidden to deviate.

While the Soviets allowed foreign tourists to visit the cities of Odesser and Kiev with permission, both a couple of hundred miles away from Uman, the city of Uman itself was completely off-limits to foreigners because it was home to a Soviet army installation. Anyone illegally caught there would be interrogated, imprisoned—and perhaps even killed.

The Rav once commented that during this period, each time he set off for another clandestine attempt to visit Uman, he went in the full knowledge that he could literally be killed in the attempt if the Soviets caught him.

The first few times the Rav tried to get to Uman, he was caught by Communist officials and prevented from even crossing the border into Russia. Undeterred, he kept trying different schemes and different routes until finally he succeeded. Nine attempts—and many tens of thousands of dollars later—he finally achieved his dream.

At this period of time, Rebbe Nachman's grave was located in the back garden of a private home, directly under the back window. Its location was known to just the handful of practicing Breslover *chassidim* who remained trapped behind the Iron Curtain, including Rav Michel Dorfman, who stayed loyal to Rebbe Nachman's teachings despite the ever-present risk of exile to Siberia, torture, or execution if he was caught actively practicing Judaism by the authorities.

When Rav Berland finally managed to get to Rebbe Nachman's grave, he prostrated himself on the tomb, recited the *Tikkun Haklali*, and then declared that now, the gates to Uman were going to be reopened.

Rav Yisrael Meir Brenner recounted that he'd once been with Rav Berland at Rebbe Nachman's *tziyun*, and the Rav had prostrated himself on the ground for a full four hours, without moving. "He did things [in Uman] that no one else could have done," says Rav Brenner.

Rav Berland by Rebbe Nachman's Tziyon in Uman, when it was still located in the outside courtyard of a local home.

On another occasion, Yosef Druck saw the Rav stay at the gravesite for almost a whole day without moving, from *chatzos* until the evening prayers: "He said to me, 'Every second at the *tziyun* is worth a million seconds of life.'"

IF NOT FOR RAV BERLAND, NO ONE WOULD HAVE GONE TO UMAN.

While other individuals also managed to clandestinely visit *Rabbeinu's* tomb, Rav Berland was the only one who sacrificed so much to bring so many people to the site, from raising money for the costly trips to arranging the foreign passports required for Israeli citizens.

Rav Shmuel Hoffman recounted that in the early 1970s, Rav Berland was making the hazardous trip to Uman every two weeks, each time taking a different route and using a different counterfeit passport, and bringing tens of new visitors with him. On each trip, Rav Berland would give all his fellow travelers careful instructions on what to say and do at the border, and also how to deal with the Communist officials so they wouldn't make any further trouble or succeed in their attempts to arrest the 'illegal tourists'.

Rav Hoffman reminisced: "If Rav Berland hadn't done all those things back then, then no one would have been able to make the trip to Uman. They wouldn't have gotten anywhere by themselves." He recalled how the Rav had tried to persuade him to join one of these clandestine tours to Uman, and he had demurred because of the danger.

THE KGB'S MOST WANTED PERSON

Rabbi Nachman Horowitz recounted that, on one of Rav Berland's clandestine trips to Uman, there were "wanted" posters of him pasted up all over town, including the hotel where he happened to be staying. But the Rav wasn't perturbed, and even stood directly under one of the posters while giving a *shiur* to his fellow travelers. Even though he was clearly the man being sought by the authorities, none of the Russians in the Kiev hotel ever connected their Jewish guest with the man on the posters.

Rav Berland's picture had been circulated throughout the region by the Communist regime, and he was also on the KGB's "most-wanted persons" list. Rav Hoffman once asked Rav Berland straight out, *"HaRav*, they already caught you once, and it's a miracle that you managed to escape from them. Aren't you scared [to go back]?"

Headlines from Israeli papers from that time, when Breslov chassidim were arrested for having a forged passport.

"Rav Berland replied that in the merit of all the trips he was making to the Ukraine at that time, a time would come when thousands of *chassidim* would start flying to Uman from all over the world," says Rav Hoffman. "I asked him how many people he thought would be making the trip in the future, and he told me 'no less than 5,000 people!' So I said to the Rav, 'Rav, the whole Breslov *Chassidus* has less than 500 people! Where are all these 5,000 people going to come from?!'

"Rav Berland replied that 5,000 was only the beginning, and there would be many, many more. Hundreds of flights filled with Jews going to Uman would take off from Israel and other places in the world."

Rav Hoffman recounts that when he first heard Rav Berland say these things, back in the early 1970s, it sounded like pure fantasy—but now, it's easy to see how the Rav truly knew what he was talking about. In 2016, an estimated 60,000 people made the trip to Uman for Rosh Hashanah!

"YOUR TRIPS TO UMAN ARE ENDANGERING PEOPLE!"

Not everyone was happy about Rav Berland's trips to Uman. At various points in the 1970s, dissenting voices were heard within the Breslov community that Rav Berland was taking unnecessary risks, and endangering people's lives with his clandestine visits to Uman.

In truth, the Rav made strenuous preparations before every trip. He didn't just organize flights, and arrange counterfeit passports, visas, and other details. Even more crucially, the Rav also used to pray profusely that the trip would succeed. It was widely known that Rav Berland would fast the whole day of the trip, until his group had crossed the border into the Ukraine, which was often the biggest hurdle.

The Rav certainly took risks to get to Uman, but made each decision with enormous *yishuv hadaas*, or spiritual clarity, as to what was needed to get the job done.

Once, Zev Frank asked Rav Berland: "How can you travel on a counterfeit passport, when it's written in *Sefer Hamiddos* that if you're able to use natural means [and not rely on miracles to travel on forged papers], then you should use natural means?"

The Rav replied, "By all means, show me the more 'natural' way of doing this, and I'll take it!"

Surprisingly, one of the more vocal critics of the Rav's clandestine trips to Uman was his spiritual mentor and guide, Rav Levi Yitzchak Bender.

Rav Yitzchak Weisshandler recounts: "Once, Rav Levi Yitzchak saw the Rav and started screaming at him that he was endangering people [by taking them to Uman, which was then still under Communist rule]. The Rav replied, 'And what about when you went to Uman, to the *kever*, and the informer was running after you? How did you get to the *kever*? That wasn't endangering people's lives?' Rav Levi Yitzchak broke into laughter, and accepted the Rav's answer.

Later on, when the path to Uman had become more established and less dangerous and Rav Berland was taking many tens of people to the Ukraine, Rav Levi Yitzchak remarked, "I'm sure that *Rabbeinu* is keeping a lot of good for Rav Lazer, who brought so many people to Uman." [XLIV]

DANCING THEIR WAY THROUGH PASSPORT CONTROLS

As the 1970s progressed, Rav Berland came up with the idea of creating a pretend "Peace Organization" that claimed to be enamored with Soviet ideas and ideals, as a pretext for bringing larger groups of *chassidim* to Uman, traveling on a variety of counterfeit passports.

The Soviet authorities were thrilled to have the opportunity of showcasing the ideal Soviet lifestyle to sympathetic foreigners, and this ruse enabled Rav Berland to start bringing much larger groups into the Soviet Union.

But, as with all matters connected with Uman, many difficulties remained. On one particular trip to Uman via Leningrad, the authorities discovered that the group was traveling with forged passports because the three "Frenchmen" in the group

---

XLIV   Heard from Rav Nachman Horowitz.

couldn't speak a word of French. Unperturbed, the Rav started dancing right there in the terminal and danced for a whole six hours, as the bemused Russian officials looked on and kept asking the three "French" passengers how on earth they could possibly be French.

But in the end, they let the whole group through. What makes the story even more remarkable is that a big "wanted" picture of the Rav was clearly hanging up in the official's interrogation room, while the Rav himself was dancing right outside the door — yet nobody paid him any attention!

THE MIRACULOUS TRIP FROM ROMANIA

On another occasion in 5747 (1987), the Rav escorted a group of 63 visitors to Uman via the Romanian city of Bucharest. Rabbi Yosef Katz was part of the group, and he describes the trip as follows:

"All of us had forged passports from a different country, with the visas and permissions we needed to enter Russia," he remembers.

"By that time, the Israeli passport control people had already figured out what was going on, so no one wanted to use their forged passports to leave Israel. We planned to hide our Israeli passports in our luggage after we went through passport control, and then enter Russia on the forged passports."

Rabbi Katz had been given the job of holding on to all the forged papers until they were required, and he'd hidden them in his *tallis* bag. The group went through passport control at Lod airport and were passing through the duty-free area when the Israeli airport authorities suddenly decided to start checking every single piece of the travelers' hand luggage, which was extremely unusual.

"They found the bundle of forged passports and all the visas, and they asked me, 'What are these?'" recalls Rabbi Katz. "I refused to answer them, and asked them to call the captain of the flight over. The second-in-command came over to speak to me and asked me what was going on."

Rabbi Katz explained that the whole group was flying to Russia and had the necessary visas to enter Russia on the forged passports. At this point, instead of calling airport security, the second-in-command started worrying about what could happen to the group if the Russians found their Israeli passports on them. "I'll let you continue, but only on condition that you don't show anyone your Israeli passports!" he told them.

There were still more obstacles. When they got to passport control in Bucharest, one of the Romanian officials started making a big fuss (correctly...) that the whole group's passports were forged. As he called over the Romanian airport security, Rav Berland got the group of travelers together and told them urgently to start learning *Likutei Moharan* with the utmost enthusiasm.

Meanwhile, some members of the group went to buy the official some hard liquor from the duty-free shop to show "goodwill," while Rabbi Katz continued to explain to the Romanians that the reason everyone had a different, forged passport was because they were on a "peace mission" to Russia and not for any sinister reasons.

After a lengthy discussion — and while the rest of the group was still avidly learning *Likutei Moharan* — the Romanian officials came back to the group and told Rabbi Katz, "Listen, we don't want to disturb your peace mission. We want to help you — but on one condition: You have to leave your Israeli passports here with us, and pick them up again when you leave the country."

Rabbi Katz explains dryly, "Naturally, we were very happy to abide by their condition. See what amazing *siyatta dishmaya* we had! The whole time we'd been worrying about what to do with our Israeli passports, because we knew if the Russians caught us and found out we were Israelis, they'd send us straight to Siberia! *Hashem* sent us these Romanian policemen, and they took care of the problem for us. If that's not an open miracle, then I don't know what is."

OTHER BRESLOV GREATS WHO TRAVELED TO UMAN WITH THE RAV

Almost every single Breslov *chassid* or Breslov Rabbi who traveled to Uman during the 1970s undertook the trip with Rav Eliezer Berland. Some of the Breslov greats who accompanied the Rav to Uman at this time included:

RAV YAAKOV MEIR SHECTER (5748)

In 5748, Rav Yaakov Meir Shecter traveled to Uman together with Rav Berland and another 18 students, on his first trip to Rebbe Nachman's grave[XLV]. The Breslovers were very keen to dip in the *mikvah* before making the trip to Uman. Often, the caretaker of the old Jewish synagogue in Kiev would allow Jewish guests to dip in

---

XLV   Rav Shechter subsequently visited Uman again in 5778, when he attended the Rosh Hashana *kibbutz* in the Ukraine.

the synagogue's *mikvah* (for a small fee), but on this occasion, the group was told that the *mikvah* was out of order.

The travelers were heartbroken about the prospect of traveling to Rebbe Nachman's grave without first dipping in a *mikvah*. Like most of those on that particular trip, Rav Shecter was visiting Uman for the very first time, so it was a particularly meaningful occasion.

Rav Berland then spoke up, and said that he had a personal *mikvah* in the area. To everyone's surprise, he took them to a freezing river and tried to break the thick ice in order to allow them to dip in the natural stream of water.

When Rav Yaakov Meir saw the great effort Rav Berland was expending to break the ice, he said, "There is no power that can stop Rav Lazer." He used the expression of Ben Azzai, who said about Rabbi Akiva in *Brachos* 58, "All the Sages of this earth, all the strength of Israel, are the same to me as a garlic peel, apart from this bald one." [*Kerei'ach* in Hebrew means "bald one." Rav Shecter changed the expression to "*kerach*," meaning ice.]

RAV SHMUEL SHAPIRA (5749)

The renowned Breslov elder Rav Shmuel Shapira made a famous trip to Uman on Rosh Hashanah in the last year of his life, in 5749 (Rosh Hashanah, 1988). By this point, the elderly Rav Shapira was very ill and wheelchair-bound. His doctors and carers told him that he was endangering his life by making the trip, because he was so sick and weak. Rav Shapira replied, "It's preferable for me to die traveling to the *Tzaddik*."

During the connecting flight from Israel to Cyprus, Rav Shapira took a turn for the worse, and it seemed very unlikely that he'd have the strength to continue the journey to Uman. The family members who were accompanying him to Uman were in a real quandary about what to do: Rav Shapira was in no state to fly anywhere — not to Uman, and also not back to Israel.

At that point, Rav Berland came and sat very close to the deathly ill Rav Shapira and started to gently talk to him about the greatness of *Rabbeinu*. Rav Berland continued on in this vein for a quarter of an hour, praising Rebbe Nachman, as Rav Shapira slowly regained his strength. By the end of the conversation, Rav Shapira looked like a completely different person and had regained the energy he needed to complete the trip to Uman.

Some of the people on his flight suggested that he should still return to Israel, but Rav Shmuel got very stubborn and reiterated that he'd rather die on the way to the *Tzaddik* (Rebbe Nachman) than return to Israel[XLVI]. After all, Rav Shapira knew the teaching that one who merits to die on the way to the *Tzaddik*, when he arrives in *Shamayim* he goes straight to the *Tzaddik*.

After his conversation with Rav Berland, Rav Shmuel remarked to his son, Rabbi Mendel Shapira, "Do you know where he gets all his strength from? From *Likutei Halachos!*"

EVERY BRESLOVER NEEDS TO SHOW GRATITUDE TO THE RAV

Commenting on the Rav's efforts to open the path to Uman for the wider public, Rav Shalom Arush once said: "We're obligated to show *hakaras hatov*. Every Breslover *chassid* needs to show gratitude to the Rav [for opening the path to Uman.] Everyone used to scream and shout at him, that he was taking people on forged passports to such a terrible country like [Russia], behind the Iron Curtain.

Rav Shalom Arush during one of the first trips to Uman in 1989, praying at the grave of the Baal Shem Tov.

"The Rav once told me: 'Every journey that I take [to Uman], I prepare myself for the possibility that I won't be coming back.' The Rav demonstrated a lot of *mesirus nefesh*. He opened the path, while everyone was screaming at him and laughing at him. But he stuck to his guns, and he had the merit of opening the path [to Uman].

"We need to show him gratitude! Today, everyone can go to Uman, but it's the Rav's self-sacrifice that opened the way. "

FIRST, UMAN

Rav Berland made a huge effort to get as many people to Uman to visit Rebbe Nachman's grave as possible. These trips only became legal for Israeli citizens in 1989, when the Soviet Union finally collapsed into the trash bin of history. Before that, the Rav played an instrumental role in encouraging the Breslov *chassidim*, including his own students at Shuvu Banim, to make the dangerous and costly trip to Russia on counterfeit foreign passports.

The cost of obtaining a false passport, plus the prohibitive cost of the flights and arranging the visas required to enter Russia with the Soviet authorities, was often beyond the modest means of many of the students at Shuvu Banim. So on many occasions, the Rav simply covered the cost of these trips out of his own pocket.

"The Rav used to really push his students to fly out to Uman—even when there was officially no Uman," says Rav Moshe Shavili. "The Rav pushed me to go to Uman with my sons, and to do whatever it took to get there. In the merit of the Rav, I was in Uman at least four or five more times than I otherwise would have been, because he encouraged me to make the effort to go even when it seemed impossible.

THE LAST TRIP BEHIND THE IRON CURTAIN

By 1988, the Soviet Union was on its last legs, and *perestroika* was in the air. Although many hundreds of people had managed to visit Uman by this time, albeit on counterfeit papers, the Soviet authorities still hadn't given permission for the annual Rosh Hashanah *kibbutz*, or gathering, to be reinstated, and they still hadn't made their peace with the tens of people who were clandestinely flocking to Uman.

Rabbi Baruch Sharvit recalls the last trip the Rav made to Uman, when it was still behind the Iron Curtain:

"The Rav isn't afraid of anything," he begins. "The Rav used to say that fear is *tumah*, and that when a person is afraid, he gives power to the forces of evil. All the problems come from the fact that people are afraid.

"Before the last trip that he made to Uman before the Soviet Union crumbled, the Rav announced: 'On this trip, we're going to destroy Russia!' The other side [referring to the Russians] sent American messengers to Breslov to tell us, 'We know that you want to come [to Uman], but if you come one more time, we're going to immediately send you to Siberia!'

"When we heard this, we started to feel really scared and no one wanted to make the trip. But the Rav said that it was all nonsense, and that nothing at all would happen. Nevertheless, most of the people still decided not to go. But some of us wanted to go with the Rav, come what may. He then told us that we'd be traveling to Uman by way of Moscow.

"At that point, we started arguing with the Rav and told him, 'No way! That's like entering the lion's den!' So he acquiesced, as is always his way, and agreed to travel by a different route."

In the end, the group spent two long, arduous weeks traveling by train through Galicia, in very difficult conditions. "We got to the border with Russia, and the officials started abusing us," recalls Rav Sharvit. "I just kept reciting the names of the *Tzaddikim,* and I also decided to fast. One member of our group by the name of Blatt was the only person with a genuine American passport. The Russians told him his passport was forged, and wouldn't let him enter.

"Then they got to me, with my French passport with a picture of someone who didn't look anything like me, and they told me that I could cross the border. That time, they also didn't let the Rav enter, and they sent him back to Greece.

"I think this happened because we got scared, and we didn't listen to the Rav. The Rav always used to tell us: 'Fear is what gives them [i.e., the Russians] their power.'"

THE FRENCH PASSPORT WITH NINE NAMES

The group traveled on to Uman, and managed to pray by the *tziyun,* but the So-viet authorities caught up with them again on the way back and accused every-one of having a forged passport. "They put us all in the interrogation rooms, and then at the end they announced they were freeing everyone—except me!" recalls Rav Sharvit.

"I had a French passport with nine names, and it was too much for them to swal-low. So I was kept in detention until it was time for my trial. The Russian judge asked me, 'Are you French?' and I told him 'yes'. Then he asked me if I understood French, and I told him 'no'. He wanted to know how that was possible, and I told him that we were very sheltered people, and we didn't really have any connection to the outside world. We didn't look at women, we didn't hang out on the streets, and we just studied all day.

"Then the judge asked me, 'Do you know what all of your names are?' and I told him 'no!' He asked me again if it was really my passport, and this time I told him 'no!' The judge asked me if I was afraid, and I started laughing out loud. 'What? Me be afraid?!' The judge said to me, 'Why aren't you afraid?' So I told him that anywhere else in the world, I'd be really frightened, but because I was in Russia, which is such an honest, just country, with such honest, just people, I had no reason to be scared, because I knew I was in a just country. That's the sort of thing the Rav had taught us to say.

"The judges questioning me were completely shocked by this. They conferred with each other, then told me to get out of there immediately. I flew back to Israel via Greece, and there I met up with the Rav and the rest of the group. The Rav was really happy that we'd made it to Uman, and we danced a long while. Then the Rav said, 'This time, we destroyed Russia!'"

By the time the Rav was organizing his next trip to Uman, the Soviet Union had crumbled into dust.

THE BRESLOV *MACHLOKES* REARS ITS UGLY HEAD

The same year that the path to Uman opened up, the last of the three Breslov elders who'd been shielding the Rav from his opponents died. Rabbi Y.K. takes up the story:

"On *Chol Hamoed Succos*, in the year when the path to Uman was finally opened, it was the *yahrtzeit* of Rebbe Nachman. Rav Michel Dorfman, *zt"l*, one of the Breslov elders who spent many years behind the Iron Curtain before finally being allowed to make *aliyah* and settle in Meah Shearim, said publicly, 'Everything is in the merit of Shuvu Banim! Everything is in the merit of Reb Lazer!' And then he continued to praise the Rav very much for opening the path to Uman for everyone.

"People came to the Rav and told him what Rav Michel Dorfman had said about him, because they thought it would make him very happy to hear these good tidings. But the Rav said, 'What? He really said those things?' His expression resembled that of a person who'd just received the worst possible news.

"Immediately after that, the huge *machlokes* against the Rav erupted. People started complaining that the Rav had taken too much money for the trips and so on. Suddenly, everything was turned around.

"Later on, a few of the people who'd insulted him came to the Rav and asked for his forgiveness. He told them with a big smile on his face, 'I forgive you for what you did in the past, what you do in the present, and what you will do in the future!'

"When another one of the Rav's detractors later came to ask for his forgiveness, the Rav told him, 'I'll only forgive you on one condition.' When asked what the condition was, the Rav responded, 'That you'll continue to insult me in the future!'"

ROSH HASHANAH WITH
THE TZADDIK

"My Rosh Hashanah is greater than everything! I can't understand how it is that if my followers really believe in me, they aren't all careful to be with me for Rosh Hashanah. No one should be missing! Rosh Hashanah is my whole mission. The whole world depends on my Rosh Hashanah."

"Whether you eat or don't eat; whether you sleep or don't sleep; whether you pray or don't pray[XLVII]; just ensure that you are with me for Rosh Hashanah, no matter what!"

Rebbe Nachman of Breslov, quoted in Chayei Moharan

Writing in *Likutei Eitzos*, Rav Noson Sternhartz, the Rebbe's main pupil and redactor of his teachings, stated:

"It's customary to go to the *Tzaddik* to celebrate Rosh Hashanah. Rosh Hashanah is above all the Day of Judgment. But no matter how big the judgment, and no matter what place in the world is threatened by it, everything is sweetened when Jews gather around the *Tzaddik* on Rosh Hashanah. When so many Jewish souls gather together and merge in abundant love, a wonderful happiness and delight come to the world."

THE FIRST ROSH HASHANAH GATHERINGS IN UMAN

During his lifetime, Rebbe Nachman was very particular that his followers should gather and be by him on Rosh Hashanah. But in the last year of his life, 1810, he made it clear that the Rosh Hashanah gathering, or *kibbutz*, as it came to be known, should continue after his passing, too.

Rav Noson Sternhartz organized the first Rosh Hashanah *kibbutz* after Rebbe Nachman's death in 1811. Initially, only a few followers made the journey to participate at the Breslov *kibbutz* in Uman, but as the ranks of the Breslov *chassidim* continued to swell over the following years, Rav Noson realized that he had to build a dedi-

---

XLVII   With *kavanah*.

cated Breslov synagogue in Uman to house all the many followers who had started to come from all over Eastern Europe.

"The Kloiz", as this Breslov synagogue came to be known, was officially opened in 1834. It served the community for almost a century, until the Communists took over and eventually turned the Kloiz into a munitions factory, in 1936.

After the Bolshevik Revolution in 1917, Russia's borders with the neighboring countries were sealed, and foreign citizens could no longer legally make the pilgrimage to Uman for Rosh Hashanah. However, some brave souls still tried. One of the last people to successfully cross the border into the Ukraine was Rabbi Shmuel Horowitz, who managed to spend three years in Uman before being discovered and arrested by the Soviet authorities. The first Chief Rabbi of Israel, Rav Avraham *HaKohen* Kook, intervened with the Communist authorities to free Rav Horowitz and get him sent back to Israel.

In the following years, the Soviet persecution of religious Jews only mounted. Twenty-eight Breslov *chassidim* were given permission to travel to Uman for Rosh Hashanah in 1934, but it turned out that this was just a ruse by the Soviet authorities to flush them out of hiding. Sixteen of the Breslovers were murdered in Uman, while a further 12 were exiled to Siberia. Only four of them ever returned.

Yet despite the life-threatening circumstances, the Rosh Hashanah *kibbutz* continued clandestinely right up until 1938—the year before World War II broke out. Twenty-seven *chassidim*, including Rav Levi Yitzchak Bender, risked their lives to participate in this gathering.

THE SOVIETS STOP THE ROSH HASHANAH *KIBBUTZ*

After the war, the *kibbutz* resumed, but in secret and on a very small scale. A handful of *chassidim* within the USSR would risk their lives every year to participate in the clandestine Rosh Hashanah gathering organized by Rabbi Michel Dorfman. (Rav Dorfman was eventually permitted to leave Russia in the 1970s, and he settled in the Breslov community of Meah Shearim.)

Apart from 1975, when 12 American Breslovers led by Rabbi Herschel Wasilski were granted permission to spend Rosh Hashanah in Uman, the Rosh Hashanah *kibbutz* remained a distant dream over the following decade. Throughout the 1970s and 1980s, Rav Berland led many clandestine trips to Uman that often coincided with Rosh Hashanah, but the Soviet authorities wouldn't allow any foreign visitors to stay overnight in Uman until 1988 - which was the first year that the Soviet authorities permitted 250 *chassidim* to be in Uman for Rosh Hashanah.

The following year the USSR imploded, and the gates to Uman and the Rosh Hashanah *kibbutz* were finally flung open to all. In 1989, around 800 *chassidim*—many of whom came with Rav Berland from the Shuvu Banim Yeshivah—gathered in Uman for Rosh Hashanah. By 1990, the number of participants had already doubled to more than 2,000. By 2016, an estimated 60,000 people were making the pilgrimage to Uman for Rosh Hashanah. Rebbe Nachman's *kibbutz* had returned with a vengeance.

SHUVU BANIM'S FIRST ROSH HASHANAH IN UMAN, 1989

Rabbi M.H., one of the more senior students in Shuvu Banim, describes the yeshivah's first communal trip to Uman for Rosh Hashanah, 1989:

"Many people traveled to Uman from the yeshivah during 1989, but due to the difficult financial situation Shuvu Banim was in at that time, most of these trips were financed by the Rav himself, out of his own pocket," he explains.

"Many of the students had also borrowed money to pay for their tickets, so by the time Rosh Hashanah 1989 came around, the yeshivah couldn't afford to pay for all the *avreichim* to fly out to Uman. Many of the students wanted to take out an additional loan to cover their travel costs, but the Rebbetzin didn't allow it. She already knew from past experience that in the end, the Rav and the yeshivah would end up having to repay the money.

"So eventually, they came to a decision that half the yeshivah would go to Uman that year, and the other half would travel to Uman for the next Rosh Hashanah. They held a big lottery to see who would have the merit of traveling to Uman first, and everyone committed to abide by the agreement that had been made.

"By the time the next year's Rosh Hashanah rolled around, the yeshivah was already in a much better financial situation, and a few of the students who'd traveled the first year were now able to pay for their own tickets to go again in the second year. They didn't want to miss out on spending Rosh Hashanah with Rebbe Nachman but, at the same time, they'd made an agreement not to go the second year if they traveled to Uman the first year.

"Some of the members of the first year's group called a meeting with the second group, and asked them to annul the agreement they made. They all happily agreed to do that, and even signed a confirmation that the agreement had been annulled. They went to tell the Rav about it—but the Rav didn't agree. He told them, 'You made an agreement, and you need to see it through to the end!'

"So that year the whole Breslov *Chassidus* arrived in Uman for Rosh Hashanah—minus a big chunk of people from Shuvu Banim who had to stay in *Eretz Yisrael*."

UMAN IS ONLY *MESIRUS NEFESH*

Rav Moshe Tzanani once heard Rav Berland say that, even if a war is in the air or in the world, a person still shouldn't be scared to travel to Uman. When he spoke in Lavin (in South Africa), the Rav said that Uman is only *mesirus nefesh*. It wasn't shopping; it wasn't duty-free; it was only self-sacrifice.

When the Twin Towers were attacked in New York, shortly before Rosh Hashanah 2001, Rav Berland praised Rav Eliezer Shlomo Schick and other Jews who had somehow managed to get to Uman for Rosh Hashanah from the West. Some people paid almost $10,000 to make the trip to Uman that year, as so few planes were flying immediately after 9/11.

The Rav explained that spiritual light in Uman is recreated anew each year, in the merit of the self-sacrifice undertaken by the people who travel there. He said, "Whoever comes to Uman, and who is then worried that he's going to be thrown out of his yeshivah as a result, or that he won't have a home to come back to after Rosh Hashanah, all of Uman is in his merit. And in that person's merit, all the light comes down to the world that year, and there is no doubt that afterwards he'll see revealed miracles and everything will work out for him."

Once, a yeshivah student from a *Litvish* yeshivah saw his *Rosh* Yeshivah in Pushkina Square in Uman on *Erev* Rosh Hashanah, walking toward him among the crowd. The student approached his teacher and said to him emotionally, "*Rosh* Yeshivah! What are you doing here?! I thought you would throw me out of the yeshivah because I came to Uman!" The *Rosh* Yeshivah replied, "Please, just don't tell anyone else you saw me here..."

ROSH HASHANAH BELONGS TO REBBE NACHMAN

Rav Shalom Abergel[XLVIII] was one of the people who fought together with Rav Berland to let people continue visiting *Kever Yosef*, in Shechem. Even after many of the holy graves in the Shomron were deemed too dangerous to visit after the Israeli government handed control of these areas to the Palestinian Authority, Rav Abergel would continue to visit them, trusting that *Hashem* would protect him.

Once, a soldier stopped him and said that he'd let him continue his visit only if he was armed. The Rav told him he was armed, so the soldier left him alone. As he was leaving, the soldier asked to show him his weapon—and he whipped out his *tzitzis* and said, "This is my weapon!"

Every time Rav Abergel would see Rav Berland at the *Kosel*, he'd tell him, "Let's go to Shechem, to *Kever Yosef*!" Rav Abergel had the custom of going to *Kever Yosef* every Rosh Hashanah, until one year he related that *Yosef HaTzaddik* had appeared to him in a dream and told him, "Rosh Hashanah belongs to Rebbe Nachman." So, from that point on, Rav Abergel made the trip to Uman instead.

OPPOSITION TO LEAVING ISRAEL FOR UMAN

When masses of people started leaving *Eretz Yisrael* to travel to Uman, not all the *tzaddikim*—Breslov or otherwise—were thrilled with this development. For example, Rav Mordechai Ifargan[XLIX] was initially against it. But when he traveled to Uman to spend Rosh Hashanah there for the first time, he also felt the incredible spiritual light at the *tziyun* and the yearning for greater spirituality.

After that, he said he was no longer against the practice of traveling to Uman for Rosh Hashanah, and from then on he traveled there every year. After one trip to Uman, when Rav Ifargan saw how men with earrings and ponytails got rid of them and did *teshuvah* out of love, he said, "What takes *Arachim* months of time and effort to encourage people to do *teshuvah*, in Uman it happens automatically. You don't need to speak to people at all; they just get such a light of *teshuvah* from the *tziyun* that they immediately return to God."

XLVIII   Rav Shalom Abergel was a communal Rabbi in Petach Tikva who was also known as 'the Rav of Shechem'. As head of the *Agudat Orchot Tzaddikim* organization, he was active in keeping *Kever Yosef* in Shechem open, making every effort to help Jews visit the site, sometimes at great personal risk. He passed away in 2014.

XLIX   Rav Ifargan is a well-known Israeli lecturer from Morocco and head of a very successful outreach organization called "Return Israel with your whole heart," which includes more than 30 institutions.

He also said that, when he came back to Israel, he would tell everyone who wanted to do *teshuvah* that first they should go to Uman, to receive the spiritual light they needed.

"THIS YOU DON'T HAVE IN BELZ!"

One time, Rav Shalom Sabag wanted to take a Belzer *chassid* friend of his to Uman. The friend agreed to make the trip, but he still wanted to know, "What do you have in Breslov that I don't already have in Belz?" They got to the *tziyun*, and they saw a Jew there with a ponytail who was crying and reading the *Tikkun Haklali* with a broken heart. Rav Sabag turned to his friend and told him, "This you don't have in Belz!"

WITHOUT THE RAV, NOTHING WOULD BE LEFT OF BRESLOV

Rav Arush once said he was amazed that so many people out there still had no idea that the whole Uman phenomenon had come about only in the merit of Rav Berland. "Without Rav Berland, there wouldn't have been anything left of Breslov," he said. "I know that he really did everything. I know very well what he did."

Rav Levi Yitzchak Bender once said that Rebbe Nachman would repay all the kindness that Rav Berland had done for him, because he was constantly thinking up ways to get even more Jews to go to Uman with him.

But when Rav Berland was asked if he was happy about all the thousands of people who had flocked to Rebbe Nachman's grave since the fall of the Iron Curtain, he replied, "I'm happy. But I was hoping that many more people would go."

Rav Berland was familiar with the teaching from *Likutei Moharan* that each person who made the trip to Rebbe Nachman's grave was effectively completing the global soul of the *Tzaddik*. Each person there was a spiritual "spark" of the *Tzaddik's* soul. The Breslov elders told their students that at the gathering in Uman on Rosh Hashanah, you could *mamash* see the holy part of a person's soul - the *Tzaddik* part - shining brightly, if you would only look for it.

Rebbe Nachman himself famously taught that no one should be missing from the annual gathering, from the biggest Jew right down to the smallest. Everyone has a part to play in the spiritual rectification of the world; everyone has a spark of the *Tzaddik's* soul to contribute to the effort in some way. So it was that Rav Berland was keen to get as many people as possible to Uman for Rosh Hashanah.

Even in his recent years of exile, he continued to staunchly advocate for his students, and for all of *Am Yisrael* to be at the grave of Rebbe Nachman in Uman on Rosh Hashanah. Once, while in Uman, he explained to his students that being in Uman for Rosh Hashanah was like getting a visa for a year of good health, life, and open miracles, and to be written in the book of *tzaddikim*, all in the merit of Rebbe Nachman.

EVERYTHING DEPENDS ON YOU

Rav Berland said the following during a *shiur* he gave in Elul 2014:

"Rebbe Nachman said that everything depends on you — you who are traveling to be by the true *Tzaddik*. You have the power to return; you have the power to bring every Jew back. The secular people aren't guilty of anything. We're the guilty ones, us, that there are still secular people in our country. If we were just a little more spiritually aroused, if we had more love for our fellow Jew, then everyone would have already seen God's light. Everyone!!!

"Anyone who does *teshuvah* for real can lift up the whole generation, all of this generation and all of the other generations, too, including the generation of *Moshiach*, and the generation of the Revival of the Dead. Even then, until the time when *Rabbeinu* gets up and leaves his tomb alive and well, we will still be obligated to travel to his holy grave, and even Moshiach will travel to Rebbe Nachman's holy grave, because only he can raise up all of the generations."

When Rav Berland told Rav Shmuel Hoffman back in 1972 that 5,000 pilgrims would be "just the beginning" of the Uman phenomenon, who could have imagined the huge numbers of Jews flocking to Uman in our times? And as Rav Michel Dorfman announced in the Breslov *shul* back in 1989, it's all in the merit of Rav Eliezer Berland.

Rav Berland as a boy, with his father, Chaim, and brother, Yehezkel.

Rav Berland on his barmitzvah

Rav Berland on his wedding day

In the KGB HQ

With Rav Levi Yitzhak Bender, zt'l

At Rebbe
Nachman's grave

Crossing the Berlinski River close to
Uman, with R' Weisshandler

An early
passport photo

The early days of the Shuvu
Banim Yeshivah, Bnei Brak

The early days of the Shuvu
Banim Yeshivah, Jerusalem

Trying to break
the ice in Uman

Rav Yitzhak
Dovid Grossman

Rav Yitzhak Tuvia
Weiss, HaGavad

Rav Shmuel Auerbach

Rav Moshe Halberstam, zt"l

Rav Chaim Kanievsky

Rav Yankele Galinsky, zt"l

Rav Elyashiv, zt"l

Rav Shalom Arush

Rav Eliezer Schick, zt"l

Rav Michel Dorfman, zt"l

Rav Elazar Mordechai Koenig

Rav Nachman Rosenthal

The Gerrer Rebbe

The Sanz-
Klausenberger Rebbe

The Spinka Rebbe of Bnei Brak

Rav Dovid Chaim Stern

Rav Shmuel Rabinowitz, the Rav of the Kosel

Rav Yitzhak Meyer Morgenstern

Rav Berland is the sandek at the
bris of Rav Dov Kook's grandson

The Tolner Rebbe

The Savraner Rebbe,
Rav Berl Hagar, zt"l

The Gerrer Rebbe

The Belzer Rebbe

Rav Ovadia Yosef, zt"l

Rav Dovid Batzri

Rav Shlomo Amar

Rav Nachman Horowitz

Rav Ofer Erez

Rav Yehoshua Dov Rubinstein

Rav Shmuel Stern

Rav Moshe Bransdorfer, zt"l

Rav Yehudah Leib Frank, zt"l

The Tolner Rebbe

Rav Wiener

Rav Yitzhak Kolitz, zt"l

In Eilat, January 2018

2

THE REBBE OF
WAYWARD PEOPLE

EARLY YEARS OF OUTREACH

The Gemara in Maseches Sanhedrin 99b states that the main definition of an apikorus, or heretic, is someone who doesn't believe in the true tzaddikim, and who humiliates and shames them. This holds true even if the person claims he still believes in the Creator of the world and complies with all the other halachos down to the finest details; because of him the Beis Hamikdash was destroyed and the third Beis Hamikdash is not being built[L].

Few things have caused Rav Berland more problems with the established *frum* community—or brought him more joy—than his work to bring people back to God and *Yiddishkeit*. From the moment the Rav learned that *kiruv rechokim*, or outreach, was a key factor in the authentic Breslov path, he threw himself into reaching out and returning Jews to the path of Torah and *mitzvos*.

One of his students from that time recalls: "In the earliest years when they started to organize *Shabbasos* and other events for people who were beginning to return to their Jewish roots, the Rav wasn't one of those who sat and waited for people to come to him—he went to them!" he says.

"He went to some of the lowest places imaginable, like anti-religious *kibbutzim*, and *moshavim* that had no Jewish character at all, and those streets in Tel Aviv where the worst things happened.

"The Rav didn't skip any place, and he went without an invitation. He would just go, stand on some corner, close his eyes, and start talking words of Torah in such a fiery way that he started to light up his listeners. People would initially come over to listen to him out of pure curiosity, and in this way he transformed thousands of people into servants of *Hashem*.

"The Rav wasn't just speaking to intelligent people or nice people; he went out of his way to talk to the people society rejected, and these difficult individuals who were deeply sunk in the gates of impurity."

L   As taught in *Rosh Hashana 17a* (see Haga'os of the Chofetz Chaim).

RETURNEES TO RELIGION

Rav Yehoshua Dov Rubinstein recalls that when the Rav had just started learning at the Breslov Yeshivah in Bnei Brak, he would go with his *tallis* and *tefillin*[LI] to Tel Aviv: "to the lowest places there, like outside the bars and the discos, and he'd go and talk to people with long hair, piercings and tattoos, and he'd bring them closer, one after another, and bring them back to Bnei Brak."

Rav Rubinstein explains that at that point in time, long before any formal *baal teshuvah* movement had started in the Jewish world, many of the people in Bnei Brak didn't know how to handle all these *baalei teshuvah*. "They'd never seen people like this before in their lives!" he says. "But Rav Berland would explain how these people were coming closer to *Yiddishkeit*, and how they were starting to learn more."

THE RAV REACHES OUT TO SECULAR JEWS IN YAFFO

Rav Moshe Shavili, one of the Rav's first students, accompanied him on many of these trips. He recalls: "Sometimes we'd go to Yaffo, where the clubs and bars were open in the evening, and the Rav would go and stand in the town square there, and just start talking Torah.

"We can't know how many people were inspired to start checking into their *Yiddishkeit* more, or were somehow brought back to *Hashem* more as a result of the Rav's Torah lessons in the middle of the street. All the other Rabbis at that time were much more formal, with long beards and ties, but Rav Berland dressed like a normal, more approachable person—albeit with a big beard and *payos*.

"The Rav would walk into these pubs, and just give over the most *pashut*, regular Torah about believing in *Hashem*, and other things that would just go straight into people's hearts. Even the drunks would sit around him, repeating, 'Yo man He's right! He's right!'" says Rav Shavili.

Rav Yosef Assulin also used to accompany the Rav on some of these visits. "Sometimes, we'd go out to the nightclubs in Yaffo," he recalls. "The Rav would start talking Torah, and groups of people would start to gather around him as he just kept on talking and talking. Who knows how many people did *teshuvah* as a result of those talks?

LI   The Rav followed the tradition of the *Gr"a* from the time he moved to Bnei Brak and always wore his *tallis* and *tefillin*, while being very careful to ensure he didn't have hesech hadaas.

"Those nightclubs used to be pretty disgusting places, but the people there would come and sit around him and listen to him, and show him respect. The Rav used to talk to them about *emunah*, and about talking to God. Simple things, but these simple things achieved some wondrous outcomes. When I was in one of the nightclubs, I heard someone in the Rav's audience tell his friend, 'Wow! Listen, this guy is the real deal and what he's saying is true!'"

DANCING WITH THE HIPPIES

Another student, Rav Yaakov Reicher, explains how the Rav was somehow able to meet people at the place where they really were, without compromising his own holiness in the slightest: "I used to go with him to Kiryat Yovel, where he'd go and start dancing with the people there, and strengthening them, and he brought a lot of the hippies that were there closer, in this way."

Rav Abish Dichter recalls that the Rav's house in Bnei Brak became like a second home for many of these hippies. "He used to travel down to Eilat, and he'd even meet the hippies on the bus and bring them back to Bnei Brak," he recalls. "And that's how he started Shuvu Banim!

"One time, he brought two hippies to his house in Bnei Brak and some of his *Litvish* neighbors started talking about it and whispering about what was going on in his home. They started gossiping about him and they decided to shun him—they wouldn't even let him use the *mikvah*!

"He sacrificed so much to bring these people closer to Judaism — he really wanted to bring the whole world back to *Hashem*."

GOING FROM HOUSE TO HOUSE

As Rav Berland himself said, he's a person who likes order. Before long, he'd worked out a methodical approach of covering whole swathes of Tel Aviv and Jerusalem with his outreach activities.

Rav Zevulun Dachbush takes up the tale: "At the beginning of my *teshuvah* process I still had a car, and I used to drive the Rav around a lot. One time we'd drive over to an army base, and walk into a hall full of soldiers.

"Then there was a time when I was going with the Rav from house to house in Tel Aviv, speaking to people and doing outreach. When we finished Tel Aviv, we moved over to Jerusalem, and again started going from house to house. Hundreds of people returned to *Yiddishkeit* because of these visits.

"The Rav does everything with self-sacrifice. I remember one time when we went around for three days straight, from house to house. I dozed off here and there, but after three days I fell over in the street and went to sleep. People wanted to come and wake me up, but the Rav told them to leave me alone, because he knew how tired I was. But the Rav had also gone three days straight without sleep, visiting one house after another."

THE RAV'S HOUSE IS OPEN TO EVERYONE

Long before the Rav opened his yeshivah, everyone in Bnei Brak knew that if someone needed food, or even a place to sleep, he'd find it at the Rav's house. The young students at the Breslover Yeshivah in Bnei Brak also knew that if they needed anything, the Rav's home was the address to go to for all of their needs.

Rav Moshe Goldberger used to learn at the Breslov Yeshivah in Bnei Brak: "I was an orphan, so during *bein hazmanim* when everyone else went back to their homes, I went to stay with the Rav," he says. "I used to eat there, and the house was open to everyone. There was plenty of food, and you could go and eat whenever you wanted.

"The *gaon* and *tzaddik* Rav Yaakov Moshe Salmanovitch also used to eat by the Rav, often on Shabbos. The Rav also used to arrange *shidduchim* and marriages for his students, so the house was really used like a second home for the boys at the Breslov Yeshivah in Bnei Brak, and later on, by all the *baalei teshuvah* who were coming back to *Yiddishkeit*. They would sleep at the Rav's house, and he would help them with anything they needed."

Rav Shmuel Isaac Zucker, the Rav's grandson, recounts that his mother told him how one Pesach, the Rebbetzin and her daughters searched for old mattresses the neighbors had thrown out as part of the Pesach cleaning, to use them for the people who came to their home in need of a place to sleep.

"I used to be at the Rav's home on Shabbos and *chagim*, and no one ever told me anything like, 'We're a big family, you can't come today, there's no room. Come a different time,'" adds Rav Moshe Shavili. "That just never happened! It was always okay to come. I don't know about things like that happening these days."

A CLASH OF CIVILIZATIONS

The secular kibbutzim established by the HaShomer HaTzair organization were ferociously anti-religious from their inception.

The ideologically anti-religious stance of the secular *kibbutzim* led to many shocking scenes, for example, when secular kibbutz members would deliberately cook and eat pork products on Yom Kippur, in order to underline how far they'd travelled from keeping the faith of their fathers.

Between the 1930s and the 1960s, these secular *kibbutzim* were closely aligned with what became the State of Israel's Labor Party, and continued to maintain a hardline stance against Jewish religious observance.

During this time, the Labor Government sent many of the children from newly-arrived religious families to these strongly anti-religious *kibbutzim*, in order to 're-educate' them and tear them away from their Jewish roots and observance.

In recent years, as many of these *kibbutzim* have fallen on hard times economically and struggled in the face of an aging population, the anti-religious stance has softened. Some secular *kibbutzim* have permitted orthodox synagogues to be built on their grounds, and many others koshered their communal dining halls.

GIVING CLASSES IN SECULAR *KIBBUTZIM*

Rav Berland's search for lost souls took him all over the country, and he made a special point of teaching classes at the many secular *kibbutzim* and *moshavim* around the country.

He was often given what's politely called a "rough welcome," as many of these communities took pride in their anti-religious, secular stance. But the Rav didn't let that deter him. One year, he didn't sleep for an entire *Chol Hamoed Succos,* as he traveled from one *kibbutz* to another, trying to bring people close.

Rav Berland often explained to the people who questioned his outreach activities that the secular people today shouldn't be blamed for not keeping the Torah. In a theme he would return to on many occasions over the decades that followed, he explained that secular Jews just needed to be prayed for; then the Torah would reach them and light up their lives, and they would do *teshuvah* in a moment.

ENLIST THEM IN THE RANKS OF TORAH SCHOLARS!

The Rav recalled how he'd known a secular *kibbutznik* who was so anti-Torah, he used to boast that he was going to take his car and run people over in Meah Shearim. "Today, that man himself lives in Meah Shearim," explained the Rav. "If we only pray for them enough, all the secular people will do *teshuvah*, and instead of enlisting us in their IDF, we'll enlist them in the ranks of Torah scholars."

Rav Moshe Shavili drove the Rav all over the country for two years, to give talks at some of the most hardcore, anti-religious *kibbutzim*, like Tel Hashomer, Tal Shachar and Shomer Hatzair. "They used to invite him to come," explains Rav Shavili, "but there were always some other people in the *kibbutzim* who didn't want anyone to come and speak about *Hashem* or *Yiddishkeit*. Once, when the Rav finished speaking at a *kibbutz*, some *kibbutzniks* started throwing stones at our car as we were leaving."

MEETING RAV YITZCHAK DOVID GROSSMAN

On one of these many trips, almost 50 years ago, Rav Berland first met his lifelong friend Rav Yitzchak Dovid Grossman, who today is Rav of the Migdal Ha'emek region of Israel and President of the Migdal Or institutions. "I heard there was a saintly *avreich*, a man devoted to his *avodas Hashem*, who was coming regularly to do outreach in Mercaz Shmuel, on *Kibbutz* Nachalal in the north," recalls Rav Grossman. "I went to see for myself who this *avreich* was, and it was Rav Berland."

OUTREACH HAPPENS VIA STUDYING TORAH

While the Rav frequently took his students along with him on his outreach visits to the secular *kibbutzim* and *moshavim*, he forbid them go by themselves to these places.

"The Rav never let us, the students, go to *kibbutzim* to do outreach," recalls one of his students from this time. "The Rav used to say that a person could go out to do outreach and end up being destroyed himself. He used to say that the main outreach happened through studying Torah for its own sake, *lishmah*, and by praying with a genuine yearning for *Hashem*.

"When a person learns Torah from love, and prays with yearning, these things influence the whole world, and that's how secular people really do *teshuvah*."

THE TURKEY PRINCE

Two hundred years ago, Rebbe Nachman gave over the famous story of the Turkey Prince, the tale of a prince who went mad and spent his days pecking at scraps under the table, because he believed himself to be a turkey. This prince was healed by a wise man who had to get under the table with him and also pretend to be a turkey.

Rebbe Nachman was hinting that sometimes, the true *tzaddikim* also had to "go under the table," in a manner of speaking, to try to rescue all the souls who had somehow fallen to those low places, in order to try and lift them up. The issue of "outreach" was one of the main disputes between Yosef the *Tzaddik* and his brothers. Yosef's older brothers would see him playing with the sons of the maidservants, as a prelude to bringing them closer to holiness—and they didn't agree with his approach!

More than 3,000 years later, the controversy over outreach continued to rage, as many of the Rav's religious neighbors in Bnei Brak went on the warpath over his attempts to bring secular Jews closer to *Yiddishkeit*.

PLAYING CHESS FOR GOD

Despite the controversy it often entailed, the Rav was happy to lower himself again and again to meet his potential students at the places where they were currently holding, and then to work patiently and gently to slowly lift them up to a level where they could truly start to walk on *Hashem's* path again.

For example, one of the Rav's earlier followers was a chess champion. When this man first became interested in *Yiddishkeit*, he challenged the Rav to a chess game. The Rav won the game hands-down—and from that point on, the man become a devoted follower of the Rav, and eventually a committed Breslover *chassid*[LII].

JOINING THE RAV ON AN OUTREACH MISSION

On another occasion, Rav Nachman Rosenthal, the *Mashgiach* of the Breslov Bnei Brak Yeshivah, came to visit and unexpectedly found himself joining one of the

---

LII   Something similar occurred to Rebbe Nachman, who used to play chess with the secular leaders of the Haskalah movement in Uman, toward the end of his life. After Rebbe Nachman passed away, these *maskilim* were shattered that they had lost such a good friend, and one of them even remarked to Rav Natan that if Rebbe Nachman had lived, he would have done *teshuvah* and become a God-fearing Jew.

Rav's outreach missions. "Rav Lazer told me that he was going somewhere, and asked me if I'd like to join him," he recalls. "But he didn't tell me where we were going! We were traveling for a long time, until suddenly, we arrived at a huge, beautiful villa. I was very curious to see who Rav Berland was going to meet there.

"Suddenly, the door opened, and this tall, handsome man with a very long ponytail came out. I was shocked! I started wondering what Rav Berland was doing here, talking to this completely secular man in this far-out place. But Rav Berland was completely unperturbed, and went over to the man and spoke to him for quite a long while.

"Many years later, I met that secular Jew again — but now he had a long beard and *payos*, and he'd become a serious Breslover *chassid*, a big Torah learner with real *yiras Shamayim*. This is the power of Rav Lazer, to take a person from one extreme to the other!" concluded Rav Rosenthal.

"RAV BERLAND CAN HELP YOU"

Rav Moshe Shavili recalls: "When I first started out, over 40 years ago, I had no idea what was wrong or right, or what was good to do. At that point, I was already a *baal teshuvah* and I was keeping Torah and *mitzvos*, but it wasn't yet entrenched deep in my heart and I didn't really know what I was doing or why.

"I had no one to show me the path. When I was learning with the other Rabbis, I could only really ask them questions about Torah like, 'Is this kosher or not?' But I couldn't really ask them deeper questions about how to really find your way back to Torah, or how to really believe in *Hashem*.

"Back then, you just didn't really come and spill your heart out before a Rav. You didn't tell them that you weren't feeling so good about your *Yiddishkeit*, or that you were feeling lost and had no idea what you were doing religiously. That sort of thing just wasn't done back then. So I mentioned the problems I was having to someone, and he told me to go to Rav Berland, and that he would help me. This was before he'd even opened Shuvu Banim, and had become more well-known."

At that point, Rav Berland and his family were living in a first-floor apartment on Rashbam Street, in Bnei Brak.

"I went to visit Rav Berland in the evening, around 8 p.m., and the Rav greeted me very warmly and immediately started learning with me," continues Rav Shavili. "He just took me straight into his home without asking me what I was doing there or what I wanted. He just sat down and started learning Torah with me. By Rav Berland, every time you came to visit him was a good time. Evening, morning, afternoon — whenever you came, he never told you he had no time now, or needed to go to sleep, or so forth; he always had time for you.

"I just knocked on the door and it opened! The Rav's wife opened the door, and she told me that I just needed to wait a bit because the Rav had stepped out, but that he'd be back soon. The Rebbetzin was also a very holy, special, amazing woman. Then the Rav came back and immediately started learning with me *Likutei Halachos.*"

THE CONFUSION DISAPPEARS

While they were learning together, Rav Shavili suddenly realized that the Rav was actually answering all the questions and problems he had through their learning together. As they continued to learn, all of Rav Shavili's questions and confusion started to disappear.

"When Rav Berland used to see someone, even for the first time, he'd immediately know why this person had come to see him and how to help him," recalls Rav Shavili. He asked if he could come back again the next day, and the Rav happily agreed. The next night, they learned all through the night.

"People came in the morning, and they saw I was still sitting with the Rav and talking. I was shocked when I realized how much time the Rav had spent learning with me. I decided right then that the Rav is not a person, but an angel. At that time, I didn't really think much of myself, yet Rav Berland—a big Rav—had spent a whole night talking to this 'nothing' and teaching him the most sublime Torah ideas! Rav Berland knew how to teach things so that it went straight into your heart," says Rav Shavili.

TAKING ON THE CHURCH

Rav Berland didn't give up on any Jewish soul, however far from *Yiddishkeit* they appeared to be, and he wasn't scared to venture even into the heart of darkness itself to try to pull them out.

Rav Nachman Horowitz recalls: "One time, I met a French Jew who told me that he'd been caught up in a very strong *klipah* of idol worship, and that the Rav used to talk to him every day, giving him strength and encouragement.

"One day, the Rav told this French Jew that he was going to come with him to the place of idol worship—a place that no Rav would ever want to go of their own accord, because the spiritual impurity of the priests is so strong. He spent an entire half an hour arguing with them in English before leaving. Six months after the Rav's visit, the place shut down and all the Jews they'd caught in their net left and did *teshuvah*.

"Another time, a fellow from Haifa told me that he'd been studying in university, and the Rav would sometimes come to the university grounds to do *hisbodedus*," continues Rav Horowitz. "One day, the Rav showed up and told the students that he wanted to give them a class about *Yiddishkeit*. They agreed, and the Rav started enthusiastically reading them a story from Rebbe Nachman's *Sipurei Maasios*.

"The fellow told me, 'We were so amazed, we told him to come back again.'

"So the Rav did come back, and a short while later the fellow left university and did complete *teshuvah*. He told me how the Rav used to take them to the fields near to Arab villages, and how he was so scared of the dogs there, he used to cling to the Rav's *gartel* from sheer terror. But the Rav was never afraid.

"Another time, I met a righteous convert who told me he'd become a Jew because he listened to some of the talks the Rav gave at the university, and he'd grasped the truth of Judaism from the Rav's words. He told me, 'The Rav doesn't even know that he encouraged me to convert, just by listening to his words.'"

SELF-SACRIFICE FOR THE *BAALEI TESHUVAH*

Rav Moshe Tzanani once asked the Rav why he'd stopped going out to the *kibbutzim* to do outreach like he used to. The Rav replied, "When I bring someone closer, I take all of their reality upon myself.[LIII]"

Rav Yosef Asulin concurs, and explains that the Rav's outreach activities went far beyond making pretty speeches or guest appearances. "You have to understand that the outreach of the Rav didn't just involve Torah classes and inspiring lectures—the Rav really sacrificed himself for his *baalei teshuvah*," he says.

"The Rav once said, 'When I bring someone closer, I give everything I have to them. I give them the credit for all my spiritual work so that they'll be given the merit to

---

LIII   I.e. Rav Berland would take the spiritual judgment associated with all of the person's past sins, confusion and doubts upon himself, in order to make it easier for the person to do *teshuva*.

come closer to *Hashem*. I give over all the merit of my prayers, my Torah learning and my *tzedakah* for that period of time to the person I'm trying to bring closer.'"

Rav Moshe Levinson adds: "I don't know if there's a single person at the yeshivah in whom the Rav didn't invest many hours of his time, either by talking to them or giving them encouragement and *chizzuk*," he says. "The Rav sacrificed many long hours for every single student."

THE 50,000ᵀᴴ GATE OF IMPURITY

Rav Ofer Erez is one of the Rav's better-known students, and over the years he's seen firsthand how the Rav worked extremely hard to bring so many people back to their Jewish roots. "The biggest wonder is the self-sacrifice the Rav made for these lost souls," he begins.

"There was someone who was in such a difficult place—really, in the 50,000ᵗʰ gate of impurity. The Rav used to call him up every morning and wake him up and ask him if he'd already prayed *Shacharis*. He did this every day for a few months!

"The Rav used to tell him, 'I'm going to call you after the morning prayers, and I'll tell you what to learn today.' The guy was embarrassed, after all the Rav's efforts on his behalf, not to make some effort, and that's how he started praying and learning some Torah. After a few months, he turned over a new leaf.

"That sort of self-sacrifice on behalf of your fellow Jew is really not common. From where did the Rav get the spiritual strength to involve himself so deeply with all the personal problems of other people?"

Rav Ofer continues: "A few times, I brought people to meet the Rav and got to sit in on their meetings. These were people who were coming from a very low place, from the 50ᵗʰ gate of spiritual impurity. I saw then that the main work of the *tzaddik* is to be able to shine light into the lowest places.

"We're talking about people about whom it's easier to believe that the sun will shine in the middle of the night than that they'll come closer to holiness and Torah. The most amazing thing is that people like this would meet the Rav for just a few minutes, and then completely change their life around and do *teshuvah*. It's like they got a new soul."

INSTILLING A LOVE FOR TORAH

Rav Naftali Biton acted as the Rav's gabbai in his later years, at a time when the Rav was a virtual recluse in his home. At that time, the Rav developed a different method of trying to bring more Jews closer to their Creator.

"In those days, the Rav only did outreach through his *kabbalat kahal* sessions, the personal meetings he has with people in his home," says Rav Biton." But the spiritual *koach* of the Rav is so great, that secular people come to ask him for some miracle, or some blessing, and he says a few words to them—and they want to do *teshuvah*! Thousands of people turned into *baalei teshuvah* just from coming to the Rav's *kabbalat kahal*.

"One man came to see the Rav, and the Rav told him, 'What an amazing light you have in your face! Have you heard of Rav Stern? You have to meet him!' The Rav can grasp everything about a person in the first second he meets them—what his situation is and what would be good for him. So he sends people to the places that would suit them best — and they go on to do *teshuvah*.

"Usually, the Rav tries to instill some Torah learning in everyone he meets. Completely secular people come to him, and the Rav will tell them to read a couple of pages of *Gemara* every day! 'Only read the things printed in big letters,' he tells them. I heard him tell secular people this a few times. He'll say, 'Read this, it's all just stories of how Reuven did this, etc., and everyone can read it.'"

Rav Biton continues: "The Rav doesn't only talk the talk, he also walks the walk, and makes things happen. Once, a man came to see him from Rishon Letzion, and the Rav said to him, 'How can you be living in Rishon Letzion?! Why aren't you having pity on your children; they don't even know what *Shema Yisrael* is! This week, you need to move!'

"This man started telling the Rav that his wife would never agree to move, so the Rav said to him, 'What's your telephone number at home? I'm going to talk to her!' The Rav called her up there and then, started talking, and got things to move."

THE DANGEROUSLY CHARISMATIC RAV BERLAND

As the Rav's success in outreach spread, his reputation for being a "dangerously charismatic" individual grew in the secular press in Israel. The secular media were amazed at how the Rav could talk to an individual for barely a couple of minutes, and then the person would completely turn his life upside down as a result and return to God.

The secular media started to come up with all sorts of theories and ideas about why the Rav was so successful, ideas that were usually far, far off the mark.

"A newspaper once decided to send a couple of their journalists to interview the Rav, but they warned them beforehand, 'Keep it short. This man is very charismatic, and he can influence you to do *teshuvah*, or something. So don't spend more than a few minutes with him,'" explains Rav Rachamim Bracha.

"The Rav spoke to them for a few minutes, and they were frankly blown away by what he said. They got so excited that they told him, 'We see that you're right, and we want to do *teshuvah*.'

"According to their editors, the Rav was so 'charismatic' he could make people into *baalei teshuvah* in just five minutes. But we understand that it wasn't the Rav's charisma that was doing this, but his light, the light of truth, which was illuminating the path for *Am Yisrael* to do *teshuvah*."

THE RAV OF WAYWARD PEOPLE

While nearly all of the nation's true religious leaders and Rebbes were sympathetic to the Rav's attempts to bring secular Jews closer to their religious roots, others in the religious community were highly suspicious of the Rav's actions and were openly hostile to his attempts to bring these strange-looking, secular outsiders into the sheltered streets of Bnei Brak.

Rav Yisrael Meir Brenner recalls that when the Rav first started seriously working to bring secular Jews back to *Yiddishkeit* and all these *baalei teshuvah* started visiting him in Bnei Brak, some of the locals started calling him "the Rav of Wayward People" — and it wasn't meant as a compliment.

THE PETITION TO EVICT RAV BERLAND FROM BNEI BRAK

Rav Natan Hiller, one of the Rav's old neighbors on Rashbam Street in Bnei Brak, remembers: "When the Rav started his outreach work with people who were far from *Yiddishkeit*, he used to travel to Eilat and other various places. He'd bring these hippies with long hair home with him, and bring them closer to Torah and *mitzvos*.

"There were a lot of complaints against the Rav for doing this, from the neighbors on Rashbam Street, where many *Gedolim* lived. [The Steipler and his children all lived on Rashbam Street, as well as many other Torah leaders of the time.] And here was the Rav bringing hippies into the neighborhood, and some of them were even publicly smoking on Shabbos and so forth.

"The neighbors started a petition, which was even signed by some of the Rabbis there, to have the Rav kicked out of Bnei Brak. They took this petition to the important people in the neighborhood, and they also brought it to the Steipler, *zt"l*. The Steipler read the petition, gave the people who had brought it to him a scathing look, and then told them in Yiddish, '*Reb Lazer az ir agroiser, groiser yarai Shamayim!*' (Reb Lazer is a tremendous God fearing [Jew]). He refused to listen to another word they said, or to have anything to do with their plans."

As Rav Berland had the support of Rav Kanievsky, the *Gadol Hador*, there wasn't much more his detractors could openly do to prevent him from bringing more and more secular people closer to *Yiddishkeit*, and into the hallowed halls of the yeshivos in Bnei Brak. But they still weren't happy about it.

THE CIRCUS AROUND THE RAV

One of the Rav's earliest students, Rav Yitzchak Weisshandler, spent a lot of time at the Rav's home during this period. "I used to go a lot to the Rav's house in Bnei Brak, on Rashbam Street, and I used to bring things to the Rav for all the *baalei teshuvah* who were staying by him," he says.

"At the time, the Rav was surrounded by quite a circus of people. They'd be smoking drugs and falling asleep in the stairwells. The Rebbetzin used to do their laundry for them—and Bnei Brak was up in arms about it all. They were stirring things up on Rashbam Street, where everyone on the street was a *talmid chacham*, and had fear of Heaven and was full of Torah, and turning it into a hangout...There were a lot of complaints against the Rav then, but the Rav didn't give up on his *baalei teshuvah*, and he continued to help them with everything they needed."

THE RAV PAYS HIS ATTACKERS

During another period of controversy over the Rav, word got out that someone had donated an extremely large sum of *tzedaka* to the Rav, which made the individuals who were 'anti' the Rav extremely jealous.

They got so riled up it that they decided that the Rav needed to be "taught a lesson", and they received permission from a Jewish authority to hire two Jewish ruffians to beat up the Rav. At this time, the Rav was going out every night to do personal prayer in the field near to the kever of Shmuel Hanavi in the Jerusalem suburb of Ramot. These individuals told the two hired thugs that the best time to catch the Rav would be when he went to this forest.

When the Rav went out to the field that night and began to walk into the forest, the two ruffians jumped out and started to attack him. They hit him and pushed him over, and the Rav fell to the ground. The Rav was accompanied by some students, but they had no time to react.

One of the ruffians began to tell the Rav who had sent them, but before he could say the names, the Rav jumped up, brushed himself off and said, "Thank you so much, I really appreciate it! Here is 100 shekels for each of you, for all your work. And if you do it again, I'll have another 100 shekels for each of you." The Rav braced himself for another round of beatings - but it didn't come.

Bewildered and embarrassed by this bizarre turn of events, the two thugs turned around and ran off. Later on, the two showed up on Rav Nachman Horowitz's doorstep, and they told Rav Horowitz that they'd each been given 20 shekels to beat the Rav up, which was a large sum of money at that time.

When Rav Berland gave them five times that amount to 'reward' them for attacking him -- which was considered to be a small fortune--they did *teshuvah* on the spot.

THE BOILING-HOT *MIKVAH*

Violence aside, the Rav's neighbors also tried to find many other ways to show their displeasure to the Rav, and to make his life as difficult as possible. But the more they persecuted the Rav, the more his greatness began to shine through.

"In the early years, when the Rav was busy with *kiruv* in and around Bnei Brak, he was at the center of a lot of controversy," begins another of his students from this time. "His neighbors, and others in the area, couldn't stand the fact that the Rav was bringing all these different types of people into Bnei Brak, the city of Torah and *Chassidus*.

"We used to go out every night at *chatzos* to the fields, and then around 3 a.m., when we came back to the yeshivah, we usually went to use the *mikvah* at one of the places nearby. One day, the people who owned that *mikvah* decided to give us a nasty surprise: They heated the *mikvah* to the hottest temperature possible, so that by the time we got to the *mikvah* the water would literally be at boiling point, and we wouldn't be able to use it.

"We got there, and we could immediately feel that the *mikvah* waters were far too hot—they were like a pot of boiling water that had been left on the stove. We tried to dip our fingers in, but we immediately took them out, and despaired of using the *mikvah*.

"The Rav carried on as usual, and wasn't at all alarmed. He went into the *mikvah* completely calm and composed, without any delay or any screaming, dipped as usual, then came out as though he'd just immersed in lukewarm water.

"There is no way of explaining what happened according to the laws of nature, because a person's body gets scalded by boiling water. But by the Rav, there are no laws of nature! I still have no idea how the Rav did that."

BUILDING A NEW BRESLOV COMMUNITY

As the months and years passed, Rav Berland found himself at the center of a fledgling *baal teshuvah* movement in Bnei Brak that was starting to number many hundreds of people. While some of them had successfully managed to integrate into the yeshivah world, many more really had nowhere to go when it came to upgrading their Torah learning and embracing a more observant lifestyle.

In a fundraising letter that Rav Berland wrote to a potential donor on 6 Tammuz, 5737 (1976), he explained:

"We have tens and tens of *baalei teshuvah* coming to us, and we have nowhere to place them. And they *davka* want to come and learn with us, and to be drawn closer [to *Hashem*] by us, but many of them are being lost, because there is no yeshivah that is suitable for them.

"We tried to get them into other *yeshivos*, but they weren't always received so nicely, and experienced whatever they experienced. Last year, I had one person with me in my home for two whole months, eating and drinking by me. Afterwards, he enrolled in a yeshivah where he was treated so badly, [literally: 'broken'] that he ran away and completely disappeared from the scene. We've been looking for him for a few months, and we still have no idea where he is.

"Tens and tens of people, and in truth it's already close to 200 people, if not more [are coming to us], and if we had a suitable institution, with God's help we could save hundreds and even thousands of people...as every *baal teshuvah* immediately attracts another, and another.

"The awakening to do *teshuvah* at this present time is enormous, and is sweeping over every layer of the Jewish people. There are many people looking for a suitable institution [of Torah learning], and there are many who aren't finding one, which means that their spiritual awakening could be for naught.

"I have pulled together a few *avreichim*, and we've started to make plans to build a synagogue, but at the moment we're caught up in so many different things, and we want to move forward with this holy work.

"We've also made connections with many *kibbutzim* and *moshavim*, both secular and a little religious, and we've already had many, many groups from these different *kibbutzim* come and spend Shabbos with us. They are also experiencing an enormous spiritual awakening, and everyone wants to come closer [to *Yiddishkeit*]. There's an enormous awakening happening in the Jezreel Valley, and in Beit She'an. One person already left his *kibbutz* and went to study in yeshivah in Jerusalem, and he's learning *b'chavrusa* in the evenings with Rabbi Moshe Beninstock.

"With God's help, we've been able to accommodate them in Bnei Brak on a few *Shabbosos*, but a lot of people don't understand the concept [of bringing people back to Torah], so we don't really have where to put them. The places that kindly helped us out in the past and offered accommodations can't accommodate these groups every Shabbos. This is why we've arrived at the idea of building a synagogue, although in truth, the main point is really, with God's help, to found an institution for *baalei teshuvah*..."

It can be assumed that Rav Berland might have hoped that once he'd brought people back to the Torah world, others would open their doors to them and help them adjust to a life of Torah and *mitzvos*, while he would be left to his studies and other *avodas Hashem*.

Indeed, Rav Shalom Arush shared: "The Rav told me once that he wanted to stop doing outreach work, and just sit and learn Torah instead. But as soon as he started down that path, he contracted pneumonia, so he promised *Hakadosh Baruch Hu* that he would return to doing outreach—and immediately afterwards he regained his health."

Much as Rav Berland loved his Torah learning, it appeared that *Shamayim* had other plans, and was readying the reclusive Torah genius who hated the limelight for the next stage of his life, as a world-famous *Rosh* Yeshivah with tens of thousands of followers.

THE BEGINNING OF SHUVU BANIM

RAV BERLAND NEVER WANTED TO LEAD HIS OWN *KEHILLAH*

Rav Berland never wanted to be the leader of his own community but, as his outreach attempts continued to be so successful, Bnei Brak started to fill up with hundreds of formerly secular Jews who had a real thirst to learn Torah and develop in their *Yiddishkeit*—and nowhere to go.

Recognizing the problem, a number of Bnei Brak's spiritual leaders started coming to the Rav to entreat him to start his own yeshivah — but he firmly refused.

For a man who'd spent the best part of four decades avoiding any hint of honor or recognition, the thought of heading his own Torah institution was a very bitter pill to swallow. But, as the number of people returning to Judaism increased, the pressure only continued to mount, with more and more people asking the Rav to open his own yeshivah and begin his own community.

Eventually, the Rav saw that this was being ordained from Heaven, and that he had to agree. But he made it clear from the very beginning that he was only prepared to open the yeshivah if the people who wanted to back it would agree to his terms; namely, that the yeshivah wouldn't compromise on one iota of teaching and living the path of Rebbe Nachman and Breslov *Chassidus*, and that the focus wouldn't be on building a large institution, but rather on encouraging even a small number of people to take their Torah seriously.

THE YESHIVAH IS ONLY FOR OUTREACH PURPOSES

Right from the start, Rav Berland made it clear: "This yeshivah is only for *kiruv* purposes, and to enable people to get closer to the path of *Rabbeinu*, as set down by the Breslov elders."

He continued: "If there is any suggestion that we in the yeshivah will start to consider ourselves better than others, or to look down on other Jews, then it's better not to start in the first place! I would prefer to sit here with just five students who have simplicity and innocence, because with those five students, I could get a lot more done in the world than if I had the 24,000 students of Rabbi Akiva, who were obsessed with their own honor and status, and thought they were better than other people!"

The final push to open the yeshivah came when the Rav returned from a truly miraculous trip to Uman in October 1977, where he'd been caught, interrogated, and finally released by the KGB. On the way home to Bnei Brak, the Rav pondered on the many miracles he'd just experienced, and decided that it was finally time to agree to open his own yeshivah.

THE YESHIVAH GETS A NAME

Original sign in the yeshiva in bnei brak saying "bei knishta chada". (the sign moved to Jerusalem with the yeshiva)

Initially, Rav Berland wanted to call his nascent yeshivah " Knishta Chada[LIV]", in reference to the saying in the *Zohar* that the final redemption would only be in the merit of a very small group of people, and not because of any large communities or big institutions. For a short while, the fledgling yeshivah was also called "Roni Balayla" ("I sing to *Hashem* at night"), until it was decided that it sounded too much like a seminary for women.

Finally, the decision was made to change the name of the yeshivah to "Shuvu Banim" ("Return, Children"), because this name most accurately portrayed the yeshivah's main purpose of bringing people back to their Creator. But in truth, the Rav's initial redemptive vision for the yeshivah was still alluded to by the new name, as the *Gemara*[25] says, "As soon as the people do *teshuvah*, they will be redeemed. As the verse says, 'Return, you wayward children, and I will heal you.[26]'"

The new yeshivah of Shuvu Banim officially opened its doors in the summer of 1978, in Bnei Brak.

NOTHING WILL BE ACHIEVED WITHOUT UNITY

When the doors first opened, the Rav told his followers: "I don't want this to be just another yeshivah, because *baruch Hashem, yeshivos* and holy, learned people are not lacking in the nation of Israel, as I've seen for myself all the years I've lived in Bnei Brak. The main reason I'm opening this yeshivah is in order to have a yeshivah that's full of tremendous unity so that we can work to bring the redemption. God forbid, if we won't have unity in our yeshivah, then we won't accomplish anything!"

AN UNUSUAL *ROSH* YESHIVAH

From its inception, the yeshivah stood out as an unusual institution, and the *Rosh Yeshivah*, Rav Eliezer Berland *shlit" a*, stood out as a most unusual leader. If anyone thought that opening a yeshivah would make a dent in Rav Berland's praying, *avodas Hashem* or other outreach activities, they were about to be proven completely wrong.

Rav Avraham Chananya was one of the first students at the nascent Shuvu Banim Yeshivah in Bnei Brak. He recalls: "Once, I had the privilege of driving the Rav somewhere in my car, so I took advantage of that *'eis ratzon'* to ask him how he'd merited to attain everything that he had. The Rav told me, 'I went out to the field for every single thing. I did *hisbodedus* on every single thing, I prayed about everything.'"

The veterans of Yeshivas Shuvu Banim relate that the Rav would disappear for weeks to go and do *hisbodedus* in the fields, but when he came back to the yeshivah, he would return with such a fire that his lectures would ignite everyone to much greater *avodas Hashem*.

"When the yeshivah was still in Bnei Brak, there was a time when the Rav would immediately leave the yeshivah after prayers and go alone to the field," remembers Rav Meir Malka. "We saw that the Rav was yearning for *Hashem*, and that he wasn't satiated by his prayers, and that had a huge influence on us, his students.

"The Rav always used to say that the only true *hisbodedus* was lengthy *hisbodedus*, and that the whole point of *hisbodedus* was to get to the stage where you'd completely nullified your ego."

THERE ARE NO REAL BRESLOVERS HERE!

Doing regular *hisbodedus* was an integral part of the Rav's understanding of what a true Breslover *chassid* should be, and he made every effort to drum that into his students.

Rav Moshe Shaul was another of the earliest students at Shuvu Banim. He recalls: "One time, the Rav was giving a *shiur* when he suddenly stopped and told us, 'I permit all of you here to take a *Sefer Torah*, and to swear on it that you're not a Breslover! There are no real Breslovers here! We're all very far from really being Breslovers!'

"Someone asked the Rav how we could get to be true Breslovers, and the Rav responded, 'Only with a great deal of *hisbodedus*!'

"When the yeshivah was in Bnei Brak, the schedule was that we'd all go to sleep right after *Maariv*, and then we'd get up at *chatzos* and go out to the fields and the orchards that were owned by the Katz family," explains Rav Shaul. "When we moved to Jerusalem, we used to go to the field by the grave of *Shmuel Hanavi*. Even today, most of the people going out to Kever Shmuel Hanavi to do *hisbodedus* are students of Shuvu Banim."

PUTTING THE EMPHASIS ON *AVODAS HASHEM*

Another student, Rav Shlomo Gabbai, recounts: "In the early years of the yeshivah, the Rav invested a huge amount into implanting *avodas Hashem* into his students, like getting up for *chatzos*, praying with fire, doing *hisbodedus*, etc. It was only after a couple of years that the Rav really turned his attention to learning in depth *Gemara* at the yeshivah. Of course, we learned Torah right from the beginning, but the emphasis initially was on the *avodah*.

"Once, we asked the Rav, 'Why didn't you immediately start with intense *Gemara* learning?' After all, we knew that the Rav always used to say that the main point was learning *Gemara*.

"The Rav responded that of course learning *Gemara* was the main goal and nothing else was worth much without the *Gemara*, but if he'd started us off immediately learning the *Gemara*, we would have found the learning so sweet that we wouldn't want to hear about anything else.

"It was only after he'd inculcated us with the amazing *ruach* of *chatzos*, praying and *hisbodedus*, that the time was ripe to move us over to learning the *Gemara* more seriously. If we didn't do *hisbodedus*, and we didn't request *Hashem's* help in our learning, the *Gemara* by itself wouldn't change us."

Rav Meir Malka adds: "The Rav would explain that learning was not the final destination; rather, its purpose was to bring us to prayer and to self-nullification, and to yearning for *Hashem*. Without the learning, it's impossible to truly pray and to nullify yourself. This only comes through learning in depth, both in quality and in quantity."

Rav Gabbai continues: "In the early days of the yeshivah, the Rav would give *shiurim* for six hours straight on *Likutei Halachos*. But in practice, it wasn't just *Likutei Halachos*, because in the same *shiur* the Rav would add in teachings from *Chazal*, from all the sections of *Shas*, the *Zohar Hakadosh*, and the writings of the Ari, too.

"When the yeshivah began, we used to have tests on every subject: on *Likutei Moharan*, on *Sipurei Maasios*—and the tests would be checked and the results passed on to the Rav, who would also go through them.

"This continued until very recently. An *avreich* would go and tell him about his learning, and the Rav would say to him, 'Bring me your conclusions and *chiddushim*,' and then the Rav himself would go through the *avreich's* conclusions and *chiddushim* for many long hours."

GET UP FOR *CHATZOS,* OR LEAVE

Rav Yoram Yaish was one of the first *Mashgichim* at the new Shuvu Banim Yeshivah in Bnei Brak, and he describes how the Rav's vision for his students set him on a collision course with some of his backers.

"When the Rav first founded the yeshivah, he was convinced that the students needed to immediately start getting up for *chatzos*, do *hisbodedus*, and follow the rest of Rebbe Nachman's advice," explains Rav Yaish.

"The Rav's associates thought that we needed to go step by step because after all, the main point was to learn *Gemara* and *halachah*. They didn't want to overload the newly observant students, who were coming from places that were very far away from a Torah lifestyle, with things like *hisbodedus* and *chatzos* right at the beginning. But the Rav didn't listen to them.

"The Rav made a general announcement that whoever didn't get up for *chatzos* wouldn't have a place in the yeshivah. If someone occasionally missed it because they were too tired, the Rav wasn't strict about it. But if someone was missing *chatzos* on a regular basis, and he didn't even *want* to get up for it, that person wouldn't have a place in the yeshivah.

"The Rav said then: 'We want to found a yeshivah that follows the path of *Rabbeinu*, and *Rabbeinu's* path is *hisbodedus* and getting up for *chatzos*. Whoever can't do it doesn't need to stay here. There are lots of other yeshivos in Bnei Brak.'

"One of the students was a *baal teshuvah* who was very close to one of the Rav's associates, and he got advice from this person that he didn't need to wake up for *chatzos*. The Rav saw that he wasn't waking up, and he told me to tell that student that he couldn't continue in the yeshivah.

"This associate came to speak to the Rav about it, and told him that he was still a good student, even if he didn't wake up for *chatzos*. But the Rav wasn't persuaded, and the student ended up leaving. After that, all the associates slowly left the yeshivah, until the Rav was left to manage everything by himself.

"Today, 40 years later, when tens of thousands of people have rediscovered the Jewish spark in their soul thanks to all the words and the work the Rav invested into his yeshivah back then, we're not convinced that the same thing would have happened if the Rav had listened to the words of his associates.

"The Rav grabbed onto *Hashem's* hand, and he succeeded in making things happen, to bring a whole generation closer to their Father in *Shamayim*," concludes Rav Yaish.

ONLY BY EXAMPLE

While things like getting up for *chatzos*[LV] and *hisbodedus* have become almost commonplace in many Breslov circles today, back in 1978, when Shuvu Banim first opened its doors, these practices were considered to be only for the elite.

The practice of *shmiras einayim* was another *mitzvah* that Rav Berland managed to instill in his students, at a time when it was falling out of favor in even the most

---

LV   Many *chatzos* (or midnight) *kollels* have now opened up across the religious world, as a result of Rav Berland's efforts to reintroduce the practice of waking up for *chatzos*.

religious circles. How did Rav Berland manage to instill the will and ability to undertake these challenging practices in his newly observant students?

Rav Meir Malka offers an answer: "The reason the Rav was so successful inculcating in his students the *mitzvah* of *shmiras einayim* is that he lived it himself. He was the real thing. That's how he could radiate it and transmit it to such a big community. That was serious spiritual work.

"When we're talking about the Rav's *shmiras einayim*, we're not just talking about avoiding forbidden sights; we're also talking about avoiding all the pointless vanities of this world, like the weather forecast and other pointless predictions and speculations. The Rav constantly told us not to pay any attention to this world.

"Together with the Rav's high expectations of his students, he also had incredible patience. His patience gave all the newcomers the space they needed to start drawing closer to Judaism, for real."

THE PRAYERS AT SHUVU BANIM

One of the earliest students at Shuvu Banim recalls that: "At the beginning, the yeshivah's way was to pray with a lot of crying out and fire, from the depths of the heart. People who were walking in the street would be certain that the yeshivah contained hundreds of students, judging from the noise and the voices that were coming out of the *beis medrash* during the prayers. But in truth, there were barely more than 30 students in the yeshivah at that time."

Another student from the yeshivah's early days in Jerusalem remembers: "The prayers were long and with a lot of crying out. And every night, we were in the field for a number of hours. There was a period of time when we came from Shuvu Banim to the *shiurim* of Rav Levi Yitzchak, and after the *shiur*, we'd daven *Minchah* with such loud voices, you could hear us from the end of Meah Shearim.

"The *Tzaddik* Rav Binyamin Zev Cheshin said afterwards in his *shiur*, 'There is a yeshivah that *davens* such prayers that have never been heard before in the world! Prayers like these, with such devotion, have never been heard before!'"

A little later on, the Rav modified the way the yeshivah prayed a little, to introduce more melody.

"In the first stage of the yeshivah, we prayed with a lot of crying out and shouting," recalls one of the students. "Afterwards, the Rav changed it a bit and sweetened the prayers with more *niggunim*. We prayed most of the service out loud and together, with beautiful melodies, word for word, without any rushing or quickly mumbling the words."

BRESLOV IS ALL ABOUT LEARNING TORAH

Together with *hisbodedus*, prayer, and personal holiness, the Rav also put a lot of emphasis on learning Torah. One Purim, he commented: "Breslov is only about learning *Gemara* and Torah... Learning *Gemara* is the secret of the Shuvu Banim Yeshivah."

The Rav continued: "We don't learn *Gemara* with a cup of coffee! Anyone who tries to learn *Gemara* while drinking a cup of coffee is never going to be a *talmid chacham*, he's never going to understand the *Gemara*, and he's never going to really understand what he's learning. Also, he's never really going to acquire *yiras Shamayim*.

"People don't understand that it takes a lot of strength to learn *Gemara*! In *Torah Alef* of *Likutei Moharan*, [*Rabbeinu* says that] if a person doesn't learn their Torah with strength and determination, then they're not going to be a Breslover! Anyone who isn't learning without even speaking about all the other things they're doing, is really wasting their time.

"If a person doesn't learn their Torah with strength and determination, then the Rebbe tells us that they won't be able to overcome the *yetzer hara*, and then they won't have spiritual grace, and their prayers won't be accepted. Also, their prayers won't rise up to Heaven in the same way.

"When a person learns *Gemara*, he starts to see that he doesn't understand anything. But when he learns *Likutei Moharan*, then he starts to think that he's going to be the next Breslover Rebbe. When you learn *Gemara*, it shows you where you're really holding. You can struggle to even understand a single line!"

NO MORE COFFEE

Every *Rosh* Yeshivah has high expectations of his students, but one of the more notable things about Rav Berland is that in so many instances, his students rose to the challenge of meeting them.

Rav Avraham Chananya relates: "There are things that we just can't achieve by ourselves, but thanks to our being connected to the *Tzaddik's* people, we receive a strength that is really above nature.

"For example, the Rav once told me to stop eating fish and meat during the week, and to just eat vegetables. He told me only to eat fish and meat once a week, on Shabbos. It was very hard for me to break my eating habits, but slowly, slowly, I managed to do it.

"I was also used to drinking a cup of coffee after the morning prayers, after I'd woken up at *chatzos* and not tasted anything. After *Shacharis*, my body felt weak, and I needed something strong. I was so used to my coffee that one time I even prayed about it at the end of *Shacharis*, because the coffee wasn't always available.

"Suddenly, the Rav came over to me after the prayers and said to me, 'Stop drinking coffee after the prayers. If you're prepared to even start praying about your coffee, then you really need to stop drinking it.' How he knew that I'd been praying about it, I have no idea."

"THE STARTING POINT HAS TO BE *SHAS*"

As *Rosh* Yeshivah of Shuvu Banim, the Rav spent 20 years drilling this message into his students, over and over again: "Breslov is only about learning *Gemara*!" It got to the point where some people in the wider Breslov community started to complain, and turned the Rav's approach to Torah learning into another axe to grind against him.

Undeterred by his detractors, the Rav continued to teach *Torah Alef*—Rebbe Nachman's very first lesson in *Likutei Moharan*—which states that the main point and foundation has to be Torah learning.

The Rav once explained: "I spent 20 years arguing with some yeshivah students who kept telling me that learning Torah was the same thing as learning *Likutei Moharan* or *Likutei Halachos*. Now, they're 50 years old and they still don't understand what's written in Lesson 3 of *Likutei Moharan* [which describes how a person has to learn the Talmud and the Oral Torah].

"I don't understand how they missed that lesson! We need to reprint *Likutei Moharan* and makes sure Torah Gimmel is included—because the starting point has to be the study of *Gemara* and *Shas*. The Rebbe told us that it's impossible to make spiritual rectifications if a person isn't learning *Gemara*.

"If a person doesn't study the *Gemara*, he won't understand the *Zohar*, or *Likutei Moharan*. If you want to beat your *yetzer hara*, you can only do that if you study *Gemara*!"

THE HOME VISITS CONTINUE

As the Rav now had the additional responsibilities of running the yeshivah, he started encouraging his pupils to take over some of his outreach efforts, going door to door in secular neighborhoods and spending some time with the people there, many of whom would open up to them and start discussing matters of faith. Sometimes, the students would get so many people interested in their ideas that the Rav would encourage them to open a local *kollel* in the area, where more people could come and learn.

(In later years, Shuvu Banim would successfully maintain a number of *kollelim* around the country, eventually even expanding internationally, with new communities in North America and other parts of the world.)

The Rav used to tell his students that their home visits would lead to the redemption of *Am Yisrael*. On one occasion, he singled out one of his students, Rav Shalom Arush, praising him for making such an effort to go from city to city and door to door, trying to spread the light of Rebbe Nachman.

"He's a personal example of how I'd like all of my students to be," the Rav exclaimed, and then described how often he and Rav Arush would drive from one secular *kibbutz* to another, trying to reach out to secular Jews. "It was worth all the time and effort, even to encourage just one *Yid* to do *teshuvah*!"

RABBEINU'S MESSENGERS

The students who went out on these visits were nicknamed the "*Shadarim*," short for "*shluchei d'Rabbana*[LVI]". The Rav told these messengers: "The fact that you're going from house to house all over the place, from Eilat to Metulla, is only in order to bring *Am Yisrael* back, and to help them do *teshuvah*." He told his students that they were asking for *tzedakah* just as a way of getting the conversation started, and to give the people they were meeting the opportunity and merit of participating in some of the yeshivah's Torah and *mitzvos*.

LVI   This is a standard term used in the Orthodox world for people who go out collecting money for *yeshivos*.

"The moment they see people with beards and *payos* who are graceful and charismatic, who truly have good character traits, and who are full of holy spirit, they'll immediately want to stay in touch with them. Even if it only results in a single, fleeting thought of doing *teshuvah*, or a single moment of spiritual awakening, for that alone it's worthwhile to travel to the ends of the world."

He continued: "All we need to do is speak to people, to say something to their soul. Everyone is thirsty, and is waiting for someone to say something to their soul. There is nothing greater than to speak with a Jew. And in the end, everyone will do *teshuvah*." He also explained to his students that everyone possessed the ability to bring someone else closer to *Hashem*, and he'd always remind them: "Don't worry! The *Tzaddik* will come with you, everywhere you go!"

Rav Yosef Assulin, one of Rav Berland's former *gabbaim*, recalls: "The Rav used to really energize us to go out to do *Shadarut*. He always used to tell us: 'We don't need to go out on *Shadarut* for money. Money will always come somehow. Money comes from studying Torah and guarding the eyes, and from honoring our wives. We go out on *Shadarut* so that the Jews who live in the cities will see Jews with beards and *payos*, Jews who are *bnei Torah*, and hear a few words about *Yiddishkeit*.'

"The Rav had many millions of dollars passing through his hands over the years — many times more than anything we ever made by doing *Shadarut*," continues Rav Assulin. "He used that money for the institutions and he also distributed most of the money to other people who needed charitable funds. This was one of the most notable practices of the Rav.

"Hundreds, if not thousands, of people did *teshuvah* thanks to the *Shadarut*. They came to learn at the Shuvu Banim Yeshivah, or one of its branches, or at Rav Stern's yeshivah, or at Rav Arush's yeshivah, or other places. There are whole families today who are learning day and night just because of the *Shadarut*."

THE RAV'S HOLY STUDENTS

As the years passed, Shuvu Banim continued to attract many people who would go on to become some of the best-known Breslov Rabbis of our times. Rav Shmuel Stern once said: "Each one of the Rav's senior students, from the *baalei teshuvah* he brought in, could be an *Admor* for hundreds of their own *chassidim*"—a view shared by many others in the Orthodox world.

Some of these students came yearning for Torah. Others were inspired by the Rav's personal example and caring. Still others showed up at the yeshivah because they'd been brought there by friends, unsure of who or what they'd find at Shuvu Banim. But many of those who stayed at Shuvu Banim blossomed into some of the biggest names in Breslov *Chassidus* and the Orthodox Jewish world.

THE STUDENTS' SPECIAL FOCUS

"It's impossible to say which part of the Rav's *avodah* is the most important, because he does everything wholeheartedly, whether it's learning Torah, doing *hisbodedus*, giving charity, and so on," begins Rav M. Z., one of Rav Berland's older students. "The Rav throws himself into everything, and does it all with complete self-sacrifice.

"But his students each adopted their own special focus where they really excel. One Rabbi really excels in the *mitzvah* of 'v'ahavta l'rei'acha kamocha,' (love your fellow as yourself), for example. If someone doesn't come to the yeshivah for two days in a row, he'll get a phone call from this Rabbi to find out if he's okay, along with lots of words of *chizzuk*.

"Another Rabbi excels in the area of *shmiras einayim*. Less than a month ago he married off a daughter, and he spent the entire six hours in the wedding hall with his eyes closed. For years already, he'll only open his eyes when he's in his own home or at the yeshivah. Where can you find other people like this?

"Another Rabbi excels in learning Torah; another in visiting *kivrei tzaddikim*, where he'll do *hisbodedus* for a whole month straight; Rav Arush excels in *avodas ha'emunah*, which expresses itself in every word he says.

"Of course, everyone is also doing all the other things too, like learning Torah and guarding their eyes, but it's clear that each student took one aspect of the Rav's own *avodah* to really invest in the most."

Rav M. Z. concludes: "The Rav always told us in the yeshivah that if we really had *achdus* and unity with each other, then he wouldn't have needed to go into exile, or to be persecuted so much. He used to explain how each of us has qualities that weren't in the others, and that when we serve *Hashem* together, the good qualities of each person are included in all of us."

RAV DOVID BUBLI

Rav Dovid Bubli was one of the founding students of the Shuvu Banim Yeshiva in Bnei Brak, and also held an administrative position there. He recalls how many of modern Breslov's biggest names got their start at the Shuvu Banim Yeshivah in Bnei Brak:

RAV MICHAEL LASRY

"We were visited by a young man by the name of Michael Lasry," he begins. "He was about 17 years old when he came [to Shuvu Banim]. His father was very anti-religious. [But Michael] got connected, he grew in Torah observance. One day he asked me, 'Look, I'm thinking of finding work, choosing a profession so I can provide for my future.'

"I told him, 'If you choose a life of Torah, your future will be bright. You're talented.' I could see that he was very talented. He said, "Okay, then, let's get started.' He got married, and then I started employing him in a national network of Torah lectures. I sent him to teach at a place in Bat Yam. He ran the Torah lecture network there and discovered where his talents lay. He began peppering his lectures with the sort of humor that audiences enjoy, until he got to where he is today.[LVII]"

RAV SHALOM ARUSH

Next, Rav Bubli recalls how another of Rav Berland's famous students arrived at Shuvu Banim. "Rav Shalom Arush arrived with long hair and a huge dog, and asked to be accepted," he says. "So Rav Moshe Beninstock told him, 'If you want to be accepted into our yeshivah, you first have to give up the dog. Secondly, you have to cut your hair.' Rav Arush agreed and did it.

"We then saw that he was also talented, so we let him take on responsibilities. He started bringing people closer to *Hashem*, to emulate Rav Berland. He got very close to Rav Berland and, thank God, from toiling in Torah, he elevated himself."

Rav Arush describes what brought him to Shuvu Banim: "There was a Jew who told me that there's an amazing Rabbi in Bnei Brak. He said that even if you come to him in the middle of the night and ask him to come with you somewhere—he'll come with you! I was laughing and joking a bit with my friend about this, but then

---

LVII   Rav Michael Lasry is today one of the most popular and entertaining speakers on the outreach circuit in Israel, and regularly appears at Arachim seminars and Hidabroot events, amongst others.

he took me to see Rav Berland. We got there around 8 p.m. at night, and Rav Berland immediately started to teach us Torah."

TIME TO GO TO THE FOREST

Rav Arush continues: "I started asking him a whole bunch of questions about Torah and *Yiddishkeit*; why do we do this, and why do we do that—for a whole hour! Rav Berland sat there and answered all my questions in a very nice way—and then it was midnight. Rav Berland interrupted the discussion to tell me it was time to drive out to the forest.

"I said to him 'Forest!? What am I meant to be doing in a forest?' But the Rav told me not to worry and not to think; I should just come and speak to *Hashem* there—all my questions and problems, whatever it is I don't know, whatever I want to know, I should just come and ask *Hashem*, there in the forest.

"While we were traveling there, he told me about the concept of *hisbodedus* and the idea of talking to *Hashem* all the time—and I really liked that idea! It really lit me up! So, we went to the field, and I turned into a different person.

"I went back to Rav Berland a few more times with my friend, and each time I got stronger and stronger. I started to leave everything that wasn't good for me, and I really started to get into the Breslov Jewish world. We would just sit there, the three of us, learning Torah, and then go out to the field to do *hisbodedus*. We did that for a year."

HE NEVER TOLD PEOPLE THEY WERE WRONG

"Whenever a new guy was coming back to *Yiddishkeit*, the Rav would never tell him what he was meant to be doing. He wouldn't tell him, 'Do this or do that.' He just kept quiet, and he never told someone they were wrong," continues Rav Arush.

"For example, there was this one Russian who was trying to come back to *Yiddishkeit*, and he was at Rav Berland for Shabbos. Then, in the middle of Shabbos, he suddenly decided he needed to go to work, and he told Rav Berland, 'Listen, I have to go to work now, work is the most important thing. A person has to worry about making a living...' So, the Rav told him, 'Fine! Do what you need to do.' He never tried to scare people by telling them they were going to *Gehinnom*, or acted strictly with other people—never.

"It was only after a few weeks and months, when the Rav saw that people were now ready to listen, and after he'd opened the yeshivah, that they started to learn a *halachah* class in the morning, and slowly, slowly, the Rav started turning people in the right direction.

"In the beginning, people didn't know anything. They were coming to pray with the Rav with their long hair and their weird clothes, and the Rav saw that they weren't ready to start doing everything yet. So he started slowly, slowly, like with a baby. You don't come and put a steak in a baby's mouth; you start with the milk first, slowly, slowly."

HE KNEW WHAT EACH PERSON NEEDED

"Rav Berland knew how to approach each person in the best way. He knew how to talk to them, and what was troubling them, and what to do to try to fix it. He knew what situation everyone was in, and when it was a good time to talk to someone, or not—he knew everything. When he took people to the forest, he'd tell them that they were going to talk to the One Who could help them with everything they were worried about, and not to relate to *Hashem* as though they were going to talk to some scary King who held the power of life or death.

"Rav Berland encouraged everyone to talk to God as though He was your best friend and you wanted to tell Him everything that was on your mind. Just talk to Him like a friend! Later, when he opened the yeshivah, things got a little stricter and some rules were introduced, but even then, everything was a request, not a command. You were asked nicely."

Once, Rav Arush actually got a little upset at Rav Berland for not telling him that he needed to ritually wash his hands every time before eating. He asked him, "Why didn't you tell me?!" But now, Rav Arush says that he learned from the Rav that this is the only way to bring Jews back to *Hashem* in a way that will actually last, and so that they'll stay observant. "Just by loving them and smiling at them, and without telling them how to behave," he observes. "In the end, they'll be 100 percent religious. But if you're always telling them what to do and what not to do, they can burn out quickly and leave the correct path."

RAV MOSHE TZANANI

Rav Moshe Shavili, one of the Rav's earliest *baal teshuvah* students, recalls how Rav Moshe Tzanani first came to Rav Berland in Bnei Brak:

"When I was in the army, I met someone called Dror Tzanani, who had a very exalted *neshamah*. (Now he's known as Rav Moshe Tzanani, but back then he was plain 'Dror.') He was looking for something more spiritual, more meaningful in life. So Dror got connected to an Indian guru and was considering flying out to India to follow this spiritual 'master'—but his father was very unhappy about what was going on.

"Dror's father had a friend who was newly religious and who was close to Rav Berland, and he kept asking this friend, 'Please, come and save my son! He wants to fly out to India to be with this guru!' So this friend tried to convince Dror to change his path, but Dror argued and told him, 'No, what I've found is good. It's the right path for me and I like it. Please leave me alone.'

"But his father's friend wouldn't leave him alone, until eventually Dror said to him, 'Come with me to this ashram, where this guru's followers gather in Tel Hashomer, and see for yourself how good it is. And if you come with me to Tel Hashomer, then I'll come with you to your Rav Berland!'"

PLANS TO MOVE TO INDIA

"Dror was so enamored with his guru that he actually did fly out to visit him in America one time, and he was making plans to fly out to India after he finished his army service to go live near the guru. In the meantime, Dror's father was going crazy, and he kept begging his friend to find a way to save his son. Eventually, the friend agreed to come with Dror to the ashram in Tel Hashomer, on condition that Dror would then come with him to visit Rav Berland.

"So the religious guy is sitting in this ashram that's full of *avodah zara*, and he's looking around, and everyone looks like they're high on drugs. He says to Dror, 'This is the "amazing spirituality" you were telling me about?! Come on, let's get out of here.' So Dror says to him, 'What?! Look how much everyone loves each other and is smiling at each other!' But in truth, everyone was laughing or crying because they were totally stoned; they were all just high as a kite.

"Then the religious guy came back to Dror and told him, 'I came to your ashram. Now you promised to come with me to Rav Berland.' Dror tried to push him off, saying, 'Listen, I really don't have time...' But the friend wasn't taking no for an answer. He'd already prepared Rav Berland for the visit and told him that he was bringing a friend who was one of the smartest, deepest people he'd ever met—but that he wanted to go to India. He asked Rav Berland to try to do whatever he could, with God's help, to try and stop that from happening."

THE FIRST MEETING WITH RAV BERLAND

"Rav Berland told him to come, and they got there at 8 p.m. in the evening. As soon as they walked in, Dror started asking the Rav about the funny boxes he was wearing on his head and hand, with the funny straps, and what they're for. Then he started asking questions about the other *mitzvos*, but not in such a nice, respectful way, even mocking a bit.

"Rav Berland gave it to him straight, and whatever question he asked, the Rav responded in such a way that there was no choice but to acknowledge the truth of the Rav's words. Dror couldn't argue and was left speechless. The visit came to an end, and Dror and the religious friend left.

"When the friend saw Dror the next day and asked him what he thought, he told him, 'It was okay. But I think I need to go back again a couple of times, just to make sure it's the real deal.' The friend thought to himself, 'If Dror is willing to go back, then the Rav's already got him and he won't leave.'

"Each time Dror returned, Rav Berland shattered some more of his beliefs in the guru and all his high-as-a-kite followers. After a few more visits, Dror turned to his friend and told him, 'Listen, I think I'm going to stay here. I'm leaving my job, I'm leaving my friends and I'm leaving the guru. I'm just going to stay here with Rav Berland, and I'm not going back to that nonsense anymore.'

"And that's what happened. He continued to learn with Rav Berland and to grow in his *Yiddishkeit* more and more, until he got to where he is now. Rav Moshe Tzanani, as he's now known, is on such a high spiritual level, it's almost impossible to grasp. And it's all in the Rav's *zechus*."

Rav Tzanani has now been studying at the Shuvu Banim Yeshiva for over 40 years, and is renowned for starting his full day's learning at the Shuvu Banim Yeshiva in the Old City at midnight. Today, many people come to Rav Tzanani for blessing and advice in his own right.

RAV ELIYAHU SUCCOT

Rav Eliyahu Succot has been one of Rav Berland's closest student for almost 50 years. He opened Jerusalem's 'House of Love and Prayer' in the 1960s, before becoming a life-long follower of the Rav.

"People think that Shuvu Banim started with Israelis, but really it started with Americans," begins Rav Eliyahu Succot, whose came back to observant Judaism after he happened to see a young Rabbi called Shlomo Carlebach at a music festival in California. "Over the following weeks and months, Rav Shlomo would often talk about the *heileger* Rav Nachman, and that's actually how I first began to feel a connection to Breslov," he says.

RAV BERLAND AND THE MOTORBIKE RIDE

Rav Succot first met Rav Berland at Reb Dovid Kramer's bris, being held in the Old City of Jerusalem in 1969, at a time when Rav Berland was still living in Bnei Brak. "The Rav was wearing a kaftan and just kind of shining all over." remembers Rav Succot. "He came over to me and started talking to me in English. He was talking to me the whole time during the *bris*.

"That bris was on a Friday, so the Rav asked me if he could come for Shabbat. Our house in Kiryat Yovel used to overlook Yad Vashem, and the Jerusalem forest, and we were used to all sorts of people coming for Shabbos, so of course I said "yes". The Rav then told me that he wanted to get more food likvod ha Shabbos (in honor of the Shabbos). My friend took the Rav on the back of his motorbike to Machane Yehuda market. Years later, the Rav told me that that was the first time he'd ever been on a motorcycle."

At that time, in 1969, the infrastructure of Jerusalem was still being rebuilt after the Six Day War in 1967, so the transportation available and the roads were very basic. There were very few cars in Eretz Yisrael in those days, and most of the Jerusalem roads were still just white dust, so people got around however they could.

Rav Succot continues the story:

"So the Rav came for *Shabbos* and he spent 26 hours just singing and dancing and speaking words of *Chassidus*. I honestly don't know if the Rav slept at all."

THE RAV SERVES HASHEM AROUND THE CLOCK

From that point on, Rav Succot became very connected to Rav Berland, and would frequently see him both in Jerusalem and also at his home in Bnei Brak. "The Rav's schedule has always been around the clock serving Hashem and that was even more so when the Rav was in his early thirties," he recalls. "The Rav was very chazak (strong) - he just didn't sleep! He would occasionally fall asleep for a few quick minutes.

"Once, I was with the Rav for two or three days and we spent a lot of time in the citrus orchards across the road from Bnei Brak. At that time there were little houses and trees there. Today, there are the huge buildings of Givat Shaul."

"I was doing *hisbodedus* there with the Rav and some other Americans when we all just collapsed into the red sand there, and fell deeply asleep. We were completely exhausted. But the Rav just kept on going."

EVERYTHING WAS WITH *NIGGUNIM*

In the early years, Rav Berland would meet Rav Succot and his friends and then go with them to Kever David, in the Old City, before going over to use the *mikvah* in Meah Shearim. Sometimes, they'd drive up to Kever Rochel, which in those days meant going straight through the middle of Beit Lechem, then from there, the Rav would head out to schools, synagogues and any other place where he'd been invited to give *shiurim*.

"He'd sing and I'd play *niggunim* on my guitar," recalls Rav Succot. "Everything was with *niggunim*. Sometimes, the Rav would dance and do somersaults in the street in Meah Shearim. You have to remember that this was before the big wave of the *baal teshuvah* movement had begun, and it was a very different Meah Shearim than it is today. The old-world community of Meah Shearim were very suspicious of the newcomers."

In 1971, Rav Succot and his family left Jerusalem to set up home in Migdal in the North of Israel, and only returned to Jerusalem and Shuvu Banim around six years' later, in 1976, when Rav Succot started attending the shiurim of Rabbi Levi Yitzhak Bender, z'tl, in Meah Shearim.

"I'd been learning with Rav Gedalya Koenig, and he was very kind to me and to other 'late beginners'," recalls Rav Succot. Rav Koenig first gave shiurim in Yiddish that were translated, then he moved on to giving his classes in Hebrew for *baal teshuvahs*, and then he began teaching *shiurim* for women.

"He endured a lot of opposition because of this," recalls Rav Succot. After Rav Gedalya died at young age of 59, Rav Succot started attending Rav Levi Yitzhak's shiur instead, at the Breslov shul in Meah Shearim. "I became addicted to his incredible *shiurim*," he recalls. "I never merited to have a personal relationship with him, but his words went straight into my heart.

"He'd say: '*vatikin* is *vatikin*; *hisbodedus* is *hisbodedus*; *chatzos* is *chatzos*; you daven *Shacharis* in the morning...' He straightened out so many things in my head with his simplicity and *temimus*, and the way he gave over Rabbenu's path."

From that time, Rav Succot has barely left the side of Rav Berland, and he continues to be one of the Rav's closest students even today.

A MESSENGER OF GOD

"I've known Rav Berland for over 40 years, and even back then he was an angel; even then, he was a messenger of God," continues Rav Bubli. "[Take] his *davening*— three hours of prayer with devotion to *Hashem*. I was with him [at Shuvu Banim] all day long, morning until night, and all he did was speak Torah. He would reveal hidden esoteric concepts to me. These were all very deep concepts that no one can understand even on the simple level. A regular person could go on like this for a day, or two, or three. He went on like this for years, growing like an ever-increasing wellspring.

"He knows so much and is constantly giving it over," continues Rav Bubli. "He never rests. He would always say, 'Let's learn *halachah*! Let's learn this, let's learn that!' He wouldn't let me rest. Every day, I was with him until 1 or 2 a.m. No one can do what he does.

"Someone once went to the Steipler and asked for his blessing. The Steipler asked him, 'Where do you learn?' He replied, 'By Rav Berland.' The Steipler replied, 'And you're coming to me? Do you know who he is? A blessing from him is enough; you don't need me.' I was there, and I heard it straight from his mouth.

"This is a person who, when I understood who he was, is a Divine angel, a messenger who receives transmissions from On High all the time. In my opinion, there's no one like [Rav Berland] in our generation today. He is the number one in this generation.

"No one is more devoted than he is. No one. Devotion like this you don't find anywhere else. I've never seen such a thing, and I know many pious *tzaddikim*. Devotion like this—24 hours a day—he'd forget to even eat. Once a day, he'd grab a morsel of food. You know how he looks, all skin and bones? He's always looked like this! He doesn't eat at all. I once saw him go three days straight without eating. Rav Beninstock once grated a carrot for him and fed it to him with a small spoon, slowly, after he hadn't eaten for three days. We were afraid for him.

"He just learns and learns and learns Torah. He pays no attention to food, has no earthly desires, nothing. Just the Creator and His Torah that He commanded us to keep, and that's all. There is nothing else besides [God], nothing," finishes Rav Bubli.

THE RAV CONTINUES TO WORK ON HIS HUMILITY

Despite the fact that he was now the head of a flourishing yeshivah—or perhaps specifically because of the great success he was enjoying at Shuvu Banim—Rav Berland continued to go to extraordinary lengths to maintain his humility.

"When Shuvu Banim had already started in Bnei Brak, the Rav still spent some of his evening at the Vizhnitz Yeshivah," recalls Rav Moshe Yosef Haas. "At Vizhnitz, everyone knew him as 'Reb Lazer the *Meshugganer*.' At that time, I was a Vizhnitzer *chassid*, and I remember there used to be groups of people standing around him, and he used to let them make fun of him and he'd laugh at himself, too.

"They used to stand there mocking him, and he'd just encourage them. The Rav used to walk around the streets with holy books, and he'd go up to people and enthusiastically say to them, 'Do you see what's written here?!' At the bus stop, on the bus itself, in all different places, he'd start reading sections of *Likutei Halachos* or some other holy book out loud to the passersby, and they'd start to laugh at him. He did this for many years.

"So I always knew him as someone who wasn't 'normal,' and who hung out with the crazy people."

SEEKING OUT INSULTS

Rav Haas continues: "After I got married, I started to get into Breslov, and there were a few people from Breslov who wanted to introduce me to the Rav. As soon as they told me his name, I started telling them that, to my great misfortune, I already knew exactly who he was, and he was not anything like the great Rabbi they were describing.

"A little while later, I read Torah 6 [in *Likutei Moharan*, where the Rebbe talks about seeking out insults and humiliation] and the thought suddenly occurred to me that maybe the Rav really was normal after all, and he'd just been acting crazy. Shortly after that, I heard a recorded *shiur* by the Rav, without knowing who had given it, and it really blew me away. I had to find out who'd given it—and they told me it was Rav Berland."

YOU'LL ONLY CATCH THE RAV WITH PRAYERS

"I was amazed at his breadth of Torah learning and I decided I had to clarify things for myself, so I tried to visit him at the yeshivah 18 times in a row. Every time I got there I was told the Rav had just left. Finally, they told me, 'You'll only catch the Rav with prayers.' So I prayed.

"The day after I prayed to see him, someone from the yeshivah contacted me and told me that there was going to be a *bris* and the Rav was going to be the *sandak*. I went over there, and that was my first meeting with the Rav. It was just after the *bris* had finished, when the Rav was meeting the public. Rav Yosef Assulin was standing outside, and he told me that the Rav had to leave soon and wasn't seeing anyone else.

"I told him, 'The Rav can't leave until I've seen him!' After a few minutes, he said the Rav was going to the *Kosel* to pray. Someone was going to be talking to the Rav on the way there, but I could accompany him back from the *Kosel* to his house. At the *Kosel*, the Rav asked me if my being a Breslover was something I revealed to other people, or something I kept hidden. He immediately hit the nail on the head.

"At that time, I was still hiding the fact that I was into Breslov from my friends. The Rav gave me his hand and started to dance with me. Afterwards, I got into Rav Assulin's car with him and the Rav told him where to drive. He spoke to me in Yiddish so that Rav Assulin wouldn't understand what he was telling me.

"The Rav basically spoke about all the different thoughts I had going on in my head for a whole hour, and I really didn't say anything! I suddenly felt so ashamed: I was so transparent, what was I trying to hide, anyway? The Rav told me that I should come and visit him from time to time. I used to come to the yeshivah for a few days to recharge my batteries and strength, and that gave me the ability to endure that tough period of time until I was able to move to Jerusalem."

TURN YOURSELF INTO A FOOL

"Once, I told the Rav about all the persecution I was enduring as a result of my coming closer to *Rabbeinu*," continues Rav Haas. "I cried as I told him that I couldn't take it anymore. The Rav told me: 'Turn yourself into a fool, who doesn't understand or know anything! That way, people will leave you alone and you'll save your soul.' He added that this is what Dovid HaMelech did, in the years when he had to flee from his persecutors, and that this is what he himself had also done, all those years in Bnei Brak, so that people would leave him alone.

"That's when I realized that the Rav had fooled a whole city for decades. It was really a miraculous thing, because he was already a *Rosh* Yeshivah and also the Steipler's regular *chavrusa*. Yet despite all that, people in Bnei Brak believed he was a *meshugganer*.

"In the Shuvu Banim Yeshivah, people had no idea of what was really going on. The Rav would make it seem as though he was going straight to bed after the evening prayers, the same as the students, but then he'd go over to the Vizhnitz Yeshivah and play the fool—and he'd done it so cleverly, for all those years!

"I started to understand that, as well as being part of his spiritual work to deliberately seek out humiliation, it had also been a strategy to get people to leave him alone so they wouldn't argue with him about the new path he'd chosen. Now, when I think about it, it's truly a wondrous thing: How could someone run his own yeshivah, learn with the Steipler, and still get people to believe he was *meshugger*? The Rav is simply a genius at hiding his greatness from other people."

SHUVU BANIM MOVES TO JERUSALEM

Even though Shuvu Banim continued to grow by leaps and bounds in Bnei Brak, it was common knowledge among the students that Rav Berland was really yearning for Jerusalem, and specifically, the Old City of Jerusalem.

"The Rav used to talk about Jerusalem and the Old City all the time, with great yearning," remembers one of the students. "When we finally got into our building there, the Rav exclaimed, 'I was praying for this day for more than 20 years!'"

THE ALL-NIGHT *SHIUR*

For a couple of years before his dream of reunifying the Shuvu Banim yeshivah in the Old City of Jerusalem came to pass, Rav Berland was dividing his time between the two branches of the yeshivah, in Bnei Brak and Jerusalem.

Rav M.T. takes up the story: "A few years before the yeshivah was established in Jerusalem, the Rav used to come to Jerusalem every Thursday night, to Rav Levi Yitzchak's *shiur*; and then in the evenings after *Maariv*, he'd go and give a *shiur* the whole night long at Rav Gavriel Grossman's home in Sanhedria.

"The Rav used to talk straight through the night, until the time for the dawn prayers. Everyone used to come to that *shiur*: secular people, *baalei teshuvah*, *bnei Torah*, even *chassidim* and old-school Jerusalemites.

"Most people didn't stay for the whole thing; they'd come and go throughout the night. Sometimes, they'd doze off in the middle, but the Rav didn't see anything and wasn't bothered by anything. He kept talking all night, without any sign of being tired or exhausted.

"A few students from the Ohr Somayach Yeshivah started coming to that *shiur*, including Avi Katz, Arik Gur-Arieh and a few others, and they quickly become dyed-in-the-wool Breslovers. One day, they decided they wanted to leave their old yeshivah and found a new yeshivah under the auspices of the Rav. They got the Rav's agreement, and that's how the Jerusalem branch of the yeshivah began.

"We started learning in 'the *Shul*' in Meah Shearim, before moving to Salant Street, and then to an apartment on Lapidot Street. The Rav spent most of the day at the yeshivah in Bnei Brak, and then after *Maariv* he'd come to Jerusalem in Baruch Sharvit's van, where he'd try to grab a bit of sleep before *chatzos*. At midnight, he'd wake us all up; then we'd go to the field around the *kever* of Shmuel Hanavi to do *hisbodedus*. Afterwards, the Rav would give a *shiur* until the morning. After *Shacharis*, he'd give another *shiur* on *Likutei Halachos*, and then he'd return to Bnei Brak."

CRYING OUT WITH OUR SOULS

Rav Yalon Yitzchaki continues: "I joined around the same time as the group from Ohr Somayach, and we decided to get something going ourselves, as Shuvu Banim still didn't have a budget at that point and they were squeezing out every shekel they had to try and help us cover the cost of setting up a branch of Shuvu Banim in Jerusalem.

"When we were on Salant Street, the place was a dining room in the morning. At night, we said *Tikkun Chatzos* there, and in the afternoon, it was a factory of *Yiddishkeit*. It's impossible to describe the praying that used to go on there. *Shacharis* would last for three hours every day, *Minchah* was an hour and a half, and so was *Maariv*—and we were crying out with all our souls. It's impossible to describe it.

"Everyone got up for *Tikkun Chatzos*. Everyone went out to the field. A little later, Shuvu Banim formally opened a branch of the yeshivah at 4 Lapidot Street that was called 'Derech Emunah,' at the suggestion of Rav Levi Yitzchak Bender.

"The faces there would change all the time. People would come to the yeshivah for a week or a month, and then go somewhere else. There are literally tens, if not hundreds, of Rabbis and spiritual leaders today who got their first taste of *teshuvah* at Shuvu Banim."

EVEN THE RAV NEEDS TO SLEEP

The rigors of running one full-time yeshivah would fill every spare moment for most *Roshei* Yeshivah, particularly when there was so much emphasis on lengthy *davening*, lengthy *hisbodedus* and in-depth Torah learning. When Shuvu Banim became two yeshivos—one in Bnei Brak and one in Jerusalem—the Rav struggled valiantly to meet the spiritual needs of both sets of students without compromising his own very high level of spiritual devotion.

It helped that the Rav barely slept more than an hour a night, and barely ate—but ultimately, it became clear that even for a *Rosh* Yeshivah as tireless as Rav Berland, having a yeshivah split across two different cities was exacting a significant toll.

"In 5742 (1982) the Rav's family told him that the situation couldn't continue any longer," explains Rav N. T. "The Rav was spending 24 hours a day at the yeshivah, by day in Bnei Brak, and by night in Jerusalem. Despite the Rav's great willingness to sacrifice himself for his students, the fact of the matter was that he had no time to sleep, he had no time to eat, and he was constantly traveling back and forth. We could all see that something had to change, so we started looking for a building where the whole yeshivah could be reunited in Jerusalem.

"By Pesach [of the same year], the Rav and the Rebbetzin were still going to look at different locations to see if they were suitable, until we got to that day, the 28th of Nissan."

THE MIRACULOUS MOVE

The story of how Shuvu Banim came to be in its present location on Maale Haladia Street in the Muslim Quarter of the Old City of Jerusalem, is nothing less than miraculous.

Rav Yalon Yitzchaki explains how it all began:" The night when the story began we were sitting and learning *Likutei Halachos* with the Rav, before praying *vasikin* and eating breakfast," he recalls.

"That day, one of the students of the Rav from Bnei Brak, Rav Zevulun Dachbash, was sitting at the *Kosel* and praying the morning service. Suddenly, he heard a man sobbing bitterly right next to him. He saw a well-dressed *Sephardi*-looking man, crying his eyes out.

"Rav Dachbash was shaken by the sight, so he went over to the man and said to him, 'Tell me what happened, maybe I can help you.' The man in question was Reb Avraham Dwek, the scion of an extremely rich family of Syrian Halabi descent. He owned a factory which made him very wealthy. He was also a very spiritual man and knew all of *Tanach* and a lot of *Gemara*, too, and he tried to explain to Rav Dachbash why he was so upset.

"Reb Dwek had come to Israel because he was trying to fulfill the *mitzvah* of 'cherishing' the stones of Jerusalem. He'd been going around the Old City until he found a place in the Muslim Quarter that was called the Chayei Olam courtyard, which was half in ruins. At the entrance to the building there was a house that was being illegally occupied by Arabs, but inside there were two vacant floors. The lower floor contained many different rooms.

"He explained that he'd checked into why it was abandoned and half-ruined, and discovered that the local Arabs believed the place was haunted by demons and ghosts. It was the only place that was still in ruins in the Old City after 1948. He discovered that the building had once been owned by the Chayei Olam Yeshivah, and that now it had fallen under the control of Atara L'Yoshna, an organization that had quasi-governmental status, whose stated goal was to rescue buildings from Arab owners.

"They'd redeemed the house, despite the fact that the Arab terrorist organizations threatened to kill any Arab caught selling their house to the Jews."

THE ISRAELI GOVERNMENT BREAKS ITS PROMISE

"Reb Dwek knew the man who was the head of the organization, and he'd made an agreement with him to put up the money to buy this building back from the Arabs, on condition that it would be turned into a shul for the *ilui neshamah* of his grandfather, the *tzaddik* Rabbi Shaul Dwek HaKohen.

"They promised him that they'd turn it into a shul, and he'd given them a large sum of money so they could start building.

"After a year and a half, he returned to Israel to see what was happening with his synagogue, and he discovered they were planning to use it for something else. They'd turned it into apartments! He met the head of the organization and asked him, 'How could you do such a thing?! We agreed that you would build a synagogue! And apart from that, this place is suitable for something very holy!' [The building has a stunning view of the Temple Mount from the upper floors.]

"They didn't know what to tell him, so he came down to the *Kosel*, and he was crying about all the money that he'd donated to the Israel government that he couldn't get back, and about the fact that there was very little hope of seeing a synagogue being built there now."

BRING ME 30 STUDENTS TODAY!

"After he finished telling his story, Rav Dachbash asked if there was anything he could do to help. He answered him, 'There's only one thing left to do, and that's to try to establish a yeshivah there, this very day! If you could bring me a *kollel* of at least 25 or 30 students, we could house them there today and establish our rights to the building. That's the only way of saving the situation.'

"Rav Dachbash told him, 'Take heart! I can get you 30 students here *right now!*' He knew that the Rav had been praying to be in Jerusalem all of his life. He took Reb Dwek to 4 Lapidot Street, where the Rav was giving a *shiur* while everyone was eating breakfast.

"The Rav stood up, gave Reb Dwek a big smile and a seat, and acted like he knew him already from somewhere. He didn't ask him any questions about why he was there. He opened up a copy of the *Likutei Halachos* and asked Reb Dwek to start reading.

"A little later, the Rav stepped out of the room with him. Ten minutes later, he re-appeared in a whirlwind of activity and told everyone to *bentch* and get their things together: They had to hit the road!

"I saw how the Rav had been expecting Reb Dwek to come. He wasn't in the least surprised by the whole story. He told one student to contact all the others in Bnei Brak and tell them to come, too. He told another student to go and rent a moving truck. And he told us in no uncertain terms, 'By 11 a.m., we're all going to the Old City!'"

"I'VE GOT A GUN!"

"By 11 a.m., we'd loaded everything onto the moving truck and we reached the place. The moving truck reversed back toward the building—and then we realized that the head of the organization had gotten wind of what we were trying to do. We got to the steps leading up Chevron Street, where the building was located, and the head guy was there waiting for us. He started yelling at us, 'You're crossing the line! I'm going to call the police! I've got a gun; you better watch out!'

"The Rav told us, 'Don't listen to him.'

"The guy saw what was going on, so he ran up the stairs of the building and locked the door. He started yelling at everyone, 'I've got a gun! I've got a gun!' Then he fired a shot into the air to try to scare us.

"The Rav told one of the students to climb in through a window and open the door. The head guy was so shocked by that, and so unnerved by the Rav's appearance, that he fell on the floor. The Rav went over to him, lifted him up, brushed him off and gave him a big hug. Then he continued on to the second floor."

ONLY IF THE TORAH ALLOWS IT

"The Rav told us clearly, 'If this isn't okay according to Torah law, we're going to leave immediately. God forbid that we should benefit illegally from the money of others.' The place was filthy, but we settled in. After *Maariv*, the Rav disappeared again, and the following morning the police showed up to talk to him—but he wasn't there, so they left us in peace.

"The Rav returned on Friday night and, after delivering a *shiur*, he told us that if we started to get arrogant about what had just happened, and how we'd made it to the Old City with all the miracles, it wouldn't be worth anything in the end.

"Two weeks later, we received notice that legal proceedings had begun against us in the name of the Chayei Olam Yeshivah, the Jerusalem City Council, and the City Engineer. The Jerusalem Mayor Teddy Kollek[27] was trying to evict us, and he'd even brought the matter as far as the Knesset. When someone asked him why, he replied, 'This is damaging the status quo, and we need to get them out.'"

THE ARMY TRIES TO EVICT SHUVU BANIM

"One day, the whole *Kosel* plaza filled with soldiers under orders to use whatever force was necessary to break into the Shuvu Banim Yeshivah and put an end to the story once and for all. They told everyone that we *chareidim* were all '*meshugga*', and spread a lot of false stories about us.

"As the soldiers gathered, the Rav was giving over a *shiur* on *Likutei Halachos*, about Rebbe Nachman's Lesson 5 in *Likutei Moharan*, describing how we get our life force from being attached to the *Tzaddik* of the generation. The Rav told us we were going to put the lesson into action by breathing deeply and having the intention of connecting to Rebbe Nachman.

"Just as we were in the middle of doing that, the army commander entered the building with a few of the soldiers and walked into the yeshivah's main study hall. He looked around, saw tens of people breathing very deeply — and suddenly got very confused. He turned on his heel and yelled out that the mission was canceled. He told all the soldiers to leave the building.

"The Rav said afterwards that we really saw the power of the *Tzaddik* clearly. In the merit of *Rabbeinu* Hakadosh, we got to stay in the yeshivah.

"Over the following weeks, the Rav tried to appease the head of the organization and showed him a lot of honor. For his part, he apologized to the Rav for his behavior. For a long time after that, the matter was investigated in the courts, and the yeshivah was given the right to stay on in their new premises in exchange for paying rent."

THE MINI-POGROM

In one of those strange ironies, Shuvu Banim's move to the Muslim Quarter turned the secular Israeli government and the Arab residents of the Old City into unlikely bedfellows. Rav Nachman Rosenthal, the former *Mashgiach* of the Breslov Yeshivah in Bnei Brak, takes up the story:

"At the beginning, when Shuvu Banim moved to the Muslim Quarter of the Old City, there was an Arab family living in the same complex as the yeshivah," he says. "The yeshivah was located on the two upper floors, but this Arab family lived below them[LVIII], which meant that the students had to pass by their home whenever they entered or left the building. This led to a lot of friction."

Rav Rosenthal recounts that one time when he was in Bnei Brak, he heard that some Arabs had broken into the yeshivah, smashed all the windows and the panels, and generally caused a lot of destruction, in order to intimidate the yeshivah students into leaving the premises. As soon as he heard this, Rav Rosenthal got on the bus to Jerusalem, to see what he could do to help.

"When I got to the yeshivah, I met Rav Horowitz there in the *beis medrash* and asked him what was going on. Rav Horowitz showed me the huge mess the Arabs had made of the place, and I could see that no one knew what to do about it," he says.

LVIII   The rooms where the the Arab family lived were also part of the Chayei Olam complex which at this point legally belonged to Shuvu Banim, but the yeshivah had made the decision not to evict them.

Just then, Rav Rosenthal spotted a big guy that he knew from Bnei Brak—except now, instead of being clean-shaven, the guy had a big beard and long *payos*. He told this guy to come with him, and they went outside to the courtyard. Rav Rosenthal took a big bottle[LIX] and smashed it loudly against the partition wall that had been illegally built by the Arab family who was living below the yeshivah.

"All of a sudden, a big Arab came out of the house and asked me what was going on," recalls Rav Rosenthal. "I just stared at him and told him, 'I did it. It was me.' The Arab suddenly got scared, and started telling me that it was his little kids who made all the problems, not him. I replied, 'Don't give me stories! God is going to punish you for this! He's going to punish you for what you did to the yeshivah!'"

Rav Rosenthal told the Arab quite a few times that God was going to punish him, until he could see that the man looked really scared. Then he left the yeshivah and went home to Bnei Brak.

"Over the next three days, that Arab called the police every single day, because he told them he was scared of the students at Shuvu Banim and he wanted police protection," recalls Rav Rosenthal. "By the fourth day, the Arab had packed up his family and moved to Chevron"—which paved the way for Shuvu Banim to reclaim the whole building.

"WHAT A COMMUNITY!"

With all of Shuvu Banim reunited under one roof, the yeshivah quickly developed a reputation for being one of the most notable bastions of Torah learning, *avodas Hashem*, and of course, Breslov teachings in the whole country.

Rav Moshe Menachem Kluger, the head of Mosdos Kever Rachel, watched the Shuvu Banim community develop in those early years. He says: "There isn't a holy *chaburah* like Shuvu Banim anywhere else in the whole world. A few decades ago, when I was a young teenager and then a young married man, I remember seeing teenagers or young married men from Shuvu Banim coming to the *Kosel*. They looked like an army platoon, and not just a bunch of guys coming to say a chapter of *Tehillim*. They would march like soldiers going into battle.

"You find a special *avodas Hashem* [at Shuvu Banim] that can't be found anywhere else in the whole world. It's the long prayers; it's the intense learning; it's the long,

LIX   In another version of the story, Rav Rosenthal took a huge hammer and started dismantling the Arab's partition wall.

244

steady hours of learning *Gemara*; and all the other things that the Rav puts in. The Rav had enormous success with Shuvu Banim."

WATER THE TREES

But despite the obviously high level of Torah learning and *avodas Hashem* occurring at Shuvu Banim, many people were unaware that this was still just the tip of the iceberg when it came to Rav Berland's own devotions and practices.

"To this day, people don't know what's really going on," says Rav Yehoshua Dov Rubinstein. "In Shuvu Banim, people would show up on Shabbos morning at 4 a.m. to *daven* with the Rav, and then the prayers would sometimes take 12 hours and the people would go home exhausted and think that's it. But the Rav often hadn't finished! He'd continue *davening* for many hours afterwards, even after he'd finished walking home!"

Rav Rubinstein continues: "One Shabbos there was *sheva brachos* for my son, the Rav's son-in-law. My father, *zt"l*, went to pray at Shuvu Banim in the Old City. The prayers that Shabbos were very long, and continued on until the afternoon. They started at 3 a.m. in the morning, and only finished between 3 and 4 p.m. in the afternoon.

"My father asked the Rav afterwards, 'It's okay for you that you've reached the levels that you've reached, but why do you have to detain the congregation? After all, *Rabbeinu* said that eating on Shabbos is entirely holy.'"

The Rav replied, "And am I detaining the congregation?! If I was left to myself, I'd close myself in a room for seven years solid and learn the holy books! But *Hashem Yisbarach* told us to 'water trees' and do *kiruv*, to bring more souls back to *Hashem*. I uphold *Rabbeinu*'s words, in simplicity and innocence."

The Rav then added: "If *Rabbeinu* said that the food on Shabbos is completely holy, then what about the Torah and prayers on Shabbos? They're even more so!"

RAV LEON LEVY'S DREAM

Thanks to the intense efforts of Rav Berland, and the intense devotion his students had for living a committed, spiritual Torah life, the yeshivah's reputation began to spread much further, both within Israel and abroad. In part, it came from people seeing with their own eyes how Rav Berland's students came to the yeshivah as regular guys but often transformed into some of the biggest kabbalists, Rabbis, and leaders in their own right, fired up with *emunah*, devotion to God and palpable *kedushah*.

But as befitting any yeshivah headed by Rav Berland, its reputation also spread by more miraculous means, too. The kabbalist Rav Leon Levy, *zt" l*, once described a dream more than 20 years ago in which he'd seen Rebbe Nachman of Breslov, and described how Rebbe Nachman had appeared to him.

"Rebbe Nachman asked me, 'Why aren't you doing something for my holy yeshivah, which is on Chevron Street in the Old City? Go there and bring them some food!'" he recalls. So the following morning, Rav Leon arrived at the Shuvu Banim Yeshivah in a truck laden with boxes of food and drink, and also stayed on to give a class to the students.

"Over the years, many, many people came closer to Judaism thanks to the Rav's efforts, but some of them also left him later on," says Rav Yehoshua Dov Rubinstein. "The Rav was never even bothered by this, let alone upset by it.

"The Rav can still remember all the names of the people who left him, and recalls them with the same fondness as though they were still his students. This just wouldn't happen with regular people, but it does with the Rav, because of his humility, self-effacement and good heart."

As with all his holy endeavors, the Rav continued to approach the subject of bringing people closer to *Yiddishkeit* with his characteristic gusto, self-sacrifice and humility, as the following story shows:

THE "SHE" WHO WAS REALLY A "HE"

"I met a dear Jew by the name of Rabbi Moshe Cohen, who came from a *chassidus* that wasn't so sympathetic to Breslov," begins Rav Yehoshua Dov Rubinstein. "One time on the *yahrtzeit* of Rebbe Nachman of Breslov, during *Chol Hamoed Succos*, I saw him in the Shuvu Banim Yeshivah in the Old City. I was curious about why he was there, so Moshe Cohen explained the whole story to me."

"I usually go to the *Kosel* every night," he said. "One time, I was going on one of the back paths through the Old City when I noticed a man with long *payos* standing and talking to a secular woman. I couldn't restrain myself, and I told him off for doing that.

"The man with the long *payos* said to me, 'Honored Rabbi, you are right. I am guilty; I have sinned. Please forgive me!' After he said that, the 'woman' opened her mouth to say something, and I suddenly realized that she wasn't a woman at all, but a secular guy with long hair.

"I didn't know what to do with myself," continued Rav Cohen. "On the one hand, the man with the *payos* clearly hadn't been talking to a woman, but on the other hand, he had already told me he was guilty of everything I'd accused him of. I was so embarrassed, I wanted the ground to open up and swallow me.

"I apologized to the man with the *payos* and I walked off. It was a big lesson in trying to judge others favorably and in understanding that not everything you think you see, is what you actually saw.

"I didn't know who the man with the *payos* was, until one day I saw a group coming to the *Kosel* with this same man at their head. So I asked someone, 'Who is that?' and they told me that it was a big Rav and his students, and that he had a yeshivah here, right near the *Kosel*. I decided that I wanted to come and visit his yeshivah one time and be a part of things there, and that maybe it would be an atonement for what had happened.

"I asked when would be a good time to come, and they told me that the *yahrtzeit* of Rebbe Nachman was a good time to visit."

"YOU SEE WHAT HE DID WITH ME!"

"But the story doesn't end there," continues Rav Rubinstein. "Some time later, Rav Moshe Cohen told me that from time to time, he used to go abroad to fundraise for the yeshivah he was affiliated with. Once, he went to London to fundraise, and one evening he knocked on a door that was opened by an *avreich* with *payos* and a beard, surrounded by small children all sporting *payos*, too.

"The *avreich* greeted him very warmly, and then suddenly, the *avreich* asked him if they'd met before. Rav Cohen told him no, he didn't recognize him at all, but maybe he recognizes him from the *Kosel* since he's there a lot. The *avreich* replied, 'Yes, I do know you from there, but it's a long story.' Rav Cohen asked him to remind him and he told him, 'Do you remember when you told off Rav Berland for talking to a woman one evening? Well, I'm that woman! You see what he managed to do with me!'"

RECLAIMING HACHOMAH HASHLISHIT

If it took a miracle for the yeshivah to find its home in the Old City of Jerusalem, it required no less of a miracle for the yeshivah's students to find affordable, suitable housing close by.

Rav Moshe Shavili recalls how Rav Berland broke the news to the yeshivah students in Bnei Brak that he wanted them to relocate to Jerusalem.

"One day, the Rav called Moshe Dror Tzanani to come and see him," he says. "By this point, Dror was already one of the Rav's more senior students. The Rav asked him to go and check into a road called Hachomah Hashlishit (lit., 'the third wall') in Jerusalem, because he wanted all of his students to move with him to Jerusalem and go and live on that street."

Today, Hachomah Hashlishit is one of the most desirable residential roads for the Breslov community in Jerusalem. It's located across the main road from the Meah Shearim neighborhood, and is a ten-minute walk away from the Old City. But in the early 1980s, the reputation of Hachomah Hashlishit was so dire that even the police were scared to enter the road if they were alone, and would only go there in groups[LX].

"So, Dror goes to check out that street, and when he comes back, he told me that he really doesn't understand what's going on, because Hachomah Hashlishit is full of drunks and petty criminals, and he can't understand why the Rav would want the people from his yeshivah to go and live there, of all places," continues Rav Shavili.

"'How can Rav Berland want us to begin building a new, holy Breslov community somewhere like that?' he asked me. But I reassured him, 'If that's what the Rav wants, that's what's going to happen.' Slowly, slowly, all the lowlifes and criminals started leaving the street, and they wanted to sell their houses to the Breslov families. Rav Tzanani lived there with his family from that first year, and it was really tough—almost every night, the neighborhood would erupt in fighting and violence, and the police would be called.

"But slowly, it all changed. The people who lived there would literally accost Breslovers on the street and ask them if they wanted to buy their houses—they were desperate to leave, and they couldn't believe anyone would want to come and move into their neighborhood. But before long, it blossomed into a new Breslov neighborhood," he concludes.

LX   At this period of time, many families with mafia connections were located in this area.

Today, the apartments that the Rav encouraged his followers to buy for peanuts back in the early 1980s are worth a small fortune, showing once again the miracles that can occur when we follow the advice of the *tzaddikim*.

THE RAV'S MISSION TO LEBANON, TO TRY TO FREE ISRAELI MIAS

Rabbi Nachman Tikolski was one of the Rav's earliest students, and was with Shuvu Banim from its earliest years. He recounts that the Rav always seemed to be at the center of a buzzing hive of activity and drastic changes, right from the start. "We know from Rebbe Nachman's teachings that things are never quiet around the *Tzaddik*," he explains. "There was always a lot of dramatic things happening around Rav Berland, and it was never quiet for even a moment."

The Rav's detractors have often tried to portray the Rav and his community as completely disconnected from the concerns of the wider Jewish world. In truth, few people have had their finger more on the pulse on the issues most dear to the wider Jewish community, and few have come close to matching the Rav's self-sacrifice to help any Jew in need, anywhere in the world, as the following incredible story shows.

In the summer of 1982, shortly after Shuvu Banim had reunited under one roof in the Old City of Jerusalem and the Rav and his community had moved into their new location on Hachomah Hashlishit, Rav Berland and 12 of his students undertook a daring mission into Lebanon to try to find and rescue the six Israeli soldiers who had been captured by the Syrian army, at the battle of Sultan Yakub.

These six MIAs were: Zohar Lifshitz (killed in the battle); Ariel Lieberman and Chezi Shai (who were released by the Syrians some three years later); and Yehuda Katz, Tzvi Feldman and Zecharia Baumel, who are still missing, presumed dead, more than 30 years later.

The brother of Yehuda Katz had become close to Rav Berland, and arranged for his father, Yossi Katz, to come and talk to him. Mr. Katz had broken down in tears during the meeting, prompting Rav Berland to take a very close interest in the matter. "I said to a group of my *chassidim* that they should come with me to Lebanon, to rescue Yehuda Katz," recalled the Rav, during an interview he gave many years later to *Mishpacha* magazine.

Rav Berland believed that if his small group of *chassidim* would believe *ein od milvado*, that God was the only force in the Universe, with all their hearts, then their mission would succeed. The Rav continues the story:

"We tried to cross the border into Lebanon secretly. It was *parashas Eikev*, where it says[28], 'Every place that your feet tread will be yours, from the wilderness and Lebanon.' We entered Lebanon and reached Sidon, driving through villages looking for Yehuda Katz. The driver was Baruch Sharvit, one of the students at Shuvu Banim.

"The entire area was full of roadblocks. At first, they thought we were diplomats. When we came closer to the roadblocks we donned kaffiyehs. Then, when we approached Sidon, we changed to regular clothes. They thought we were clergymen. We passed all the roadblocks. Suddenly, they realized that we were Jews and the terrorists began shooting at us. It was a miracle we got out of there.

"We were able to reach the lookout at Rashia Al Fuchar, two kilometers from where Katz and his friends were captured in northeast Lebanon. And from there, we were able to see the exact spot where the abduction took place. That night, we were in the Rashia camp, and I gave a *shiur* for 50 soldiers in the dining room. The commander, who was also listening, said to me, 'I don't know why we have to fight this war. Soldiers are killed every day.'

"I told him, 'If you don't defend us here, they will capture Metulla.' He said, 'I don't care, let them capture Metulla.' I replied, 'They will get to Haifa.' The commander didn't care. Even when I said they would get to Tel Aviv, he didn't care. 'Why should my soldiers get killed here in Lebanon?' I told the commander, 'If you don't defend us here they will get to Jerusalem.' And then he said, 'Jerusalem? Oh no, we won't give up Jerusalem!'

"The next day, when we tried crossing the border back into Israel, IDF soldiers caught us and wanted us prosecuted. They handed us over to that same commander. But the commander gave other orders. 'Give these people immunity. Don't do anything to them. Let them into the dining room, feed them, and let them sleep. Give them the best of what we have...'"

But what of the fate of the missing MIAs, including Yehuda Katz?

"I'm sure that when we crossed the border, he was still alive," says the Rav. "When Chezi Shai was returned on a plane from Lebanon to Germany, one of the soldiers guarding him asked his friend, 'Is this Yehuda Katz?' The

Arab soldier guarding him replied, 'No, this is Chezi Shai.' Based on this exchange, we know that he was still alive.

"We did a lot to bring him back. We got the Red Cross on the case, we met with the Austrian prime minister. We did a lot. Now, it's been 30 years since his capture. Yosef HaTzaddik was missing for 22 years. I told his parents that until 22 years there's hope. Today, after 30 years, there's no hope anymore."

"IF THERE'S A *TZADDIK* LIKE THAT, I ALSO WANT TO SEE HIM!"

Perhaps the easiest way to tap into the immense love and energy Rav Berland continued to put into his students and followers is by reading their own accounts of how they came closer to him. The following three stories are very different in detail, but they really encapsulate why the Rav continues to inspire so much love, loyalty and awe from his students.

RAV AVRAHAM THALER

"I began my journey back to *Yiddishkeit* at the yeshivah of Rav Moshe Arush, in the Jerusalem suburb of Katamon," begins Rav Avraham Thaler, one of the more senior students at Shuvu Banim. "At that time, Rav Moshe Tzanani would come to Rav Moshe's yeshivah to give some *shiurim* there, and that's how I first heard about the concepts of searching for the 'true *Tzaddik*' of the generation, and that it was forbidden in *Yiddishkeit* for a person to stagnate, and to just try to stay in the same place, spiritually.

"I understood that although I'd already managed to get acquainted with Rebbe Nachman, there was also a '*Tzaddik* of the generation' who'd been tasked with the job of presenting the inner dimension of Rebbe Nachman's teachings to each generation, in a way that was relevant for them.

"By that point, I'd been working as an army guard very close to the Shuvu Banim Yeshivah in the Old City for 13 years already, but I had no idea the yeshivah even existed. It seems as though the Rav must have been hiding himself from me.

"So, I went to ask Rav Tzanani what I should do next, now that I knew all this, because I'd spent all my life trying to get close to the true purpose of life, and now it seemed as though I still had a way to go before I actually found it. Rav Tzanani told me, 'Do some *hisbodedus* and ask *Hashem* to show you who the *Tzaddik* of the generation is in our times, and that the *Tzaddik* should reveal himself to you and give you a message, or something similar,' he advised me.

"So for the next three months, I did a lot of *hisbodedus* only about this subject. I literally spent hour after hour talking to God about it. '*Hashem!* Show me the right way to go; show me the right path!' I begged Him. 'If there's really someone like this, then how come I'm not worthy of knowing who it is?' I was literally pleading with God like that every day, until midnight one Shabbos evening when I literally threw myself down on the ground in the field where I was doing *hisbodedus* and said to *Hashem*, 'Why is my life like this? If there really is a true *Tzaddik* like they're telling me, then I also want to see him!'

"Suddenly, it started pouring really hard, without stopping—and that's when I suddenly saw him, Rav Berland, as though he was literally standing right next to me, wrapped in his *tallis* and doing some unusual motions with his hands. I'd never seen the Rav before, and I had no idea who he was, so I was pretty scared. I called out, 'Mister, what do you want from me?' but he didn't answer.

"As you might expect, the very next day, Sunday, I went to find Rav Tzanani and told him the whole story about what had happened. He tried to double-check that I hadn't just seen a picture of someone or something, but I was adamant about what I'd seen and how 'real' the whole thing had felt. Rav Tzanani asked me, 'Would you recognize him again if you saw him?' When I answered in the affirmative, he told me, 'Well, if that's what you say, then meet me at the Breslov shul on Ido Hanavi Street next Shabbos.'

"The next Shabbos, I walked all the way from Katamon to Ido Hanavi, and I got to the synagogue around 4:30 a.m. As soon as I walked in the door, I saw that Rav Berland was waiting for me, and was making the same unusual motions with his hands that he'd done during my *hisbodedus* session in the field. I suddenly got it: 'Wow! It's the same Rav that I saw in the field!!' From 4:30 a.m. until 2 p.m., I didn't let the Rav out of my sight.

"From that time, I came to the yeshivah of the Rav, the Shuvu Banim Yeshivah, but it was only after another 15 years had elapsed that I actually spoke to the Rav about that first meeting. All the Rav said in reply was, 'What amazing miracles you're experiencing!' and then proceeded to change the subject.

"Indeed, I have seen many amazing miracles and wonders from the Rav, especially in connection to when I was going out to help the masses and do outreach work," Rav Thaler continues. "I saw many, many people get helped as a result of the promises I made to them in the name of the Rav."

HIDING THE MIRACLES

"One time, one of my friends asked the Rav, 'Why are you doing all these open miracles for people who are far away [from *mitzvah* observance and Torah], while with the people in the yeshivah, everything is hidden?' The Rav replied, 'You, I already brought close, but they are still far away, and they haven't gotten here yet.'

"One of my friends told me that in the days when he was first considering doing *teshuvah* and becoming more observant, he went to visit one of the *Admorim* and wanted to kiss his hand [a normal custom among *Sephardim*], but the *Admor* pulled his hand away and put on a glove. My friend was so hurt, he wanted to turn his back on *Yiddishkeit* completely, but a friend of his persuaded him to come with him to Holland to visit Rav Berland. As soon as Rav Berland saw him, he gave him a big hug and gave him a very warm, loving reception.

"This friend told Rav Berland that the other *tzaddikim* could see our faults and blemishes, but that only Rav Berland—because of his enormous love for *Am Yisrael*—could come close to us even without 'wearing his gloves', and that love could fix all of the blemishes," ends Rav Thaler.

PREVENTING A POTENTIAL SUICIDE

Rav Berland at the Dirshu siyum, engrossed in his holy books. (The Rav is at the very bottom right of the picture.)

The following story was told over by Rav Yaakov Amzaleg:

"The grandchild of the Klausenberger Rebbe, *zt"l*, married the grandchild of Rabbi Moshe Halberstam, *zt"l*, and the whole Orthodox world, including all the Rebbes and Rabbis, came to the wedding, including the Rav.

"At this time, I was teaching at one of the yeshivos, and I had a student there who was a *baal teshuvah*, who was suffering a great deal from all the errors he'd made in his past. He was being plagued by negative thoughts that didn't give him any respite.

"He used to tell me what he was going through, and I'd try to give him some *chizzuk*, but on the day that this wedding was taking place, he came to me and told me he just couldn't continue anymore. The *yetzer hara* was chasing him nonstop, and he'd reached the end of his rope. He told me, 'I want to kill myself.'

"I told him, 'Look, I can't help you any further, but I have an idea for you: The only way to get past this is to go to Rav Berland. He's the biggest expert in things like this.' The student agreed to see him.

"But we still had to solve the next problem, which was how to arrange a meeting between the two of them. At that point, the Rav was very isolated, and it was very difficult to get in to see him. So I told the student, 'There's a big wedding tonight that the Rav is definitely going to attend. Go to the wedding, and hopefully you'll be able to grab a few words with the Rav there.' He agreed to go.

"The Rav was sitting in the middle of the very long table of Rabbis and Rebbes, and there were a lot of people between my student and the Rav, including rabbinic attendants and ushers. But this student didn't let anyone put him off, and he patiently worked his way past everyone until he managed to get to the Rav, where he grabbed his hand and quickly told him why he'd come to see him."

"YOU'RE BETTER THAN ALL OF THEM!"

"The attendants were trying to prevent him from talking to the Rav, but when they saw he'd already got close to him, they decided to let him be, as they didn't want to make a big scene. If they'd known what was about to happen next, they would have probably thrown the student out immediately, but *Hakadosh Baruch Hu* is the One who runs the world.

"The Rav listened to the young man and heard everything he had to say. When he'd finished, the Rav squeezed his hand, took off his glasses, and then gestured to the whole table of dignitaries seated around him, before saying, 'You see all the Rabbis here? You're better than all of them!'

"And the Rav didn't say this quietly; he yelled it at the top of his lungs, before continuing, 'All of them [referring to the Rabbis] don't even come up to your shoelaces!' Needless to say, there was a very awkward silence for a few seconds after this happened, as everyone turned to look at the Rav. Even the people who'd been dozing off woke up to see what all the fuss was about.

"After all, we're talking about a table full of Rabbis and Rebbes, so clearly some *derech eretz* was required... Who was yelling things like that, so loudly?! Everyone looked at the Rav in astonishment.

"But the Rav didn't pay them any attention, because he knew that these Rabbis weren't about to go and commit suicide, God forbid. If it was embarrassing for the Rav, or making an unpleasant scene for him, what did he care? In fact, that would even be an extra bonus for him, if he could also manage to humiliate himself publicly...The most important consideration for the Rav was that there was a Jew standing in front of him who needed to be rescued.

"The Rav hugged the young man and gave him a kiss, and thus they parted.

"When I saw my student a little while after that happened, he was floating on air. He told me so enthusiastically, 'The Rav told me that I'm worth more than everyone else put together!' He was still floating on air for a few weeks after it happened, and that's how the Rav managed to disconnect him from his very negative, even suicidal, state of mind.

"He strengthened himself, got married, and today he's the father of a big family of *bnei Torah* in Modiin Illit. Every time I see him, he tells me again how all his success in life is because of Rav Berland," concludes Rav Amzaleg.

HELPING A *BAR MITZVAH* BOY

"The Rav is devoted to everyone's well-being," begins Rav Shalom Fuchs. "When I was a young boy, just 13 years old, I came to the Rav with a whole bunch of questions. I used to have a friend who would give me a lot of encouragement in my *avodas Hashem*, and one day he just got up and left, and that really hurt me. So I came to tell the Rav about it.

"At that time, we were praying in the house of Yaakov Cheshin on Shabbos. As soon as I told the Rav what happened, he started looking all over the *shul* for my ex-friend, to tell him that he should befriend me again. He was looking for this friend for 20 minutes, and all for a simple young 13-year-old who had no other connection to him whatsoever."

THE IMPORTANCE OF VISITING *KIVREI TZADDIKIM*

As well as its commitment to high-level Torah learning and its reputation for lengthy prayers and *hisbodedus* sessions, another practice the Shuvu Banim Yeshivah became known for was visiting the graves of holy *tzaddikim*, particularly in *Eretz Yisrael*.

Again, this was something that was heartily encouraged and emphasized by the *Rosh* Yeshivah, Rav Berland, who continued to lead by example, spending a lot of his own time visiting the different holy tombs in *Eretz Yisrael* at a time when the practice of going to holy graves wasn't widespread. When the Rav would leave the yeshivah to go and visit a holy tomb, literally dozens of cars would follow after him in a convoy, and this is how the practice of going to the graves of holy people become more widely established.

Rav Berland also composed a number of specific prayers to be said at practically every holy grave in the country. Many of these prayers are now hanging next to the graves they were written for.

Rav Moshe Shavili was the Rav's driver for two years. He recalls: "Every Tuesday, I'd drive him to *Kever Shmuel, Kever Dovid* and then to Chevron—and the whole time, the Rav would have his *Likutei Tefillos, Likutei Moharan* and *Sipurei Maasios* with him while we were driving. The Rav always spoke Torah in the car. He didn't miss a single week: Every week we'd go to different holy places, to different *kivrei tzaddikim*, or I'd take him to the *Kosel,* and the Rav would just pray there for hours."

On one of the occasions when Rav Shavili drove the Rav to *Kever Shmuel Hanavi,* on the outskirts of Jerusalem, they were confronted by two Arabs who'd illegally taken over the tomb and wouldn't let anyone in unless they'd pay them money. "These Arabs would lock the place up after 6 p.m. and wouldn't let anyone in," remembers Rav Shavili. "So some Breslov students came with hammers and big metal chains, and they broke the doors down."

The two Arabs started trying to fight the students off, and were then joined by many more Arabs from the neighboring houses. "They started fighting and hitting each other, and then the police came and it was a big mess," says Rav Shavili. "But from that point on, there were no doors on the tomb and people could go and pray there whenever they wanted."

On another occasion, Rav Shavili joined a group of some of the Rav's first students to go to the tomb of Reuven Ben Yaakov, on the way to Rishon Letzion. "There was a lot of sand there, and Bedouins had set up their tents and were camping right next to the grave," he says. "The Bedouins had a lot of dogs, and each dog was as big as a horse. They set their dogs on us and everyone got very scared and started scrabbling around to find sticks to try to fight the dogs off. But then Rav Berland told everyone to stop and said the dogs wouldn't do anything to us. He went out in front of the other men and started walking toward the dogs. He just shooed them away—"Go away!"—and miraculously, the dogs turned around and ran off," he recalls.

TIKKUN HAKLALI **AT** KEVER NOSSON HANAVI

For many long years, Rav Berland enjoyed very good relations with the local sheikh of Halhul, a town near Chevron. The tombs of the biblical prophets Gad and Natan are in Halhul, now located at the center of a local mosque.

Over the years, Rav Berland and his students would visit Halhul to pray at the *kever*. Usually, they would start praying outside the mosque, and then after a few minutes the sheikh would arrive and let the group in to the tomb himself. One time the sheikh came into the mosque in the middle of the Rav's prayers, and the Rav hugged him and told him, "We are brothers." The sheikh replied, "Yes, you are always welcome here."

On one of Rav Berland's earlier visits to Halhul, the sheikh didn't appear when the Rav was waiting outside the mosque, so after waiting a few minutes, he and his students climbed in through a window.

His students were shocked to see that the mosque was full of sleeping Arabs. Evidently, their visit had coincided with some sort of festival. What was even more shocking was that the Rav just continued to pray there for a full hour, as was his custom, while many of his students were half paralyzed with fear that the Arabs would wake up and attack them.

Miraculously, not a single Arab woke up the whole time they were in the mosque, and the Rav and his students were able to leave in peace.

After the Oslo Accords, things started to change and the town became increasingly radicalized, until it developed a reputation as a Hamas town. But the Rav still continued to pray there and to take his students to pray there, often with enormous self-sacrifice. After Rav Berland moved to Beitar Illit in 2012, he developed the custom of making nightly trips to both Chevron and Halhul -and a large convoy of cars would follow after him.

On one of his last trips out to Halhul, the Arab residents decided to try to put an end to these nocturnal visits, and set up an ambush around the mosque in anticipation of the Rav's nightly visit to the grave of Gad and Nosson. As Rav Berland and the group of people that was with him were leaving, the Arabs started tipping massive stone building blocks off their roof, and onto the Jews' cars below. Many of the cars were literally crushed by the weight of these massive stones, but miraculously no one was hurt.

Despite the open miracles, the IDF—which until very recently continued to oppose visits for Jews to the holy tombs in Halhul—was distinctly unimpressed with this turn of events.

Later, Rav Berland commented that everything that occurred—that they managed to pray at the site and leave unscathed—was in the merit of the *Tikkun Haklali* they recited at the gravesite.

THE RAV'S FIGHT FOR *KEVER YOSEF*

The Rav's fight to reopen the path to Rebbe Nachman's tomb in Uman during the 1970s and 1980s is well documented in earlier chapters. But while he was reopening the path to Uman in Russia, back in Israel he was also fighting the Israeli government to prevent them from closing access to many of the Jewish holy places located in the West Bank, particularly *Kever Yosef*.

Rav Berland had made it a regular practice to visit *Kever Yosef* after the site was recaptured from the Jordanians in the Six-Day War in 1967. "I would go there every day," recalls the Rav. "At that time, there was a tremendous fear of the Jews. I lived in Bnei Brak then, and I'd get a bus on Jabotinsky Street to Kfar Saba that would cost me three liras. Then, I would continue on to the *kever* of Binyamin ben Yaakov, and I would spend an hour alone there, before traveling to Kalkilya by taxi with seven Arabs. [The Arabs] often gestured to me as though they wanted to slit my throat, and I did it right back to them."

The Rav continues: "I would walk for five minutes by myself through the *Kasbah* in Shechem, until I reached the *kever* of *Yosef HaTzaddik*. Today, I come and I see people with M16s, and I ask them why they need them..."

When Rav Yitzchak Ginzburg opened the Od Yosef Chai Yeshivah at the site of Yosef's tomb in the 1980s, it looked like the Jews were back in Shechem to stay. The site was formally turned into a synagogue in 1997, when *sifrei Torah* were brought in.

The Israeli government, however, didn't see that the spiritual benefit of enabling Jews to regularly visit these tombs far outweighed the practical risks involved in securing these areas from hostile Arabs.

KEVER YOSEF AND THE OSLO ACCORDS

On December 12, 1995, control of the city of Shechem (Nablus) was handed over to Yasser Arafat's Palestinian National Authority as part of the infamous Oslo Accords, but the State of Israel was meant to retain control of several religious sites now under PA jurisdiction, including *Kever Yosef*.

Under Oslo, the agreement made was that: "Both sides shall respect and protect the religious rights of Jews, Christians, Muslims, and Samaritans concerning the protection and free access to the holy sites as well as freedom of worship and practice."

But that's not exactly what happened. On September 24, 1996, the Palestinians initiated a wave of riots throughout the West Bank to protest the opening of the new Western Wall Tunnels attraction in the Old City of Jerusalem. During the riots, six Israeli soldiers were killed at *Kever Yosef* and the local yeshivah located next to the tomb was ransacked.

KEVER YOSEF BECOMES A FLASHPOINT FOR PALESTINIAN TERROR

Although many Jews tried to visit and pray at *Kever Yosef*, the situation at this time was tense and complicated. The surrounding town of Shechem was now under full PA control—yet the Palestinian Authority proved time and again that they weren't interested in maintaining the safety of Jews at the holy sites under PA jurisdiction, though that was a clear condition of the Oslo Accords.

As time went on, *Kever Yosef* came under Palestinian gunfire, and was stormed by hundreds of Palestinians, prompting the Israeli army to retake partial control of the site. Thanks to Oslo, this ancient and important Jewish holy site effectively became too dangerous for Jews to visit.

Between 1999 and 2000, the IDF, Israeli Border Police, and *Shin Bet* asked the government to evacuate *Kever Yosef* and forbid Jews from visiting it—in violation of the access rights that had been negotiated as part of the failed Oslo Accords.

When the second Palestinian intifada started in September 2000, *Kever Yosef* was again one of the key flashpoints. A Palestinian mob broke into the deserted tomb and burned the adjacent yeshivah to the ground. The Palestinians also painted the dome of the tomb green as a defiant indication of their desire to turn *Kever Yosef* into a mosque.

SECULAR VS. SPIRITUAL

As the intifada continued, a large rift developed between the secular Israeli view and the spiritual/religious view of what should be done with *Kever Yosef*. After another Israeli border policeman died, the head of the IDF's southern command, Brigadier-General Yom Tov Samia, threatened to resign, and told then-Prime Minister Ehud Barak that keeping Israeli control over *Kever Yosef* was "patently illegal."

Yet the Oslo Accords clearly stipulated free and safe access for Jews to Jewish holy sites under PA jurisdiction. On October 7, 2000, Barak turned control of *Kever Yosef* over to the Palestinians. A few short hours later, the tomb was once again burned and pillaged by the Palestinians, and a resident of the nearby Jewish village Elon Moreh, Rabbi Hillel Lieberman, was murdered when he went to check on the damage.

The Palestinians continued the delegitimization of the tomb as a Jewish holy site which had begun years earlier by the secular Israeli politician Shulamit Aloni, and claimed that the site was a Muslim holy place with no historical connection to Judaism.

Rav Berland at Kever Yosef.

After intense international pressure spearheaded by the United States, which was concerned that turning *Kever Yosef* [LXI] into a mosque would spark outrage among the Israeli public and lead to abandoning the Oslo Accords, the green dome of the "mosque" was repainted white. But in the meantime, Jewish access to the site seemed to have permanently ended, at least as far as the secular politicians and IDF chiefs were concerned.

FIGHTING FOR THE RIGHT TO VISIT *KEVER YOSEF*

But Rav Berland and his students at Shuvu Banim, together with other Torah leaders like Rav Shalom Abergel, decided to fight back and keep visiting these holy places, no matter how dangerous they appeared to be.

LXI   In 1994, MK Shulamit Aloni, then-Minister for Culture and Education in Yitzchak Rabin's government, publicly claimed that *Kever Yosef* was only 200 years old, despite all the clear archaeological evidence supporting its antiquity.

They understood that Israel's greatest protection against Arab violence lay in prayer and maintaining a strong connection to the true *tzaddikim*. Rav Berland and many other spiritual leaders, including Rav Mordechai Gross, Rav Yitzchak Ginsburg, Rav Shalom Abergel and Rav Mor Golan, understood that if *Kever Yosef* or *Kever Rachel* were placed permanently off-limits to the Jewish people, as the Israeli government wanted, that would only worsen Israel's security problems in the long run.

The holy books[29] mention that, in the merit of the bones of Yosef (which were brought from Egypt), the sea split and the Jews were eventually allowed to enter the Land of Israel. Furthermore, it's only in the merit of Yosef's bones that the Jews can endure in the Land.

THE STUDENTS KEEP VISITING

Although the media and the Israeli government went to great pains to portray the Rav and his students as putting their own and the Israeli soldiers' lives at risk with their clandestine visits to *Kever Yosef*, in truth, the Rav prepared meticulously for every single visit to the site, just as he had when taking groups of *chassidim* into the USSR.

Any risk the Rav took was always calculated, prayed about, and double-and-triple-checked with *Shamayim*. Over the years, the students at Shuvu Banim knew that they could only go to *Kever Yosef* when specifically directed to do so by Rav Berland. On those occasions, the Rav always promised them that nothing would happen and that they would see open miracles—and indeed, they did.

The students also understood that, if they wanted to make the trip to *Kever Yosef* by themselves, i.e., not during times when the army was escorting the public into Shechem, they first had to ask the Rav's permission. Usually, the Rav would promise the students that they could make the trip safely and that nothing bad would happen. But there were times when the Rav specifically told his students *not* to go into Shechem alone. The only time a student from Shuvu Banim was seriously hurt going to *Kever Yosef* was when he disregarded a specific warning from the Rav to stay away.

By continuing to visit *Kever Yosef* and the other holy places in the West Bank, Rav Berland was simply complying with the stipulations set out in the Oslo Accords--and trying to ensure that the Jewish people wouldn't lose access to one of their holiest sites, dating back to antiquity.

KEVER YOSEF COMES BACK UNDER IDF CONTROL

In 2002, the IDF moved back into Shechem as part of Operation Defensive Shield. Rav Berland, his students, and the other Rabbis and visitors who had fought to maintain Jewish access, immediately requested the IDF to formally permit Jewish visits to *Kever Yosef* again.

As many of the Rav's students (and others, like the late Rav Shalom Abergel) were continuing to visit the site in any case, it can be assumed that the IDF found itself between a rock and a hard place. It reluctantly agreed to open the tomb to Jewish visits one night every month at midnight, with the aim of preventing more unauthorized clandestine visits.

If these "clandestine" visits hadn't been happening, it seems certain that *Kever Yosef* and many other holy Jewish sites would have been desecrated, turned into mosques, and placed permanently off-limits to Jewish visits without a peep of protest from the army or the government.

Indeed, a little while after the visits began, in October, 2002, the IDF again closed the tomb to Jewish visits. In 2003, the religious public began a new effort to lobby the Israeli government about the ongoing desecration and vandalization occurring at *Kever Yosef*, but the IDF shrugged the matter off, claiming that guarding the site would cost too much money.

In the meantime, *Kever Yosef* continued to be used as a garbage dump by the local residents of Shechem for the next four years.

EVEN THE MKs START TO COMPLAIN

The state of the tomb deteriorated so badly that even some Knesset members were appalled by the situation. In February 2007, 35 MKs wrote to the IDF, asking them to reopen the site for Jewish visitors. In 2008, another group of MKs wrote a letter to the prime minister, asking that the tomb be renovated.

They wrote: "The tombstone is completely shattered, and the holy site is desecrated in an appalling manner, the likes of which we have not seen in Israel or anywhere else in the world."

Initially, the Israeli government wanted the PA to cover the cost of the repairs. When that didn't happen (and the Palestinians sent some people along to burn tires inside the tomb, instead), the renovation work was finally carried out by Jewish workers, funded by anonymous donors.

It cannot be overstated how little the secular Israeli government officials and IDF chiefs valued some of Judaism's holiest sites.

REGULAR VISITS RESUME

In 2009, regular monthly visits to the tomb resumed under IDF protection. Rav Berland also instituted the custom of going to *Kever Yosef* on the night of *Yesod she'b'Yesod*, the 41st day of the *Omer*, each year. From humble beginnings, this annual visit has become a very popular event. In 2016, more than 3,000 people came to visit *Kever Yosef* on this night with the full support of the IDF. The visitors that year arrived on more than 60 buses, and included Rav Shalom Arush and the well-known *Litvish posek* Rav Mordechai Gross.

Thanks to the efforts of Rav Berland and many other individuals, visits to *Kever Yosef* are now becoming a mainstream event in the Jewish world.

THE FIGHT FOR ACCESS CONTINUES

Nevertheless, in the wake of continued Palestinian violence and vandalism at the site, the fight to save our Jewish connection to *Kever Yosef* and many other holy places continues even today.

On July 7, 2014, the Palestinians tried to burn down *Kever Yosef*, but were stopped before they could do so. The tomb was vandalized again during Chanukah 2014, and then on October 16, 2015, the Palestinians once again fire-bombed *Kever Yosef*, heavily damaging the women's section.

Two days later, on October 18, 2015, Rav Berland gave his students instructions to take paint and brushes and go clean up *Kever Yosef*. The group of 30 students arrived at the tomb at 2 a.m. They cleaned it up and painted it—before being noticed by the locals, who attacked them and left six of the group with bruises.

As the students had gone into Shechem without permission from the IDF, who were later called in to protect them from their Palestinian attackers, the IDF was very upset about the cost and manpower involved in their impromptu rescue operation.

Of course, the media painted the Rav and his students as crazy extremists who were endangering people's lives. That's the secular view. The spiritual view is as the Rav himself phrased it: It's not the IDF protecting these tombs; the tombs are protecting the IDF.

The day after this occurred, then-*Sephardic* Chief Rabbi of Israel, Rav Yitzchak Yosef, visited the tomb and ordered the site to be completely renovated after the destruction wreaked by the Arabs.

THE BRESLOV CONTROVERSY AGAINST SHUVU BANIM BEGINS

The yeshivah's arrival in Jerusalem marked a new chapter in the development of a wider Shuvu Banim community and a worldwide Breslov revival, which had been slowly gathering steam under Rav Berland's tutelage for many years. The move to Jerusalem's Old Quarter brought many of the Rav's students in much closer contact with the Breslov elders of Meah Shearim, and the more established old-school Breslov communities.

The pronounced culture clash between Rav Berland's formerly secular, often *Sephardi* "new" Breslovers and the sheltered, Yiddish-speaking Breslov community in Meah Shearim led to a number of difficulties.

Rav Berland's *baal teshuvah* students would eagerly join him for prayers in the Breslov *shul* in Meah Shearim, expecting more of the brotherly love, caring, spirituality, and acceptance they'd come to associate with Rav Berland's brand of Breslov—but unfortunately, they'd often find the opposite.

The extremists in the Breslov *shul* would yell at them, insult them, and even physically bar them from entering. More than one of the Rav's newly-religious students left the Breslov *shul* in tears, stunned at the hostile reception they'd been given by these Breslov zealots.

Rav Berland strengthened his students by repeatedly sharing Rebbe Nachman's teaching about the importance of accepting insults with love. He used to say: "When someone is putting you down it shows that *Hashem* has great mercy on you. It says in *Meseches Kallah* that a person must love those who chastise him. So love them! And despise those who honor you, because you don't need any honor. The people who are putting you down are giving you the greatest gift. If you only knew what they were giving you, you would kiss their feet and buy them gifts."

THE BATTLE FOR THE SOUL OF BRESLOV *CHASSIDUS*

Shuvu Banim's move to Jerusalem in 1982 really marked the beginning of the battle for the soul of Breslov *chassidus*. On the one side, there were the Yiddish-speaking Breslov extremists centered in the Breslov *shul* in Meah Shearim who wanted to keep Breslov small and exclusive, and free of *baalei teshuva*.

On the other side stood Rav Berland and his students, who tried to the best of their abilities to fulfill every word that Rebbe Nachman spoke.

Rav Mota Frank is a senior figure in the more established Breslov community in Meah Shearim, and was very close to Rav Levi Yitzchak Bender. He recalls of this time: "With my own eyes, I saw how many times they [the people who were 'anti' Rav Berland and his community] would go to Rav Levi Yitzchak's house and come to him in *shul*, to speak against Rav Lazer and his people.

"Rav Levi Yitzchak listened to them and listened to them, and then he said to me (and this is his exact wording): 'What do they want? I get to *shul* before dawn and who do I find there? Rav Lazer's people. Who goes to the field [to do *hisbodedus*]? Rav Lazer's men. Who do I meet in the *mikvah* before dawn? Rav Lazer's men. What do they want?'"

Perhaps, they wanted Breslov *chassidus* to stay small and effectively "dead." What they definitely *didn't* want was for Rav Berland to start bringing hundreds and thousands of outsiders in to Breslov.

THE TOSHE REBBE

As the controversy continued, one of the leading Breslov figures in America was contacted and asked to try and resolve the situation. He was extremely uncertain about whether he should get involved in the matter, so he went to see the Toshe Rebbe, Rav Meshulam Fish Halevi, *zt"l*, for advice. Without mentioning any details, he told the Rebbe that he'd been asked to urgently fly out to *Eretz Yisrael* in order to help a big Rabbi there with some sort of complicated issue, and he didn't know what to do.

The Toshe Rebbe pondered the matter for quite a few moments, and then asked, "Are you referring to the Rav who has a yeshivah in the Old City, very close to where the *Beis Hamikdash* used to stand?" The Breslov Rabbi hadn't mentioned which Rabbi he was referring to, or any other details, so he knew the Toshe Rebbe clearly had *ruach hakodesh*. He told the Rebbe, "Yes! That's the yeshivah and the Rabbi I was talking about."

The Toshe Rebbe leaned forward in his chair and told him, "Go, and God will be with you. You should know that the Breslover *chassidim* are the true *chassidim*! It's known that all the prayers of *Am Yisrael* ascend via the place of the *Beis Hamikdash*. But to our great sorrow, today the place of the *Beis Hamikdash* has been snatched by outsiders[LXII]. But you should know that every prayer of *Klal Yisrael* today is ascending via the yeshivah of Rav Lazer."

The Toshe Rebbe concluded: "Fly out to *Eretz Yisrael* and you'll see success, and you'll make a big *kiddush Hashem*."

Thanks to the pressure they came under from a number of leading Rabbis and spiritual leaders, the Breslov extremists in Meah Shearim really had no choice but to stop their open persecution of Shuvu Banim.

However, their hatred of the Rav and his students never really disappeared; it just went underground. As long as the Rav continued to be the leading light of Breslov *chassidus*, there was nothing much they could do to touch him. In the meantime, they would bide their time and wait for another opportunity to try to settle old scores. That occasion would only present itself some 20 years later.

LXII   Literally *chitzonim* (outside forces)

IDO HANAVI

s the new millennium dawned, it was greeted with a mixture of excitement and apprehension by the world at large, anxious to see whether mankind had finally arrived at that period of time known as the "End of Days".

Change was on the horizon—and nowhere more so than in the Shuvu Banim Yeshivah. After more than 30 years of selflessly working to bring tens of thousands of Jews back to their Jewish roots, Rav Berland was now the head of an organization that comprised a number of Talmud Torahs, *chadarim*, nurseries, boys' schools, girls' schools, *kollelim*, and seminaries in Jerusalem and many other locations around the country.

In October 1996, Rav Berland decided to move house from the Old City, and to take up residence in Hachomah Hashlishit instead, close to many of his followers and students. As a result of this move, the Shuvu Banim Yeshivah stopped holding its Shabbos prayers in the Old City, and started renting a hall in the Bet Yisrael neighborhood close to Meah Shearim instead.

Roughly a year later, a synagogue building was acquired on Ido HaNavi Street. From that time on, the Shabbos service was held there instead. The institutions for boys and girls all moved out of the Old City as well, and Shuvu Banim opened a new *smicha Kollel* in Meah Shearim which was headed by the Rav's son, Rabbi Nachman Berland, *shlita*.

While Shuvu Banim's Yeshivah and existing *Kollel* remained in the Old City, the Rav rarely visited between the years of 1996 and 2011. But he yearned to return to the Old City, as he himself expressed in a number of the prayers that he wrote at this time.

From the inception of the yeshivah, Rav Berland nurtured very high hopes for what he prayed to achieve with the Shuvu Banim community. Back in 1978, he'd told his first students: "The main reason I'm opening this yeshivah is to have a yeshivah that's full of tremendous unity (*achdus*), so that we can work to bring the redemption. God forbid, if we won't have unity in our yeshivah, then we won't accomplish anything!"

As Shuvu Banim continued to grow, turning out more and more Rabbis, spiritual leaders, and kosher Jews, and bringing more and more families back to the faith of their fathers, the *sitra achra* set its sights on destroying the sense of unity and *achdus* that the Rav had worked so hard to instill within the Shuvu Banim community.

With great cunning, the *sitra achra* made use of the very same traits that Rav Berland had used to build the community—his complete self-nullification to God's will, his humility, and unconditional love for his fellow Jew—to try to destroy it.

THE YESHIVAH IS TAKEN OVER

A number of individuals rose to positions of authority within the yeshivah who started demanding large sums of money from anyone who wanted to speak to the Rav of ask for a blessing. Students were often demoted or promoted on a whim, and lists were drawn up to determine who would be allowed access to the Rav privately, who could attend the Rav's weekly *shiurim* and even who would be allowed to pray with the Rav on Shabbos.

The Rav and his family were greatly pained by these developments, and begged the people responsible to stop, but in public, the Rav kept silent. He understood that on some level, he and his yeshivah had been given a spiritual test—and a great deal depended on the outcome.

The Rav became a virtual recluse in his home for more than ten years. He stopped *davening* with the Shuvu Banim community in the Old City. He barely gave classes or attended public events.

During this time, the security situation in Israel also began to worsen drastically, as the promise of "peace" offered by the Oslo Accords dissolved into the violence and murder of the Second Intifada, which began on September 2000 and lasted for six long, bloodstained years.

In the few classes that the Rav gave during this time he often said, "There are uprisings in Shuvu Banim, uprisings in the whole world." Then the Rav would allude to all the unpleasantness occurring in the yeshivah and explain cryptically: "Everything that's happening here is a puppet show."

From the Rav's words, many of his students understood that the awful, bizarre circumstances that had taken hold of the yeshivah and which were causing a huge split in the community were all part of a spiritual test that had been decreed by *Shamayim*.

STRIFE IN THE HOUSEHOLD OF THE TZADDIK

In *Sichos Haran*[30] (translated into English as "The Wisdom of Rebbe Nachman[LXIII]"), Rebbe Nachman wrote the following:

"The world is full of strife. There are wars between the great world powers. There are conflicts within different localities. There are feuds among families. There is discord between neighbors. There is friction within a household, between man and wife, between parents and children.

"Life is short. People die every day. The day that has passed will never return, and death comes closer each day. But people still fight and never once remember their goal in life.

"All strife is identical. The friction within a family is literally a counterpart of the wars between leaders and nations. Each person in a household is the counterpart of a particular world power, and their quarrels are the wars between those powers.

"The traits of each nation are also reflected in these individuals. Some nations are known for anger, others for bloodthirstiness. Each one has a particular trait. The counterparts of these traits are found in each person of the household.

"You may wish to live in peace. You have no desire for strife. Still, you are forced into dispute and conflict. Nations are the same. A nation may desire peace and make many concessions to achieve it. But no matter how much it tries to remain neutral, it can still be caught up in war. Two opposing sides can demand its allegiance until it is drawn into war against its will.

"The same is true in a household. Man is a miniature world. His essence contains the world and everything in it. A man and his family contain the nations of the world, including all their battles...

"The strife within the household of *the Tzaddik* is also the aspect of war between nations..."

LXIII   Published by the Breslov Research Institute.

"It is also the wars between the *Shvatim* (Jewish tribes) who were fighting one with the other, Ephraim against Yehudah, etc. And when the *Moshiach* comes, all strife and wars will be abolished and there will be tremendous peace in the world, as it says, "The wolf will live with the sheep and the leopard with will lie with the kid...There will be no more injuring and no more destroying [in all My Sacred Mountain for the land will be filled with knowledge of *Hashem* as water covering the sea bed][31]."

"MAKE PEACE WITH THE PEOPLE WHO HAVE HURT YOU!"

At this very difficult juncture in Rav Berland's life, when the entire Shuvu Banim Yeshivah appeared to have been turned into some sort of spiritual "war game" being played out at Heaven's request, the Rav often spoke about how everyone needed to make peace with the people who hurt them.

After 10 years of struggling with what had become a very difficult and challenging situation within his own yeshivah, on Chanukah 5771 the Rav finally decided that a new and altogether more radical course of action would be required to bring peace and redemption to the world: humiliation and exile.

IT'S EASIER FOR *TZADDIKIM* TO STAY HIDDEN

On the last Shabbos that he spent in Jerusalem before leaving for the north of Israel, Rav Berland spoke about this theme at length. He said that *tzaddikim* don't need any students, and if they had the choice, they would choose to go to a faraway country, alone, where they could serve *Hashem* without any outside interference.

The following week, the Rav began his exile from Jerusalem, which took him first to the North, and then to Beitar Illit and other places in Israel, before he left the country completely and went into exile in Morocco, Zimbabwe, Holland, and South Africa.

THE RAV LEAVES JERUSALEM

After he left Jerusalem and went up North near Tiveria for a few weeks, the Rav called some of his closest students and described some of his feelings about what had occurred over the past ten years. When he saw one of his students pushed away by the guards when trying to get close, it had caused him great anguish and complete physical breakdown, which in turn had led to him being admitted to the hospital. Here are some of his words (transcribed from a recording of the phone call): "After I ended up being admitted to the hospital three times in just four weeks... after I saw that this is now a situation of *pikuach nefesh* and that I was on the cusp of a complete physical breakdown, I decided to leave [Jerusalem]...

"It pains me to leave my family and especially my beloved wife, beloved children and my beloved grandchildren. But [understand] I left because I care for them, I care for my son that he should have a father, and for my grandson that he should have a grandfather. When I used to leave my wife for long periods of *hisbodedus* I would say to her that I left in order to bring you back a husband who is a *Rosh* Yeshivah, so now I left in order to bring you a *Rosh* Yeshivah who is alive, not a *Rosh* Yeshivah who is in the hospital every two weeks, and who every three or four days has a heart attack (God forbid). I don't want them to eulogize me in the newspaper, saying what a holy person I was, so I decided to lengthen my days...

"Now I'm in the North doing *hisbodedus* and going to *kivrei Tzaddikim*. I wish you could all be here with me. I learned more Torah on one Shabbos [up North] than I learned in almost all the last ten years...If I can't return to Jerusalem, where the threats against me are very serious and terrible; I can't go into details about them here, but the threats being made against me are increasing each moment. The situation in Jerusalem is only getting worse with each passing moment, so there may be no choice except to reopen the yeshivah in the Galilee; if the terror continues so we'll build a yeshivah here so we can all be together, and serve *Hashem*, a yeshivah that will accept all different kinds of people, an elementary school for all different kind of boys, and a girls' school for all different kind of girls so that there will no longer be a possibility that a boy or girl is asked to leave or not accepted because they don't fit certain criteria and they have to go to a school for off-the-*derech* children. There will be a place in Shuvu Banim for everyone, for every type, so we can once again raise up the glory of Torah; that's the goal of Shuvu Banim, my goal all my life, to raise up and glorify the Torah...

"I want to make a new start now. The Rebbe [Rebbe Nachman] wrote in Lesson 64 that every *machlokes* leads to a new creation of the world...Everything that has been done until now, it's for the best... The Rebbe explains that it's forbidden to condemn anyone, or to put anyone down, or to take vengeance against them. Now, we're getting ready to create the world completely anew. Shuvu Banim is going to get a new lease on life...

"In the event that we won't be able to return to Jerusalem, no one needs to become discouraged by this—in fact, the opposite. Now that they've burned down the *Beis*

Hamikdash in Jerusalem [referring to the yeshivah], that fire is going to transform into the wings of the *Shechinah*. The redemption will come *davka* from Tiveria. The *Zohar* says that the redemption will come *davka* from the Galilee...

"It could well be that we will have to continue wandering. We learn in the *Gemara*, *Tractate Rosh Hashanah* that after they burned down the *Beis HaMikdash* the *Shechinah* experienced 10 different exiles... After they burned down the *Beis Hamikdash*, I started my exile in Jerusalem [by leaving the Old City]. Now, I'm already in my third exile.

"On Shabbos I was in Chanita, and now I am in Amirim, and I intend to continue wandering onward...we are living on wheels now...until we bring to fruition the vision that we had at the creation of Shuvu Banim, and that vision finally moves from potential to actuality, 'For My House will be called a House of Prayer, for all the nations[LXIV]...'

"We're now on the cusp of creating a completely new framework...Just strengthen yourselves, and pray for me, that all the different communities should be reunited, and through being unified the verse will be fulfilled: '[And it will happen at the End of Days:] The mountain of the House of *Hashem* will be [firmly established as] the head of the mountains and it will be exalted above the hills, [and all the nations will stream to it][32].'"

Rav Berland made these comments in late 2010. Even then, he made it clear to his followers that the long, hard period of exile was just beginning--and this was two years before any libels had been spread about Rav Berland 'escaping' from Israel because he was wanted by the Israeli police.

As the Rav clearly hinted then, the underlying reasons for his exile were more profound than most people could begin to grasp. He was involved in a spiritual war, and he was determined to make a historical change that he hoped would lead to true peace and the complete redemption of the Jewish people.

The Rav would return to these themes again and again over the coming years.

"STOP FIGHTING, OR MY EXILE WILL CONTINUE!"

A few weeks later, the Rav attempted to return to his community and yeshivah in Jerusalem—.but the infighting and arguments just continued as before. In lesson

---

LXIV   A quote from *Isaiah* 56.

after lesson, the Rav pleaded with his followers to pursue the paths of peace and unity, because otherwise, he warned them, his exile would have to continue, and he would have to leave the yeshivah and go to many other parts of the world.

He told his community on more than one occasion that if they couldn't stand up to the test they were being sent from *Shamayim*, to overcome the "winds of war" being sent down to the world and sweeten them by pursuing peace and unity no matter what, the Rav would end up having to travel from place to place until he finally ended up in South Africa...

In one such *shiur*, recorded when the Rav went to say *Tikkun Haklali* at *Me'aras Hamachpelah* in the week of *parashas Pekudei* 5771 (March 5, 2011), he said the following: "I can no longer come and pray in the synagogue on Ido Hanavi, and not in Shomrei Emunim... Just now, I called South Africa, I want to build a house with 100 floors, where each floor can house a thousand people; I want to buy 10 airplanes and distribute free flights [to there]; we'll organize flights for 4,000 people [to South Africa]. All of this is being recorded[LXV]...

"If everything passes peacefully, then tomorrow we'll return here. But if not—and there will be persecution and more intense blows--then we will need to wander onward."

At the time Rav Berland said these words, many people thought he was joking or exaggerating about having to be exiled to South Africa. With hindsight, it's obvious that the Rav could see what was coming--and also, what was necessary--well in advance of what actually occurred.

While the world believed that Rav Berland only came to South Africa because he was a 'fugitive from justice', the Rav's exile occurred for much deeper and more profound spiritual reasons, and had been planned for many years in advance.

Even at this stage, the Rav continued to call for his followers to make peace with their persecutors. Again, in a theme that Rav Berland has come back to time and again, he urged his followers to forgive and forget all the insults, humiliations and strife, in order to accomplish much greater things, spiritually.

LXV   Indeed, this recording is still extant.

THE WINDS OF WAR

In that same *shiur*, the Rav reminded his students that he'd predicted long ago that he would end up with just five students, just as Rabbi Akiva did some 2,000 years before him. The Rav continued: "We're already starting to see the light of *Moshiach*." Rav Berland then mentioned a few dates in the Jewish people's recent history, including 1948 and 1967, when the light of *Moshiach* was ready to come down to the world, but didn't because the Jewish People failed their tests and missed the opportunity. The Rav then continued:

"If we'd passed the test [referring to his yeshivah, Shuvu Banim], then by now we would have been able to revive the dead and see the rebuilt third Temple that would have descended from *Shamayim*."

But the test hadn't been passed, and a different type of spiritual rectification was now required.

THE PORTENT OF THINGS TO COME

All this occurred two years before the Rav actually made good on his words and left the country. It seems he was giving his followers a number of clues about what was to follow and why, to prepare them for the dramatic and often shocking events that were about to occur.

From the time the Rav first left his home in Jerusalem, he began to speak a great deal about the need to nullify the Heavenly decree of the next holocaust, and the looming threat of a nuclear Iran. It seemed as though the Rav's exile and the Iranians' threat to drop a nuclear bomb on the Jewish state were all connected. But how?

THE KING OF PERSIA AND
HARSH DECREES

In a midrash from the Yalkut Shimoni (Yeshaya 60) it says the following:

"Rabbi Yitzchak said: The year that Melech HaMoshiach will be revealed, all the kings of the nations of the world will provoke each other. The king of Persia will threaten the king of Arabia and because of this the king of Arabia will go to the king of Edom for advice.

"Afterwards the king of Persia will destroy [most of] the world. The remaining nations will be hysterical and frantic and fall on their faces and will be seized as if by labor pains.

"And the people of Israel will be frantic and hysterical and they will say, where will we come and go? Where will we come and go? And Hashem will say to them: Do not fear, My children, do not fear. All that I have done, I did only for you. Why are you afraid? The time for your redemption has come!"

BEFORE *MOSHIACH* COMES, ALL THE NATIONS OF THE WORLD WILL PROVOKE EACH OTHER

These words were spoken by Rabbi Yitzhak and recorded in the *midrash* 2000 years' ago, but in 2013, the same year that Rav Berland left *Eretz Yisrael* to go into exile abroad, it seemed as though the words of this *midrash* were materializing before the world's eyes. Iran—the "king of Persia"—was continuing its plans to become a nuclear power, while wars and terrorist attacks continued to explode in all parts of the globe. By mid-2013, reports started to circulate that at least 12 more Arab nations, all sworn enemies of the Jewish people, had also begun to develop nuclear energy programs.

In the *Gemara* in *Maseches Sanhedrin* it states that the war of Gog and Magog will coincide with the *Shemittah* year that occurs every seven years in *Eretz Yisrael*, where the land is left to lie fallow. As the next *Shemittah* year, 5775, approached (beginning September 25, 2014), all the signs seemed to be pointing to a terrible war looming on the horizon, with Israel caught squarely in the middle.

HOW TO STOP THE DECREE OF DESTRUCTION

Rav Berland once explained that, before the time of the Second World War, there was a Chassidic Rebbe in the Jewish world (whom the Rav actually named) who could have stopped the terrible decree of destruction that subsequently materialized into the Holocaust. How could this Jewish leader have done that? The Rav explained that if he had willingly agreed to the terrible criticism, public humiliation and shame that would accompany being falsely accused of adultery and other immoral behavior[LXVI], the decree of destruction would have been overturned.

Sadly, the Rebbe in question didn't have the strength to endure this terrible test and thereby sweeten the judgments then hanging over the Jewish nation. When the Germans subsequently rose to power, the destruction of European Jewry was almost total. The Rebbe himself gave his life to sweeten the judgments as he perished in the holocaust. But had he taken upon himself the terrible humiliation, he would have stayed alive and prevented the Holocaust as well.

A HOLOCAUST EVERY 70 YEARS

The Rav's grandson, Rav Shmuel Isaac Zucker, said: "My mother told me, in the name of her father, the Rav, that in the year 5742 the Rav told her that every 70 years there should be another holocaust[LXVII] but, through insults and humiliation, it's possible to sweeten this. He said that if there had been a *tzaddik* at the time of the Holocaust who would have been prepared to accept terrible shame and humiliation upon himself, the Holocaust wouldn't have occurred."

In 2005, when Ahmadinejad, the newly-appointed president of Iran, appeared on the international scene threatening more destruction to the Jewish people, Rav Berland and many other *tzaddikim* in the Jewish world took the threats of this "new Haman" very seriously.

Sixty-seven years after the Holocaust, in 2012, the Bushehr Nuclear Power Plant had reached its full capacity, and the Iranians were very close to obtaining a full-fledged nuclear arsenal. The *tzaddikim* decided that urgent action was required to hold off the evil decrees.

LXVI   As Rebbe Nachman explains in Lesson I:260 of *Likutei Moharan*.
LXVII   The idea that there would be another holocaust in roughly 70 years' time was also passed down in the name of the Chofetz Chaim.

THE SPIRITUAL REASONS FOR THE IRANIAN NUCLEAR BOMB

Before continuing with the story of Rav Berland's subsequent public humiliation and exile, we need to understand the spiritual context. The first question to ask is: Why was Heaven so angry with the Jewish people? What had they done to spark off such harsh decrees, including the worsening security situation in *Eretz Yisrael* and the looming threat of an Iranian nuclear holocaust, God forbid?

Someone once asked the Rav why *Moshiach* hadn't come yet, despite all the predictions over the last decade that his arrival was imminent. The Rav replied: "You're asking for *Moshiach* to come, but I'm fighting to cancel the decree of the nuclear bomb that has arisen because of the internet."

After three teenage boys were kidnapped and murdered in the summer of 2014, sparking an enormous barrage of rocket fire from the Gaza Strip and the IDF's Operation Protective Edge in defense, Rav Yaakov Edes stated that he'd found the following source in the *Ramchal*: "Because of the sin of *p'gam habris* (lit., blemish of the covenant, referring to immoral conduct), holy souls from *Am Yisrael* have to be killed by the hands of the non-Jews in order to rectify this blemish."

On another occasion, Rav Shalom Arush made the following statement on Radio Galei Israel: "The internet is bringing destruction to the world, enabling people to believe they can judge other people solely on the basis of the rumors they read online. But this is not the way that true judgment is ascertained, and this is not the true Torah way, to publicize rumors, and to spill another person's blood publicly, and to break every rule of *lashon hara* simply by pressing the 'send' button. And we're not even talking about all the other types of destruction that these computers are bringing to the world."

PERMISSION TO GO TO WAR

By 2013, the year the Rav left Israel and went into exile, a mountain of spiritual claims had been stacked up against the Jewish people, and the ministering angel of Yishmael was given permission to go to war against Israel.

So, the intifadas were quickly followed by rocket attacks from Hezbollah and Hamas, stabbings and murders, and then the biggest threat of all: nuclear attack. Rav Berland and our other holy leaders foresaw all this, even decades ago.

Back in the 1980s and 1990s, the saying "We want Moshiach NOW!" became very popular in certain sections of the Jewish community, and there were many who believed that *Am Yisrael* had already begun the process of *geulah* and redemption and that all that was left to do now was to wait to greet *Moshiach*.

Rav Shlomo Gefen is a long-standing student of the Rav. He recalls that when Rav Berland first heard this, the Rav commented, "It's not so simple to say that we've already begun the redemption process. Blood is still going to be smeared on the walls of our cities, and *Am Yisrael* still needs to undergo the selection and clarification process associated with the nuclear bomb."

The Rav uttered these chilling words many years before the intifada broke out in Israel. When the terrible reports started arriving of Arabs murdering Jews in the streets, it became clear that the Rav had foreseen the current wave of Islamic terror, with Iran firmly at the heart of it, many decades previously.

THE WORSENING SECURITY SITUATION IN ISRAEL: AT A GLANCE

1971-1982: Yasser Arafat's **PLO relocated to South Lebanon** from Jordan, and staged many attacks on the Galilee.

1978: Israel launched **Operation Litani,** the first large-scale invasion of Lebanon by the IDF, to try to expel the PLO. The PLO continued to make rocket and ground attacks against Israel.

1982: The **First Lebanon War** began on June 6, 1982, with the IDF once again attempting to expel the PLO from Lebanon and create an Israeli Security Zone. Israel was drawn into a long, protracted fight against many Lebanese Shi'ite Muslim terrorist organizations in Lebanon, as part of the Lebanese civil war. The biggest threat came from the newly-formed Hezbollah, which received training, weapons, and financial backing from Iran. Israel's departure from Lebanon in 2000 only strengthened Hezbollah.

1987-1993: The **First Palestinian Intifada** began, and continued intermittently for six years.

2000-2005: The **Second Palestinian Intifada** (aka the 'Al-Aqsa Intifada') began on September 29, 2000, and lasted for five years. Approximately a thousand Israelis were killed by Palestinian terrorists during this time.

2006: The **Second Lebanon War** began on July 12, 2006, sparked by a Hezbollah ambush and attack on two IDF Humvees patrolling on the Israeli side of the border with Lebanon. The attack left three soldiers dead and two Israeli soldiers abducted into Lebanon and later killed. Hezbollah received unprecedented support from Iran during this war, where it rained down hundreds of rockets on the North of Israel, causing many observers to dub this episode the beginning of the "Iran-Israel proxy conflict." About half a million Israelis fled their homes due to the rocket attacks and 165 Israelis were killed.

2008-2009: Operation Cast Lead (aka the Gaza War) began on December 27, 2008, and lasted for three weeks, in response to the ongoing rocket attacks against Israel coming from the Gaza Strip. This was the first time that Palestinian rockets reached Beer Sheva and Ashdod, forcing hundreds of thousands of Israelis into their bomb shelters. Thirteen Israelis died in the operation. The international community accused Israel of committing "war crimes" against the Palestinians during the conflict.

2012: Operation Pillar of Defense began on November 14, 2012, when the IDF killed the head of Hamas's military wing in Gaza, in response to more than 100 rocket attacks against Israel that had been launched in the previous 24 hours. The Hamas terrorists also tunneled into Israel to attack an Israeli military patrol jeep on the Israeli side of the border, leading to the abduction of Gilad Shalit into Gaza. Three Palestinian terrorist groups operating in Gaza fired more than 1,456 rockets at Israel during this time, including Iranian-made Fajr-5 rockets and Russian-made Grad rockets. Many Israeli cities came under rocket attack for the first time since the Gulf War in 1991, including Rishon Letzion and Tel Aviv. Miraculously, only six Israelis were killed. While the Iron Dome intercepted 142 rockets, in an open miracle another 875 rockets fell on open areas. The operation ended eight days later, with the Palestinian terrorist infrastructure in Gaza still firmly intact.

2014: Operation Protective Edge began on July 8, 2014, in response to the kidnapping and murder of three holy Jewish teenagers from the Gush Etzion area, and also in reprisal for ongoing rocket attacks against Israel from Gaza. The conflict lasted for seven weeks, and this time Hamas and the other Palestinian terrorist groups fired 4,564 rockets at Israel. While 735 rockets were intercepted by the Iron Dome, more than 3,000 rockets again fell on open land in Israel, in another open miracle. The Israeli government also destroyed 34 tunnels the terrorists had excavated between Gaza and Israel, to use in surprise terrorist attacks. A cease-fire was announced on August 26, 2014, shortly before Rosh Hashanah 5775 began.

THE *GEZEIRAH* THAT GOT CANCELED

Between the years 2011 and 2016, there were many other indications and statements from other leading figures and *tzaddikim* that the situation facing *Am Yisrael* was very bleak. One such person was the kabbalist and *Rosh* Yeshivah Rav Dovid Chaim Stern.

In 2014, Rav Stern told his attendant that in the previous year, he'd seen terrible decrees being made in *Shamayim* in relation to the destruction Israel's enemies wanted to visit upon the Jewish people. These decrees were so bad, Rav Stern had even started telling the people who were visiting him that they didn't need to worry about money anymore, and that they should start giving all their money away to *tzedakah* because very soon there would be such a period of chaos and destruction descending on the world that money wouldn't be worth the paper it was printed on.

Day after day, Rav Stern described how he could see these decrees gathering steam—until Rav Berland decided to take upon himself terrible shame and criticism, leave *Eretz Yisrael*, and go into exile abroad. Rav Stern then told some of his students that Rav Berland's self-sacrifice canceled these terrible decrees.

PREDICTIONS OF REDEMPTION

Another leading kabbalist, Rav Chaim Cohen Perachia (aka the *Chalban*, or Milkman), had also made a number of predictions that the redemption was about to begin.

When Operation Protective Edge began in July 2014, the Milkman made the following statement: "They informed me from Heaven that the redemption process started today. *Am Yisrael* is going to be redeemed. No one knows how long it will take, dear brothers, but know that the complete redemption process has begun, and because of this, the troubles are not going to cease in coming. However, you should know, brothers and sisters, that you now have the chance to get on the *geulah* train. May it be *Hashem's* will that we merit this, *amen.*"

Once, the kabbalist Rav Yehuda Sheinfeld, who is one of the *Chalban's* most senior students, told a gathering at the grave of Shimon *HaTzaddik* that one of the *Chalban's* students had approached the *Chalban* and asked him why the redemption apparently hadn't begun when he said it would.

"What can I do?" replied the *Chalban*. "Rav Berland is changing everything; he's disrupting the whole timetable! I saw the decrees that they were preparing in *Sha-*

mayim, but then the Rav took upon himself to go into exile, to flee to Morocco, and to make himself the target of harsh criticism and embarrassment. By doing so, he changed everything around in *Shamayim*. Now, it seems as though the redemption is going to come with sweetness."

RAV MORDECHAI ELIYAHU

Around this time, the following story involving the late Rav Mordechai Eliyahu, who passed away on June 7, 2010, was also widely publicized:

The wife of Rav Mordechai Eliyahu was with him in the hospital before he passed away, as he was slipping in and out of a coma. His wife asked him, "The Baba Sali promised you that you were going to live to see *Moshiach*. How can you leave the world now, when we didn't see *Moshiach* yet?"

Rav Mordechai Eliyahu replied, "You should know, *Moshiach* was already supposed to come; we have reached the End of Days[LXVIII]. But there are two *tzaddikim* who are pushing him off and preventing him from coming right now, in order to give all of *Am Yisrael* time to do *teshuvah*, so that *Moshiach* should come peacefully, and not with terrible bloodshed. Once *Moshiach* comes, they won't be able to do *teshuvah* anymore."

The Rebbetzin asked him, "Who are these two *tzaddikim*?"

Rav Eliyahu told her that the two *tzaddikim* were Rav Dov Kook from Tiveria and Rav Eliezer Berland.

DEATH, SHAME, AND EXILE

The Jewish year 5772 (corresponding to 2011-2012) had long been touted as a very likely date for the redemption of the Jewish people to begin. The late Rav Yitzchak Kaduri had publicly stated on a number of occasions that *Moshiach* would come during *Av* 5772[LXIX].

Rav Yitzchak Shlomo Zilberman had also publicized the tradition he'd received that the Vilna Gaon had hinted that 5772 was the year of *Keitz*, or End of Days, as had other descendants of the Vilna Gaon's students.

LXVIII   Rabbi Eliyahu is known to have possessed the "Geula Watch" of the Baba Sali, who said that when the hands on the watch pointed to 12 o'clock, it would be time for the redemption.
LXIX   Rav Kaduri stated this directly to Rav Yehuda Moalem and Rav Yosef Chai Zakkai.

Meanwhile, Rav Yosef Scheinberger told over the story he'd heard directly from Rav Grosnas, one of the Chofetz Chaim's students, that the Chofetz Chaim had said in the year 5692 that it wouldn't take more than another 80 years for *Moshiach* to come—again, bringing us to 5772.

Over the last decade, an enormous number of sources from the *Zohar* and other holy works, *gematrias* and anecdotal traditions were amassed, all pointing to the year 5772 as the year of redemption. As more and more of this information came to light and was publicized, the religious public waited with bated breath to see *what will be* in 5772.

THE BIRTH PANGS OF *MOSHIACH*

But before *Moshiach* could come and redeem the nation, the world would first have to undergo the difficult test known as the "birth pangs of *Moshiach*," including the War of Gog and Magog. These were known to be such difficult tests that some of the Sages of *Chazal* had said, "Let the *Moshiach* come, but let me not be there to see him![LXX]"

If the Jewish people would merit it, the *Moshiach* would come the sweet way. If they didn't merit it, *Moshiach* would come with enormous wars, suffering, and loss of life. As 5772 steadily approached, it seemed increasingly clear that *Moshiach* was only going to come with tremendous pain and suffering.

The magnitude of judgments looming over *Am Yisrael* were so enormous and so imminent, particularly in relation to Iran's nuclear program, that many of the nation's leading kabbalists and Rabbis began to issue detailed warnings about the terrible events they could foresee in the near future.

Against the backdrop of Arab hostility and violence, religious persecution within and without Israel's borders, and the terrible hardship and suffering that so many members of *Am Yisrael* were experiencing in their own private lives, the great kabbalist Rav Dov Kook from Tiveria made a Heavenly agreement with Rav Berland and Rav Elazar Abuchatzeira, grandson of the famous *tzaddik* from Netivot, the Baba Sali, regarding sweetening the harsh judgments facing the nation of Israel.

At that time, the nation of Israel was at a turning point: If the three *tzaddikim* did not find some way to sweeten the harsh decrees facing the Jewish people, then unprecedented death and destruction would be unleashed on the nation of Isra-

---

LXX   Other sages said: "Let me see him, even if I sit in the dung of his donkey."

el. Rav Kook and the other two *tzaddikim* knew that the only currency that would hold enough weight in the Heavenly Court to avert these harsh decrees was *mesirus nefesh*, or self-sacrifice.

Specifically, there were three things that could sweeten these judgments: death, shame, and exile. It's taught in Lesson I:260 of *Likutei Moharan* and also in *Bava Metzia* 58b that the embarrassment of losing one's good name and reputation is akin to dying. It's taught elsewhere that when a person has no home of his own and is forced to wander from place to place, on some level that's also considered akin to dying.

Each of the three *tzaddikim* agreed to make the ultimate sacrifice, for the sake of bringing the imminent redemption the sweet way. The Baba Elazar agreed to be killed *al kiddush Hashem*. Rav Berland agreed to be slandered, humiliated, and publicly shamed. And Rav Kook agreed to be exiled from his home in Tiveria.

Except, ultimately, Rav Kook realized that he was unable to stand up to the test. So, without hesitation, Rav Berland accepted the harsh decree of exile upon himself too. If *Moshiach* was indeed going to come in 5772, these three *tzaddikim* were determined to do everything in their power to ensure he would come only the sweet way.

LESSON 260, FROM *LIKUTEI MOHARAN*

In Lesson I:260 of *Likutei Moharan*, Rebbe Nachman describes how the one *Tzaddik* who takes upon himself exile, shame, and suffering will save the whole generation from suffering terrible things. And by doing so, this *Tzaddik* will enable the redemption to come with mercy, and without wars:

The name of a person is his soul, as is taught in chapter 59, as in the verse, "A living soul is his name" (Bereishis 2). Just as we find that a person can sacrifice his soul for the sanctification of God's name and thereby sweeten harsh judgments, so too can he sacrifice his name, that is, his reputation[LXXI]. Sometimes a vast number of Jews need to be killed, God forbid, in order to facilitate a certain spiritual unification.

A person can be famous but not really be famous—that is, everyone knows about him and speaks about him, but he is not really famous, since he is not

---

[LXXI]   We see an example of this after the sin of the Golden Calf when Moshe was begging Hashem to forgive the Nation; he said, "If you will not forgive them [on Your own], erase my name from Your book". In other words, the willingness of Moshe to sacrifice his name will be enough to forgive the entire nation".

respected at all. Or, there is the person who against his wish loses his fame, which is a loss of the name, which is the soul...

But there is one person who does this intentionally and consciously, surrendering his soul for the sanctification of God's Name. He surrenders his fame—his 'name,' corresponding to the soul—and on account of this, although he is renowned, he is not famous at all.

On the contrary, everyone talks against him, conjuring stories about him that he would never have dreamed of doing. He experiences this as if he was literally being killed. He does this all intentionally, because it is a literal self-sacrifice of [his] soul, for the name is the soul, as said, and he experiences it as death.

But in this way, he saves the Jewish people from what would have happened to them in order to facilitate this unification, as said, and by thus sacrificing his name, which is his soul, he spares them.

THE SELF-SACRIFICE OF THE *TZADDIKIM*

Shortly after these three *Gedolei Hador* made their Heavenly pact, the first act of self-sacrifice on behalf of the Jewish people occurred.

On the evening of July 28, 2011 (26 Tammuz 5771), Rav Elazar Abuchatzeira (who was also often referred to as the Baba Elazar) was stabbed to death in the waiting room of his yeshivah in Beer Sheva at the end of his routine visiting hours when members of the public would come to him for advice and a blessing.

His killer, A.D., was an outwardly observant *chareidi* man from Elad who had come to speak with the Baba Elazar many times before. Eyewitnesses said that the Baba Elazar seemed to have known in advance what was about to happen and rushed over happily to meet his attacker, who then drew a knife and repeatedly stabbed him.

The Baba Elazar was rushed by ambulance to the Soroka Medical Center in Beer Sheva, but was pronounced dead on arrival. The murder of this holy man shocked the nation to its core, and many thousands of people attended his funeral the following day, when he was buried on the Mount of Olives in Jerusalem.

Speaking a few days after the event, a distraught Rav Shalom Arush told the public that a kabbalist had called him up shortly before the Baba Elazar had been murdered and told him that a terrible thing was about to happen, but that it would bring the *geulah*, the redemption of *Am Yisrael*, closer. But the true story behind the Baba Elazar's murder would remain hidden for a little while longer.

THE RAV'S EXILE BEGINS

During Chanukah 5771 (December 2010), Rav Berland's exile from Jerusalem and the Shuvu Banim Yeshivah began. From Jerusalem, the Rav went up to the Galilee for a period of time before deciding to live in the city of Beitar Illit, located to the south of Jerusalem.

The first part of Rav Berland's deal to save the Jewish people had been set in motion, and over the coming years, his exile would take him from Israel to many different locations, including Morocco, South Africa, and Holland.

The next part of the deal—being publicly shamed, insulted, humiliated, and losing his good name—only began a little while later. The second volume of this book will introduce the different groups of people who were persecuting the Rav, and the different motivations they had for doing that. But the most important thing to remember is that *Rav Berland himself agreed to be shamed and exiled, in order to atone for the Jewish people and bring the redemption the sweet way.*

Even many years ago, he knew that he would be shamed and exiled, and spent a lifetime preparing himself—and his yeshivah—to pass the test.

WHAT THE *TZADDIK* TAKES UPON HIMSELF, TO ATONE FOR THE GENERATION

On many occasions before his exile and persecution began, Rav Berland publicly spoke about how the *tzaddikim* were obliged to take upon themselves difficulties and suffering, and to travel all over the world from place to place, to return all of *Am Yisrael* to the path of Torah observance and belief in *Hashem*.

He explained that the *tzaddikim* want everyone to be "sealed in the book of life"—even the evildoers.

In *Likutei Moharan* Lesson 228, Rebbe Nachman teaches that, when *Hashem* sees a person who can bring the world to do *teshuva*, *Hashem* Himself makes sure that this person is constantly beset by *machlokes* so that he will never be at peace. This way, anyone who continues to follow this person will assuredly be doing it only from pure motives, and not to gain honor.

Elsewhere[33], Rebbe Nachman explained why the *Tzaddik* is subject to such harsh persecution and controversy. He likens the *Tzaddik* to a tree and likens *machlokes* to water, and explains that, just as a tree cannot grow without water, so too a *Tzaddik* cannot grow without controversy.

Speaking about the terrible slander and persecution he was enduring at this stage, Rebbe Nachman continued: "Believe me, if I wanted to I could end all the *mochlokes* against me, and there would not be a single person against me. But what can I do? There are levels that cannot be reached without controversy". Elsewhere[34], Rebbe Nachman explained that even people who didn't actually know him were against him, because the *Tzaddik* needs controversy even to this extent.

SUFFERING FOR THE SAKE OF THE WORLD

In Likutei Moharan 170, Rebbe Nachman explains a spiritual rule that whoever is causing another person to suffer is actually being raised up spiritually by the person he is attacking. While some people may suffer from their family members, neighbors, and business associates, Rebbe Nachman says that there is one great person who receives suffering from the entire world. And in this way, he raises up and protects the entire world.

Rebbe Nachman returned to this theme in many other lessons[35] and explained that when the *Tzaddik* sees all the suffering that the Jewish people are meant to endure because of their sins, he begs *Hashem* to bring the suffering upon him, instead. The people don't have enough *emunas Tzaddikim* to save them[36], so the *Tzaddik* of the generation has to subject himself to all sorts of abuse and shame. Essentially, this is what fixes the lack of *emunas tzaddikim* that is at the root of the problem.[37]

THE SECRET OF THE *ADMOR* OF BELZ

The book *Admorei Belz* contains the history of the *Admorim* of Belz. In that book, there's a story that was passed down the line of each of the *Admorim* of Belz, starting with the first Rebbe, the *Sar Shalom*, Rebbe Shalom of Belz, through Rebbe Aaron of Rokatch, until the current *Admor* of Belz, Rebbe Yissachar Dov.

Both the story and its moral were given over by the first Rebbe, who recounted that in a particular country the people decided to rebel against the king, and the king's minister of war escaped to another country with his soldiers. At the end of the war, this minister returned. And the moral of the story is that before *Moshiach* comes, there will be one Jew who will escape to a different country with his faithful students, and who will conceal himself with them. The first Belzer Rebbe, the *Sar Shalom*, then explained: "*Moshiach* will come in their merit."

Generally, Belz *chassidus* has not been known for occupying itself with teachings about *Moshiach*. Yet it seems the Belzer *Admorim* understood that before *Moshiach* comes, a holy Jew and his students would have to go into exile abroad, in order to break the forces of evil.

ACCEPTING AN INSULT LOVINGLY PROTECTS A THOUSAND JEWS

Over the years, Rav Berland also gave a number of talks about Lesson 260 in *Likutei Moharan*. The following excerpt comes from a *shiur* the Rav gave more than 20 years ago, where he described how accepting insults and humiliation with love could save the lives of thousands and even millions of people.

"The Rebbe says that, in the merit of those who accept upon themselves disgrace, people are saved from getting killed. It says in *Likutei Moharan* that when a person accepts an insult lovingly, he saves tens of thousands of Jews from getting killed.

"To accept an insult lovingly is the same thing as a person protecting thousands of Jews.

"It says in *Likutei Moharan* Torah 260 that when a person lovingly accepts insults and disgrace upon himself, it's the exact same thing as when a person dies for the sanctification of *Hashem's* Name. It's the exact same thing! When a person lovingly accepts insults upon himself, he can save the entire Jewish people.

"The Rebbe says that there are those *tzaddikim* who willingly and lovingly accept the insults that come their way, and there are those who are insulted against their will, and they also sweeten the judgments; they also save a number of people. But those who chase after insults, who are looking for people to insult them and disgrace them at every moment, and who are trying to give others a reason to disgrace them and insult them, these people are saving *all of Am Yisrael!* Not just hundreds and not just thousands, they are saving *all of Am Yisrael!*

"A regular person is afraid of getting insulted, because he doesn't know that through every single insult he merits rising up ten levels. The Rebbe brings here in Torah 260 that the greatest spiritual unification is when a person accepts insults with love. It's the same spiritual unification that can be achieved by dying to sanctify God's Name, but every time a person is insulted, it happens again [i.e., each fresh insult is considered a new 'death' and a new sanctification of God's name].

"The Rebbe tells us that there are many different levels. Some people don't want to be insulted but when they are, they don't answer back. That is also a level. But there are those who do all different kinds of tricks in order that they should be insulted.

"The students want an explanation! They ask, "Why are you bringing all this *machlokes* on yourself!? It's hard for us!" So [the Rebbe] says, 'It's your life insurance! It would be harder for you to be blown up in a terrorist attack or end up missing an eye, or who knows what else would happen to you."

"The big *tzaddikim* would seek different ways for people to insult them, any possible way that people should persecute them. That is how they save thousands and thousands, and cancel all of the decrees. They save the entire nation. This is why the *Zohar* says that the greatest thing is to die for the sanctification of *Hashem's* Name.

"And the Rebbe adds that this is what happens when a person takes all of the insults upon himself and does things in order that the disgrace should only continue. Even if people are saying things about him that he never did, and they are spreading a terrible blood libel against him, he accepts it even more joyfully.

"The *Zohar* says that the *tzaddikim* who take it upon themselves to die for the sanctification of *Hashem's* Name feel tremendous pleasure from doing this, as Rabbi Akiva did, whose flesh was combed with iron combs."

PRINT THIS TEACHING AND KEEP IT WITH YOU AT ALL TIMES

Over the years, Rav Berland repeated this lesson to his students many, many times, and they came to believe that the Rav was hinting to them about future events. On one occasion in 2000 the Rav made his point even more clearly than usual.

On *Motzoei Simchas Torah* in 5761 (October 21st, 2000) Rav Berland addressed a large crowd of his followers who had gathered together in the main *Beis Knesses* for *N'eilas Hachag, Melaveh Malkah,* and *Hakafos Shniyos.* The *shul* was packed and there was barely any standing room as the crowds spilled out into the adjacent courtyard.

That night, Rav Berland again began to talk about Lesson 260 in Likutei Moharan[LXXII]. For more than an hour, he talked about the terrible bloodshed that the Jewish people had experienced throughout the generations and how the *Tzaddikim* had sacrificed themselves to sweeten the judgments and cancel the evil decrees.

He explained how the greatest *tzaddikim* would take tremendous insults and disgrace upon themselves in order to cancel the heavenly decrees. At some point during the *shiur,* Rav Berland told one of the people attending, a man who was in charge of printing the Rav's teachings and *tefillos,* to print Lesson 260 on pocket-size cards and distribute it among all the students of Shuvu Banim.

The Rav explained: "A time will come when we will all need to fulfill this lesson and it will help if each one of you reviews it daily, so that when he is insulted and persecuted he will remember to remain silent. For he is preventing a holocaust of mass bloodshed!"

ALL ITS PATHWAYS ARE PEACEFUL

One of the big questions that many people ask about the Rav's persecution and exile is why more wasn't done to publicly clear his name. There are a number of answers to that question, but the first and foremost is that Rav Berland took upon himself the harsh decree of being falsely accused of immoral behavior of the worst kind in order to ensure that he was giving Heaven its full measure.

At the beginning, when many notable Rabbis and spiritual leaders, including some of the Rav's more prominent students and supporters, wanted to make a concerted attempt to clear his name, the Rav forbade them from continuing. The following is just one of the letters that was publicized at that time:

LXXII   This lesson is still extant, and was recorded and transcribed.

Erev Pesach 5773

Anyone who disgraces the sages has no share in the World to Come, and he's included in the saying: 'He has disgraced a thing of Hashem. His soul will surely be cut off from his people.³⁸'

The terrible rumors that are going around are a terrible, painful thing that shocks the heart. They are alleging matters which cannot possibly be contemplated, and which are completely disconnected from reality.

People without any restraint on their brazenness and their arrogance opened a mouth full of haughtiness against the honor of his holiness, Rav Eliezer Berland, *shlita*, a true *talmid chacham*, one of the *Gedolei Hador*, who has nothing in his world except Torah, prayer and holiness, and who is very distant from mundane matters, and strengthens the community spiritually, sacrificing himself for every Jew, no matter who he is.

Woe to those who spill the blood of the *tzaddik* in public.

The teacher and guide of thousands of students and those who listen to his teachings, all of whom have complete fear of Heaven; many have been saved in the merit of his prayers.

Woe to us that this happened in our days, that this evil, accursed culture rose up and stands like Korach and his people to speak against a holy man of God and angel of *Hashem*, through whom many people did *teshuvah* and to whom no sin has come to his hand at all.

It's well known that we're talking about people who engage in lies and empty slanders, deliberate troublemakers who are trying to slander the Rav. It's said about them[39]: "Anyone who disgraces a *talmid chacham* does not have a cure for his wound."

They have no share in the World to Come, in keeping with the laws related to heretics and those who go against the Torah[40]. They need to be excommunicated, in keeping with the law that applies to a person who disgraces a *talmid chacham* (*Shulchan Aruch, Yoreh Deah* 334:43).

The public should be aware that these matters are completely false, and woe to anyone who so much as suspects that these falsehoods may be true, even in his heart, as the *Gemara* says in *Sanhedrin* 110: "Anyone who has a thought in his heart against his Rav, it's as though he has a thought against the *Shechinah*." And this is also brought as a law in the *Rambam* and *Shulchan Aruch*.

And woe to us that in the days preceding the festival of freedom and our redemption, instead of busying ourselves with the expected redemption of Jerusalem, we are tearing *kriyah* over the destruction we're witnessing, as it says: "Jerusalem wasn't destroyed except for the disgrace of *talmidei chachamim*."[41]

Hashem, the Good, will atone for all Israel.

This letter was signed by Rav Shalom Arush, together with the leading *poskim* Rav Meir Sirota and Rav Shechnazi.

When Rav Berland found out that Rav Arush was attempting to clear his name, he immediately called Rav Arush from Morocco and urgently requested that Rav Arush should stop what he was doing, and not get involved in the matter. Rav Berland explained that he'd worked very hard to procure all these insults, and he didn't want the whole thing to be ruined prematurely.

So Rav Arush's letter, together with many other letters that were written at the time by other notable Rabbis in defense of Rav Berland, were never published, and stayed hidden within the Shuvu Banim community.

THIS IS ABOVE NATURE

Right from the start of Rav Berland going into exile, Rav Dov Kook has been unstinting in his praise of him, with many of his statements being widely publicized in the Hebrew-speaking religious media. On May 29, 2016, Mor Devorah, one of Rav Berland's students, met Rav Kook. He explains what he was told:

"On Friday, *Erev Pesach*, I traveled to Tiveria in order to get a *brachah* from Rav Dov Kook. While I was there, I had the merit of accompanying Rav Kook to the grave of Rabbi Chiya, who is buried in Tiveria. While we were traveling together, I took the opportunity to ask Rav Kook about Rav Berland.

"I asked him, 'What does the Rav say about everything that Rav Berland is going through, all of the suffering that he's enduring?'

"He replied, 'Everything that's happening with Rav Berland is above nature. It's impossible to explain this. Everything that's happening with Rav Berland is above nature.' Rav Kook repeated himself twice, in order to make this point very clear."

The Rav had a job to do, to atone for the nation's sins, and he didn't want anything to jeopardize that, despite the enormous suffering he would endure over the next four years.

What sins was Rav Berland trying to fix on behalf of *Am Yisrael*? The list is long, and is topped by *p'gam habris*, *lashon hara* and *sinas chinam*.

In Part Two of this book you will read about the incredible story of the Rav's exile and humiliation, and the terrible personal suffering the Rav had to endure as a result of his holy desire to sacrifice himself for the sake of *Am Yisrael*.

While it's hard for us to fathom that a human being would willingly put himself through such difficult hardships, let's end Volume I by reminding ourselves of the words of Rav Shmuel Shapira: "This is not a man, it's a holy angel!"

GLOSSARY

Ahavas Chaverim	To love our fellow Jew (literally, to love our friends).
Achdus	Unity.
Admor	A Rebbe in a Chassidic court.
Al Kiddush Hashem	In order to sanctify God's name.
Aliyah	Literally, 'going up--both to the Torah, and to the Land of Israel.
Am Yisrael	The nation, or people, of Israel.
Am Ha'aretz	An unlearned man; a boor.
AN"SH	Abbreviation of *Anshei Shelomeinu*, or 'our people', used in reference to other Breslov chassidim.
Atik Yoman	A kabbalistic term referring to higher worlds.
Aufruf	A celebration held by the groom on the Shabbos before his wedding.
Aveira (pl: aveiros)	Sin, wrongdoing.
Avodah Zara	Idol worship.
Avodas Hashem	Literally, '*Hashem's work*'--refers to any holy endeavours, prayers, or mitzvos, etc.
Avodas HaTefillah	Literally, 'the work of praying'--refers to praying.
Avreich	A married student who's serious about learning Torah, often full-time.
B'Iyun	In depth.
Ba'al Teshuvah	(Plural: *ba'alei teshuva*) A person who returns to God (repents).
Baal Toke'iah	The one who blows the *shofar* in synagogue on the High Holidays.

Baalei Batim	Householders who work instead of learning Torah full-time.
Bachur (pl: bachorim)	An unmarried student who's learning Torah in a Yeshivah.
Baki	Knowledgeable.
Baraisa	*Tannaic* statements that are found in the Gemara, but that have a lesser status than *mishnayot.*
Baruch Hashem	*Literally*: Bless God. *Colloquially*: Thank God.
Bat Kol	A voice from heaven.
Bein Hazmanim	Literally, 'between times'--refers to the period between the 9th of *Av* and the first of *Elul*, when Torah institutions are closed for the summer.
Beis Din	A religious, Jewish court of law.
Beis Knesses	Synagogue.
Beis HaMikdash	The Temple in Jerusalem.
Beis Midrash	*Literally:* The house of learning. Colloquially, the yeshivah's main study hall.
Bentch	To bless--usually refers to reciting the grace after meals.
B'ezras Hashem	With God's help.
Birkas HaMazon	The blessing after meals.
Birkas HaShachar	The blessings recited in the morning, from the prayer book.
Bitachon	Trust (usually refers to trust in *Hashem*).
Bitul	Self-nullification.
Biyas HaMoshiach	Hebrew for: The coming of the *Moshiach.*
Bnei Torah	*Literally:* Sons of Torah. Refers to Torah observant Jews.
Brachah	A blessing.
Bris Mila	The circumcision ceremony typically held eight days after a Jewish boy is born.
Chadar (pl: chadarim)	Religious pre-school.
Chaburah	A Torah study group.

Chai V'kayam	A biblical expression usually used to refer to a dead *Tzaddik*, as being still 'alive' spiritually, and present and acting in the world.
Chalakah	A celebration where a three-year-old Jewish boy has his first haircut.
Chalban Chaim Cohen.	The Milkman. Referring to the kabbalist, Rav
Chas v'shalom	*Colloquially:* God forbid.
Chassid (*pl: chassidim*)	A group of religious, orthodox Jews who usually follow their own 'Rebbe'
Chassidei Breslov	(or *'Chassidim'*) Devout students or followers of Rabbi Nachman of Breslov.
Chassidus	The spiritual path originated by the Ba'al Shem Tov, and followed by his students, including Rabbi Nachman. A sect of Judaism which emphasises joy in its practice and teaches that every Jew, no matter his level, can get close to *Hashem*.
Chatzos	The time of *halachic* midnight.
Chavrusa	A one-on-one study partner, when learning Torah.
Chazal	The initial letters of the following expression in Hebrew: Chachmanu Zichronam L'vracha. *Literally:* "Our Sages, may their memory be for a blessing."
Cheshbon Nefesh	Making a self-reckoning or personal accounting of our own deeds.
Chessed	Kindness.
Chevrah Kaddisha	The organization responsible for preparing a Jewish body according to *halacha*, before burial.
Chizzuk	Strengthening, spiritual encouragement.
Chol HaMoed	Refers to the intermediate days between the first day (or days) of *Yom Tov*, and the last day (or days) of *Yom Tov*, for *Succos* or *Pesach*.
Chuppah	The marriage canopy used at Jewish weddings.

Chutz L'aretz	*Literally:* Outside the land. Refers to anywhere outside of Israel.
Chutzpadik	Brazen, shameless, cheeky.
D'Oraisa	Refers to a commandment or *mitzvah* that's derived directly from the written Torah, as opposed to the Oral Torah.
Daas	Godly awareness, knowledge or wisdom.
Daf Yomi	The daily study of a specific, set page of the Gemara.
Dam (pl: damim)	*Literally:* blood, or bloods. Refers to 'blood money'.
Darshan	Someone who gives over a Torah class or lesson in public.
Dati Leumi	*Literally:* National-religious. Describes a group of more modern orthodox Jews in Israel.
Davka	On purpose, specifically.
Derech Eretz	Good manners. *'Derech Eretz kadma le Torah'* literally means that you have to put practical considerations before learning Torah.
Dveikus	Closeness or clinging to *Hashem*.
Ein Od Milvado	*Literally:* There is only Him (i.e. God).
Eis Ratzon	A favorable time.
Emunah	Trust, faith, and belief in *Hashem*. *Emunas Tzaddikim:* believing in the words of our *Tzaddikim*.
Erev	*Literally:* The eve of. *Erev Shabbos* refers to the time before candle-lighting on Friday.
Etia HaMoshiach	The time of Moshiach.
Gabbai	A person responsible for managing the services within synagogue, and/or attending a rabbi or Rebbe, in a capacity similar to a private secretary.
Gadol HaDor	*Literally:* Great one of the generation. Refers to the senior, leading figure in the Torah world.
Galus	Exile.
Gaon	Torah genius.

Gashmiyus	Materialism, materiality.
Gedolim	*Literally:* Great ones. Refers to the leading Torah personalities of a generation.
Gehinnom	Purgatory.
Gemilus Chassadim	Acts of kindness, good deeds.
Gemach	A free loan fund for money or other items.
Geula	Redemption.
Gog and Magog	The last war that's meant to occur at the End of Days, ushering in the time of *Moshiach*.
Hachnassas Orchim	The *mitzvah* of hosting guests.
HaKadosh Baruch Hu	*Literally:* The Holy One, blessed be He. Another term for God.
Hakafos Shniyos	Referring to the custom to dance with the Torah all night long on the night after Shemini Atzeres.
Hakaras HaTov	Gratitude.
Halachah (pl: halachos)	Jewish law.
Hashem	God.
Hashem Yisbarach	God, may He be blessed.
Havdalah	*Literally:* separation. The service performed at the conclusion of Shabbos, before returning to the mundane activities of the rest of the week.
Hilulah	Anniversary of a person's (usually a *Tzaddik's*) passing.
Hishtadlus	One's own personal or physical effort.
Hisbodedus	Personal prayer to God in one's own words.
Ibburim	Refers to containing sparks of a particular soul, or souls.
Kabbalas Shabbos	Welcoming the Shabbos.
Kapparah	*Literally:* Atonement. Often refers to a financial or material loss that occurs instead of something worse happening.
Kavanah	Intention.
Kedushah	Holiness.

Kehillah	Community.
Keitz	The end, usually specifically referring to the End of Days.
Kesubah	Marriage contract.
Kever	*Literally:* grave. Usually used when referring to the burial place of a holy person.
Kiddush Hashem	Something that sanctifies God's name.
Kiddush Levanah	The monthly blessing recited over the sighting of a new moon.
Kibbutz	An often secular agricultural settlement in Israel founded on socialist principles. *Kibbutznik:* Member of a *kibbutz.*
Kippah	Skull-cap.
Kisei HaKavod	*Literally:* The holy throne. Refers allegorically to God's throne in the Heavens.
Kivrei Tzaddikim	Plural of *kever Tzaddik*, or the grave of a holy, righteous person.
Kloiz	The main synagogue in Uman, originally built by Rabbi Nasan.
Korbanos	*Literally:* The Temple sacrifices. Here, it means the recitation of the sacrificial service in the morning prayers, in lieu of actually performing the sacrifices in the Temple.
Kosel	The wailing or Western wall of the destroyed Temple, that still stands in Jerusalem.
Kriyah	The Jewish custom of tearing the clothing upon being told of the death of a close relative, as a sign of deep mourning.
Kvitlach	Notes sent to a *Tzaddik*, requesting a blessing.
K'vod HaRav	*Literally:* The honor of the Rav. A respectful greeting offered to rabbinic figures.
Lashon Hara	Evil speech, gossip.
Likutei Moharan	The main work of Rebbe Nachman of Breslov.
Limmud Torah	*Literally:* Torah learning.

Lishmah	For its own sake, or for God's sake, without ulterior motives.
Maariv	The evening prayers.
Machlokes	Strife, trouble-making, discord.
Malach	Angel.
Maseches	Tractate--usually referring to the Gemara.
Mashgiach (also, *Mashgiach Ruchani*)	The spiritual guide of the yeshivah.
Masmid	Someone who is constantly engaged in learning Torah.
Masorti	Traditionally religious.
Mattan Torah	The giving of the Torah.
Mechitzah	The barrier between the men's and women's section of a hall or synagogue.
Megillah	Scroll.
Melevah Malka	*Literally:* The queen's meal. Refers to the meal that occurs after the end of Shabbos, to bid farewell to the Shabbos Queen.
Menahel	Head teacher.
Meraglim	Spies.
Meshugga, Meshugganer	Yiddish terms for craziness; a crazy person.
Mesirus Nefesh	Self-sacrifice.
Midda Keneged Midda	A measure for a measure.
Middos	Character traits.
Midrash	Stories and explanations from the Gemara and other holy books.
Mikvah	A pool of ritually pure water that cleanses a person from spiritual impurity.
Milah Deshtusa	*Literally:* Foolish words.
Milchama (pl: *milchamos*)	War, wars.
Minchah	The afternoon prayers.

Minyan	A quorum of at least 10 men required for Jewish communal prayers.
Mishnayos	Plural of *Mishna*. Refers to the *Tannaic* statements that are part of the Oral Torah.
Mitzvah	(plural: *mitzvos*) Commandment(s), good deeds.
Moranu	*Literally:* Our teacher.
Motzoei Shabbos	The night after Shabbos has ended, Saturday night after nightfall.
Navi	Prophet.
Ne'ilah	The final prayer service on Yom Kippur.
Neshamah	The Divine soul.
Netz	Sunrise.
Ovdei Hashem (also *'ovdim*)	*Literally:* Hashem's workers, people who are continually engaged in *mitzvos*, prayer, and learning Torah.
P'gam HaBris	*Literally:* A blemish in the covenant. Refers to physical immorality.
Parashah	Refers to the Torah portion for each week.
Parnassah	Livelihood.
Pashut	Simple, in all simplicity.
Pasul	*Halachically* invalid / not kosher.
Payos	Side-curls.
Pidyon HaKlali	The general redemption payment which sweetens all the judgments over a person. *Pidyon HaKollel:*
Pidyon Nefesh	A redemption of the soul (a payment made to a *Tzaddik* that is used to redeem the person's soul from where it is trapped).
Pirkei Avos	Ethics of our Fathers - a collection of aphorisms from *Chazal*.
Poskim	*Halachic* decisors. A *psak* is a *halachic* decision or ruling.

Protekzia	Influence, nepotism (often a by-product of endemic corruption).
Prutah	A coin of very low value.
Rabbenu	Rabbi Nachman of Breslov (but also means 'our teacher' when used in reference to other Rabbis).
Ratzon	Will or desire.
Refuah sheleimah	*Literally:* A complete recovery, or healing.
Ribbono Shel Olam	*Literally:* Master of the World. Another term for God.
Rosh Yeshivah	The head Rabbi of a yeshivah.
Ruach Hakodesh	Divine intuition.
Ruchniyus	Spirituality, spiritual matters.
Samech Mem	Refers to the head of the forces of evil.
Sandak	An honorable position given at a *bris*, refers to the person who holds the baby.
Seforim	Holy Jewish books.
Segulah	A practice which results in a spiritual or material benefit, which is not logically derived.
Seichel	Wisdom, intellect, brains.
Seudah shlishis	The third Shabbos meal.
Shacharis	The morning prayers.
Shalom Bayis	*Literally:* Peace in the home. Marital peace.
Shamash	Attendant.
Shamayim	Heaven.
Shechinah	The Divine Presence in this world.
Shefa	Bounty.
Sheker	Lies, untruths.
Shemittah	The seventh year of a seven year cycle, in which the land is left unworked.
Shemoneh Esrei	The central prayer, consisting of 19 blessings, that is said three times a day.

Sheva Brachos	The seven blessings that are recited for a newly-married Jewish couple on each of the first seven days after their wedding.
Shidduch (pl: *shidduchim*)	Marital match, a date with a view to getting married.
Shiur	Torah class or lesson.
Shliach Tzibbur	The one leading the prayer service.
Shlichus	Going out to do outreach; some other *mitzvah*.
Shlita	An honorific term appended to the name of holy men during their lifetime.
Shmiras Einayim	*Literally:* Guarding the eyes. Refers to the *mitzvah* of not looking at immoral, spiritually damaging things.
Shtreimel	A round fur hat typically worn by chassidim on Shabbos, festivals, and other communal celebrations.
Simchah (pl: *simchas*)	Happiness. Also used to refer to a happy occasion like a wedding, for example.
Sinas Chinam	Baseless hatred.
Sitra Achra	*Literally:* 'The other side'. The dark side or source of negative spiritual forces; also an aspect of the *yetzer hara*.
Siyatta dishmaya	Heavenly help, Divine providence.
Smicha	The process of conferring rabbinic status on an individual.
Sofer Stam	The practice of writing *mezuzahs, sefer Torahs,* and other holy texts. (Also called '*safrus*'.)
Sugya (pl: *sugyos*)	The section of Torah being learned; usually refers to Gemara.
Tallis	Four-cornered prayer shawl.
Talmid Chacham	A wise Torah student.
Techiyas HaMeisim	The revival of the dead, that will happen in the times of *Moshiach*.
Tefach (pl: *tefachim*)	A biblical unit of measurement, approximately 8-10 centimeters.

Tefillin	Black boxes containing holy texts that are worn on the arm and the forehead.
Tehillim	Psalms.
Teshuva	Repentance.
Teshuvos	Responses to *halachic* questions.
Tikkun	(plural: tikkunim) Spiritual rectification. *Tikkun Olam*--rectification of the world. *Tikkun Chatzos*--Midnight prayer, said to rectify / lament the destruction of the Temple.
Tikkun HaKlali	*Literally:* The General Rectification. The Ten Psalms (numbers: 16, 32, 41, 42, 59, 77, 90, 105, 137, 150) prescribed by Rebbe Nachman as a powerful spiritual remedy.
Tikkun Chatzos	*Literally:* The Midnight Rectification. Also known as the Midnight Lamentation, it consists of various verses and prayers mourning the destruction of the Temple, and is meant to be recited in the early hours of the morning.
Tisha b'Av	The ninth of *Av*, the date on which we remember the destruction of the *Beis HaMikdash*.
Toivel	To immerse in a *mikvah*.
Tosafos	One of the more famous groups of commentators on the Gemara, dating from approximately the 12th century.
Tumah	Spiritual impurity.
Tzaddik	(plural: *Tzaddikim*), The righteous one.
Tzedakah	Charity.
Tzitzis	A four cornered garment normally worn by Jewish men under their clothes, with fringes/strings at each corner.
Tziyun	The grave of a *Tzaddik*, e.g. Rebbe Nachman's grave.
Vasikin	Dawn minyan.
Yeshivah	Religious Jewish institution for learning Torah.
Yetzer Hara	The evil inclination.
Yirah; Yiras Shemayim	Fear of Heaven.

Yishuv HaDaas	A settled mind.
Yom HaAtzmaut	Israel's Independence Day.
Zechus (also Zocheh)	Merit, to merit.
Zemiros	Jewish songs, usually containing biblical verses, that are typically sung on Shabbos, and on other Jewish festivals and happy occasions.
Zman	Period of time.
Zt"l	Stands for: *Zichron HaTzaddik Levracha: Literally:* May the *tzaddik*'s memory be for a blessing.

LEARN MORE ABOUT RAV ELIEZER BERLAND AND SHUVU BANIM

For the latest news and updates about Rav Eliezer Berland and Shuvu Banim, please visit our website at:

www.ravberland.com

You can also listen to real-time updates, announcements, and stories in Hebrew by calling the Shuvu Banim hotline.

THE SHUVU BANIM HOTLINE:

In Israel, please call: *9148 or 02-800-8800

In the USA, please call: 845-640-0007

In the UK and Europe, please call: +44-203-807-3333

If you would like to come and learn with Lev Daniel, the English-speaking division of the Shuvu Banim Yeshivah located in the Old City, please contact us at: info@ravberland.com.

If you would like to send a name for a blessing from Rav Berland, please email: moked318@gmail.com (please include your contact details).

For all other information and queries, please contact us at: info@ravberland.com.

PLEASE SUPPORT THE IMPORTANT WORK OF RAV ELIEZER BERLAND'S 'SHUVU BANIM INTERNATIONAL' OUTREACH PROGRAMS'!

Please help us to spread the light of the *Tzaddik*, Rebbe Nachman of Breslov, throughout the world, by supporting Rav Eliezer Berland's 'Shuvu Banim International' Outreach Programs.

Suggested levels of support:

☐ $15.60 (30¢ / week)   ☐ $ 100

☐ $26.00 (50¢ / week)   ☐ $ 250

☐ $39.00 (75¢ / week)   ☐ $ 500

☐ $52.00 ($1 / week)   ☐ $ 1000

☐ Other Amount: $

If you'd like to be informed about the latest books etc. from Rav Eliezer Berland, please give us your details:

Email address:

Name:

Street address:

City, State, Zip:

Phone: (   )

Contribute via Credit Card:

Credit Card Type:

☐ Visa   ☐ MasterCard   ☐ Discover   ☐ American Express

Credit card number:

Expiration: (Month / Year)

Cardholder Signature:

Contribute online via PayPal on our website, by visiting: www.ravberland.com/donate

Contribute via a direct bank deposit to:

Shuvu Banim International

Non-profit #: 580608610

Discount Bank

Branch 67

Account Number 81373

If you have any queries or comments, please contact **Shuvu Banim International** on: 02-626-6148 (within Israel), or: +972-2-626-6148 (from outside of Israel).

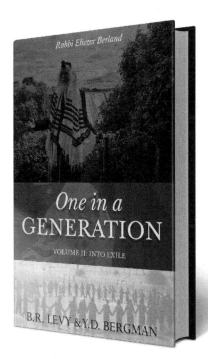

Coming Soon

ENDNOTES

1   The Berland family stems from the Davidic dynasty through Rav Eliezer Zev, the Rav of Buchetch in Romania.

2   Heard from Shlomie Berland, son of Yechezkel Berland (Rav Berland's brother).

3   Heard from Rav Berland himself.

4   "The Fire and the Light", Mishpacha Magazine, January 30th 2013.

5   Heard from Rav Nachman Horowitz.

6   From Amnon Levy, exclusive interview on Israeli TV Channel 10. Israeli television

7   Heard from Amnon Levy.

8   It's told about the Steipler Gaon that he would walk in the street with his eyes closed in order not to see women, and that one time he was seen walking into a pole and saying "excuse me" without looking up.

9   Said over by R. Aaron Lebel *shlit"a* in the name of R. Feival Lebel *ztz"l*

10   As told by his classmate Rav Shalom Tzadok *shlit"a* (today the Rav of the Ariel and Bnei Ayish settlements).)

11   The recording of Rav Koch *ztz"l* can be heard on the Shuvu Banim information line extension 43121.

12   Rav Berland was born 65 years after this statement.

13   *Bechoros* 31b.

14   See *Likutei Moharan 62*.

15   See *Chayei Moharan 401-402*.

16   See *Likutei Moharan 241*.

17   *Tehillim* 92:13.

18   *Parshas Shemos* 35:1.

19   *Parshas Shemos* 33:8.

20   Sanhedrin 110, Targum Yonasan and Baal Haturim on Bamidmar 16:10, Kiddushin 33b, Tanchuma Shemos 33:8).

21   *Parshas Vayeira*, 18:2.

22   A book full of miracle stories about Rav Berland is soon to be published in Hebrew, called *Lahavot Eish Part II*.

23   You can see Ronen Dvash telling his story here: https://www.youtube.com/watch?v=Eh5AXCRIWA0

24   See *Tractate Brachos 5a*.

25   *Sanhedrin 97b*.

26   *Yirmiyahu 3:22.*

27   Teddy Kollek was an old-school Labor politician who was ideologically opposed to religious Judaism. He was the mayor of Jerusalem between 1965-1993, and continued to harass the Shuvu Banim _{yeshivah} for many years after this story occurred.

28   *Parshas Eikev,* 11:24.

29   *Shemos Rabbah,* Chapter 20.

30   Chapter 77.

31   *Isaiah* 11:9.

32   *Isaiah* 2:2.

33   *Chayei Moharan* 401-402.

34   *Chayei Moharan* 394.

35   *Likutei Moharan* 63 and 71.

36   *Likutei Moharan* 61.

37   These lessons all stem from Isaiah 53, which talks about the suffering that the *Tzaddik* endures for the people. See also *Sanhedrin* 98 and Rashi's commentary there about how the *Moshiach* will do this in order to redeem the nation.

38   Quote from the *Shulchan Aruch, Yoreh Deah* 243:6.

39   *Shabbos* 119.

40   *Sanhedrin* 99.

41   Rambam, *Hilchos Talmud Torah,* Chapter 6.

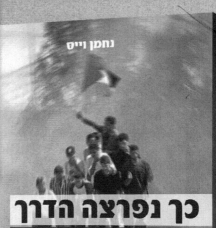